# ISSUES IN
# CONTEMPORARY ATHLETICS

# ISSUES IN CONTEMPORARY ATHLETICS

## JAMES H. HUMPHREY
### EDITOR

**Nova Science Publishers**
*New York*

**NOTICE TO THE READER**

The Publisher has taken reasonable care in the preparation of this book, but makes no expressed or implied warranty of any kind and assumes no responsibility for any errors or omissions. No liability is assumed for incidental or consequential damages in connection with or arising out of information contained in this book. The Publisher shall not be liable for any special, consequential, or exemplary damages resulting, in whole or in part, from the readers' use of, or reliance upon, this material.

Independent verification should be sought for any data, advice or recommendations contained in this book. In addition, no responsibility is assumed by the publisher for any injury and/or damage to persons or property arising from any methods, products, instructions, ideas or otherwise contained in this publication.

This publication is designed to provide accurate and authoritative information with regard to the subject matter covered herein. It is sold with the clear understanding that the Publisher is not engaged in rendering legal or any other professional services. If legal or any other expert assistance is required, the services of a competent person should be sought. FROM A DECLARATION OF PARTICIPANTS JOINTLY ADOPTED BY A COMMITTEE OF THE AMERICAN BAR ASSOCIATION AND A COMMITTEE OF PUBLISHERS.

**LIBRARY OF CONGRESS CATALOGING-IN-PUBLICATION DATA**
Issues in contemporary athletics / James H. Humphrey, editor.
    p. cm.
Includes bibliographical references and index.
ISBN 13: 978-1-59454-595-5
ISBN 10: 1-59454-595-2
1. Sports--United States.    I. Humphrey, James Harry, 1911-    .
GV583.H85                                                                    2005
796--dc22                                                          2005020557

Published by Nova Science Publishers, Inc. ✤ New York

# CONTENTS

# PREFACE

This new book tackles some of the leading issues in athletics, a world in which virtually everyone has a stake, be it as a child, parent, participant, fan, wanabee or the target of someone telling us to participate more in athletics.

In chapter one, children's athletics have developed to the extent that various estimates suggest that there are upwards of 40 million participants. This broad participation is accompanied by concerns that parents may have as their children engage in these activities. This article takes into account such major parental concerns as competition, injuries and supervision. It also carefully assesses the possible negative aspects of children's athletics.

An important factor in the success of any children's athletic program is the ability of those in charge to provide desirable and worthwhile athletic learning experiences discussed in chapter two. Taken into account here are the principles of learning applied to athletics, along with a detailed discussion of the various phases of the teaching-learning situation in athletics.

It should be obvious that the success of athletic learning will depend in a large degree upon how well the experiences are presented. Some athletic programs for children are destined to failure because those in charge do not have the knowledge and training to provide desirable and worthwhile athletic learning experiences for children. This discussion is intended to provide a more or less scientific approach to the conducting of such experiences.

The term teacher in the present discussion refers to any adult (usually the coach) who will assume the responsibility for conducting athletic learning experiences.

The teacher should be aware that every child is highly unique and that he or she approaches all learning tasks with his or her own level of motivation, capacity, experience and vitality. Moreover the teacher must by a combination of emotional and logical appeal, help each individual find his or her own way through the experience and at his or her own rate. The teacher must also help the individual understand the meaning of the experience and help meaningfully to incorporate it and its use into the childs own life.

The teacher's role should be that of a guide who supervises and directs desirable and worthwhile learning experiences. In providing such experiences, the teacher should constantly keep in mind how an athletic experience can contribute to the physical, social, emotional and intellectual development of the child. This implies that the teacher should develop an understanding of the principles of learning and apply these principles properly in presenting athletic learning experiences to children.

In chapter three the proponents of children's athletics are high in their praise of how social development can be accomplished through this medium. This is a valid assumption provided programs are conducted in a satisfactory manner. Guidelines for social development of children through athletics are provided along with various possibilities for such development. Also, methods of evaluating how athletics can contribute to social development are considered.

The first step in chapter four for developing a successful program of interscholastic athletics should be in the direction of a sound philosophy and valid objectives of the program. Considered here are suggestions for such development that are compatible with principles of total development of the student athletics who participate.

Chapter five states that the unprecedented popularity of women's athletics has been accompanied by the many problems associated with athletic programs. Not the least of these problems is the stress imposed upon women coaches and the athletes they coach. This paper takes into account the many stress-inducing factors in women's athletics including causes of such stress, the affect it has on coaches and athletes, as well as how they attempt to cope with this stress.

As restraints are imposed in chapter six, administrators within non-profit organizations, including universities and their individual departments, must make the most efficient and effective use of the resources at their disposal. The effective management of human resources, in particular, consistently has been linked to the performance and even survival of organizations in a variety of industries including banking, manufacturing, and industrial products. The purpose of this paper is first, to review previous models of the relationship between HRM and OE and second, to propose a measurement model that overcomes noted limitations of the previous models. The third purpose is to review and provide a rationale for best human resource practices that should be included in research regarding non-profit sport settings. Finally, directions for future research, extensions of the model, and practical implications are discussed.

The purpose of chapter seven is to assess the importance and relevance of market demand factors to the levels of consumption and identification of potential consumers of an NFL expansion team. Research participants (N=308) were residents of a greater metropolitan area, who were interviewed before the inaugural season of an NFL expansion team. A questionnaire was followed for the interviews, which included eight demographic background variables, 18 market demand variables under four factors (game attractiveness, marketing promotions, economic consideration, and socialization opportunity), and 14 criterion variables under two categories (consumption and identification). One-sample t-tests revealed that the overall mean scores of the market demand and the criterion factors were significantly ($p < .05$) greater than their midpoints, respectively, suggesting that there were high expectations of market demands, high intentions of consumption, and high team identifications by the potential NFL consumers. Multiple regression analyses revealed that the market demand factors were positively ($p < .05$) predictive of consumption and identification, indicating that an NFL expansion team should focus on the market demand variables when developing game products and promotional strategies.

A 92 year-old senior athlete looks back through the events leading to and including senior athletes. In his narrative in chapter eight he includes personal experiences as they relate to the changing public attitude towards the inter-relationship between aging and physical exertion.

There was a time around four decades ago that for anyone over forty to go running was rather unthinkable. The real single event that led to athletic events of all ages, including seniors, happened about three decades ago in the state of California. An attorney, David Pain, arranged a one-mile race for people over forty. The public was strongly against it. "People would be having heart attacks all along the way." Nobody did. Instead, "older people" (over 40) began clamoring for another race, a shorter race, a longer race, a track meet including throws and jumps.

The desire was there, the avalanche started, track and field events emerged, road races began from the short 3K (1.8 miles) to the marathon and beyond (ultramarathons) for all ages. The "running craze" hit the road throughout the U.S. and around the world. The clamor instigated the recording of U.S. and around the world. The clamor instigated the recording of U.S. and world records of every age from forty into the nineties for each athletic event. California became the capital of masters and senior athletics. With the fast breaking of records, the booklet, Masters U.S. and World Age Records, had to be revised every year. Road races of all distances sprang up everywhere from 3K to the marathon for all ages. The "age gaps" of earlier years began to disappear. Senior olympics sprang up in many areas. For the first time, some athletic events were "just for seniors." The first World Masters (including senior championships) occurred in Toronto, Canada in 1975 and have continued bi-yearly throughout the world.

Perhaps the most important aspect of senior athletics is the effect on the senior athlete himself or herself. As for metal effects, the author, a still practicing psychologist, has been amazed at the improvement in his elderly patients who became athletes, while physiological measurements showed anti-aging effects.

September 11, 2001 immeasurably and permanently changed the United States as described in chapter nine. The events of that fateful day have made American life more complicated and uncertain. This is true even for those who work in the sports industry, and especially true for those who own or operate sport stadiums and arenas. What was once unimaginable and unforeseeable is now reality. This new foreseeable threat carries with it legal implications for those who own or operate sport facilities. If a sport facility is the target of a terrorist attack, then there is a possibility that the facility's owners and operators could be sued and subsequently held liable. Therefore, it is crucial for sport facility owners and operators to understand how liability can be imposed on them for the actions of third-party terrorists.

Though there are several benefits to hosting a professional sport event, tangible, monetary benefits are often thought of as most important states in chapter ten. Economic impact analysis represents one method of measuring such effects. The purpose of this study was to conduct an economic impact analysis of a professional tennis tournament. Data were collected on-site from 638 spectators. Results indicate the tournament had a $16.92 million in local economic activity (sales multiplier), $8.11 million in residents' personal income (income multiplier), $11.38 million in personal income, property income, and indirect business taxes (value-added multiplier), and 203.6 new jobs (employment multiplier). The benefits and pitfalls of the various multipliers used and of economic impact analysis in general are discussed.

Within intercollegiate athletics, a popular strategy to encourage ethical decision-making and behavior portrayed in chapter eleven has been to create codes of ethics. Despite the importance placed on codes of ethics, little is known about how student-athletes feel about their codes of ethics. To better understand student-athletes' perceptions of the content and purposes of their codes of ethics, a sample of student-athletes from one NCAA Division I conference (n = 336) was surveyed. Results revealed student-athletes' general perceptions of toward codes of ethics and their positions on responsibility for conduct, enforcement, and penalties. Further, results revealed student-athletes' feelings toward important ethical ideals. Findings from this research should help conferences in writing codes of ethics that are more effective.

The purpose of this investigation in chapter twelve was to evaluate the factors that may be influential in the college selection process of baseball student-athletes. A second purpose was to investigate the differences between baseball student-athletes from each of the National Collegiate Athletic Association (NCAA) Divisions (Division I, II, and II). The participants in this study were 320 collegiate baseball student-athletes from 12 colleges and universities in the Midwest. The participants completed the Influential Factors Survey for Student Athletes (IFSSA). The IFSSA was a 32-item survey that can be separated into five sections (athletics, coaching staff, academics, social, and financial aid). Results of the study were analyzed using descriptive statistics and a multivariate analysis of variance (MANOVA). Descriptive statistics showed the five most influential factors to be a winning program, opportunity to play early in career, baseball specific facilities, coach's personality/philosophy, and tradition of the athletic program. The MANOVA revealed factors related to athletics as the most influential for baseball student-athletes. Results also showed that Division III baseball student-athletes viewed academics significantly more influential than Division I and II student-athletes. Division II baseball student-athletes viewed financial aid to be significantly more influential than Division I or Division III student-athletes.

Demographic research in chapter thirteen shows that the percentage of female spectators for many sports is growing. Some experts suggest that, as sport spectators, females differ from males. If such differences do in fact exist, then it is critical to identify them in order to develop more effect marketing schemes. This investigation examined gender differences in sport consumer behavior among a convenience sample of 484 college students (male = 225, female = 259). Ninety-three percent of the respondents self-identified as Caucasian. MANCOVA results showed that after controlling for level of respondent's team identification, the effect of gender was statistically significant ($F = 18.6$, $p < .00$; $\eta^2 = 0.19$) on combined sport consumer behaviors. Results indicated that female respondents were more likely to have purchased team merchandise in the past, more likely to purchase team merchandise in the future, and were more likely to wear team apparel than male respondents. Male respondents were more likely to read about the team and watch the team on television than female respondents. No gender differences were found for plans to attend home football games.

Issues in Contemporary Athletics
Editor: James H. Humphrey, pp. 1-10

ISBN 1-59454-595-2
© 2007 Nova Science Publishers, Inc.

*Chapter 1*

# PARENTAL CONCERNS ABOUT CHILDREN'S ATHLETICS

### *James H. Humphrey\* and Deborah A. Yow*

University of Maryland, College Park, Maryland, USA

## ABSTRACT

Children's athletics have developed to the extent that various estimates suggest that there are upwards of 40 million participants. This broad participation is accompanied by concerns that parents may have as their children engage in these activities. This article takes into account such major parental concerns as competition, injuries and supervision. It also carefully assesses the possible negative aspects of children's athletics.

The term *athletics*, as used here, means *organized interactions of children in competitive and/or cooperative physical activities*. The term *children* includes those boys and girls through the chronological age of 12 (ordinarily the final year of elementary school).

Children's athletics, as conceived here, are not a prominent part of many elementary school programs. There are some instances where elementary schools support interscholastic or varsity programs, but for the most part this is not the norm. In a majority of elementary schools, where resources are available, the major emphasis is placed on a well-balanced physical education program where all children have an equal opportunity to participate. However, some elementary schools provide athletic programs in the form of *intramural* activities. This is a natural outgrowth of the physical education program with teams organized so that one classroom may play against another. Also, some schools provide opportunities for competition in selected sports to compete with other schools. These often occur after school and is supervised by school officials.

However, the great preponderance of children's athletic programs take place outside the school and are not ordinarily conducted under the supervision of the school. They are usually sponsored by such organizations as recreation centers, business enterprises, and assorted boys' and girls' clubs.

Over the years such organizations as Little League Baseball, Midget Football, Pop Warner Football, Itty Bitty Basketball, Pee Wee Golf along with a host of others have flourished and attracted children in amazingly large numbers, which some estimates place well in excess of 40 million.

Contrary to general belief, these kinds of experiences for children are not of recent origin. In fact, educators and philosophers as far back as the early Greeks felt that such activities might be a welcome adjunct to the total education of children. For instance, more than 2,300 years ago the renowned Greek philosopher Plato suggested that all early education should be a sort of play and should develop around play situations. In the 17th century, Locke, the English philosopher, felt that children should get plenty of exercise and learn to swim early in life. Rousseau, the notable French writer, held much the same opinion, believing that learning should develop from the enjoyable physical activities of childhood. These individuals, along with numerous others, influenced to some extent the path that children's athletics were to follow through the ensuing decades.

There have been periods in our history when any type of athletic program was abandoned purely on the basis that body pleasure of any type must be subjugated because this activity was associated with a foolish or unnecessary expenditure of time and energy or even evil doing. The early American pioneers more or less typified this kind of puritanical thinking because there was little emphasis on athletics for the pioneer child, certainly organized athletics. In addition to this rationale was also the absence of free time and available athletic equipment as we know it today.

Eventually, however, attitudes changed and interest in children's athletics began to emerge. Instrumental in the movement was the establishment of the first public playground in Boston in 1885. This idea soon spread nationwide with children from one playground competing in various athletic activities with those from other playgrounds.

It was not long before enterprising merchants saw possibilities for advertising by sponsoring various teams, thus capitalizing by organizing the traditional neighborhood games of children. It certainly made any child proud to be wearing a shirt with "Sherman's Grocery" or "Morton's Drugstore" emblazoned on the back.

In more modern times a much different outlook has characterized the area of children's athletics. And much of this involves the *physical fitness* of children. In fact, over a period of several decades there have been varying degrees of interest in the physical fitness of children and youth. In the early 1950s the publication of the results of six physical fitness tests (named after the authors, Kraus-Webber Tests) stimulated a great deal of concern about the physical fitness of American children. These tests had been conducted with numbers of European children and comparisons made with the results of the tests administered to a sample of children in Westchester County, New York. The fact that this geographical area at the time was considered to be one of the country's highest socioeconomic levels made the results of this comparison all the more appalling to the citizens of the United States.

The validity and reliability of these tests, as well as the conditions under which they were administered, tended to arouse criticism among some of the skeptics of that time. Nonetheless the results did serve the purpose of alerting American educators and laymen alike to the alleged physical status of the nation's children.

As a result, then President Dwight Eisenhower appointed Shane McCarthy, a Washington, DC lawyer, to head a committee on Fitness of American Children and Youth. Among others, this committee consisted of assorted professional boxers and a famous racehorse trainer. While the intentions of these individuals were not necessarily questioned, at the same time their knowledge and understanding of childhood fitness was of concern to many. And since that time the various Chairpersons of the President's Council on Physical Fitness and Sports have been appointed to some extent because of their public name-recognition rather than their knowledge of fitness of children.

Since its early emphasis, childhood fitness through athletics has experienced various degrees of success. Interest has continued to a point that now children's athletics are enjoying almost unprecedented support, development and enthusiasm. Without question this enthusiasm has been accompanied by certain concerns that parents might have with regard to their children's participation. There are a number of factors that parents might be concerned with when they become involved in children's athletics. In this regard, the issues dealt with in this paper are competition, injuries, supervision, and unfortunately the negative side of children's athletics.

## COMPETITION

The positive and negative aspects of athletic competition have been debated for decades. In fact, some decades ago the second author was the chairman of the national committee on "Competition for Children." After studying the matter with some degree of thoroughness, the "experts" on the committee decided that the success or failure of such competition was dependent upon the type of supervision provided for overseeing such programs. (As mentioned, supervision of children's athletics will be discussed later.)

There has always been a concern for the emotional stress that competition can have on a child. And, of course, such emotional stress can impact on the child's physical well-being. In fact, a new policy from the American Academy of Pediatricians states that children should be discouraged from specializing in a single athletic activity before adolescence to avoid physical and psychological negative effects.

When we asked 200 5$^{th}$ and 6$^{th}$ grade children the question, "What is the one thing that *worries* you most in school?" there were a variety or responses. However, the one general characteristic that tended to emerge was the emphasis placed on competition in so may school situations. Although children did not state this specifically, the nature of their responses clearly indicated this sentiment.

Most of the literature on competition for children has focused on athletic activities. However, there are many situations that exist in some classrooms that can cause competitive stress. An example is the antiquated "Spelling Bee" which still exists in some schools, and in fact, continues to be recognized in an annual national competition. Perhaps the first few children "spelled down" are likely to be the ones that need spelling practice the most. And, to say the least, it can be humiliating and embarrassing in front of others to fail in any school task.

It is interesting to note that the terms *cooperation* and *competition* are antonymous. Therefore, the reconciliation of children's competitive needs and cooperative needs is not an easy matter. In a sense, we are confronted with an ambivalent condition which, if not carefully handled, could place children in a state of conflict, thus causing them to endure distress.

This was recognized by Horney (1937) many decades ago when she indicated that we must not only be assertive but aggressive, able to push others out of the way. On the other hand, we are deeply imbued with ideals which declare that it is selfish to want anything for ourselves, thus we should be humble, turn the other cheek, be yielding. Accordingly, society not only rewards one kind of behavior (cooperation) but also its direct opposite (competition). Perhaps more often that not our cultural demands sanction these regards without provision of clear-cut standards of value with regard to specific conditions under which these forms of behavior might well be practiced. Thus, the child is sometimes placed in a quandary as to when to compete and when to cooperate.

It has also been found that competition does not necessarily lead to peak performance, and in fact may interfere with achievement. In this connection, Kohn (1986) reported on a survey on the effects of competition in sports, business, and classroom achievement and found that 65 studies showed that cooperation promoted higher achievement than competition, 8 studies showed the reverse, and 36 studies showed no statistically significant difference. It was concluded that the trouble with competition is that it makes one person's success depend on another's failure, and as a result when success depends on sharing resources, competition can get in the way and therefore inhibit the process.

An example of research in this area was a study conducted by Scanlan (1984) several years ago. She used an athletic environment to identify predictors of competitive stress. She investigated the influence and stability of individual differences and situational factors on the competitive stress experienced by 76 9-to-14-year-old wrestlers. The subjects represented 16 teams from one state and reflected a wide range of wrestling ability and experience. Stress was assessed by the children's form of the Competitive State Anxiety Inventory and was measured immediately before and after each of two consecutive tournament matches.

The children's dispositions, characteristic pre-competition cognitions, perception of significant adult influences, psychological states, self-perceptions and competitive outcomes were examined as predictors of pre- and post-match anxiety in separate multiple regression analyses for each tournament round. The most influential and stable predictors of pre-match stress for both matches were competitive stress anxiety and personal performance expectancies, while win-loss and fun experienced during the match predicted post-match stress for both rounds.

Pre-match worries about failure and perceived parental pressure to participate were predictive to Round One pre-match stress. Round One post-match stress levels predicted stress after Round Two, suggesting some consistence in the children's stress responses. Sixty-one percent and 35 percent pre-match and 41 percent and 32 percent of post-match state anxiety variances was explained for Rounds One and Two, respectively.

On the basis of the available evidence with regard to the subject of competition, it seems justifiable to formulate the following general concepts.

1.  Very young children in general are not very competitive but become more so as they grow older.
2.  There is a wide variety in competition among children. Some are violently competitive, while others are mildly competitive, and still others are not competitive at all.
3.  In general, boys are more competitive than girls.
4.  Competition should be adjusted so that there is not a preponderant number of highly experienced and skilled competitive teams against others who are grossly lesser in experience and ability.
5.  Competition and rivalry can sometimes produce results in effort and speed of accomplishment.

Parents involved in children's athletics might well be guided by the above concepts. Whether one is a proponent or critic of competitive athletics for children, it has now become evident that such competition may be "here to stay." Thus, positively controlling it might be our greater concern. This might perhaps be done by concentrating our efforts in the direction of educating both parents and children regarding the positive and negative effects of competition.

# INJURIES

The thing that concerns parents, particularly mothers, the most about their children's participation in athletics is the possibility of injury. And rightly so, because it is estimated that upwards of one million children report to a hospital every year because of such injuries. This could actually be much larger because many injuries are not reported. Add to this the fact that a number of such injuries are very serious or fatal. In fact, the National Youth Sports Safety Foundation (2000) reported 276 deaths from athletic injuries for a 14-year period, 1984-1998. Key findings of the report included: The number one cause of death involved trauma to the head; 45 percent of these deaths occurred in just two athletic activities; the number of deaths per year are fairly consistent at approximately 22 per year; four of the five top activities where the most deaths occurred are among the most popular sports – baseball, football, basketball, and soccer.

It should be kept in mind that contrary to popular opinion, accidents resulting in injury do not "just happen." More than 90 percent of such accidents are caused. Although injuries do occur, many of them can be avoided if proper precautions are taken. Thus appropriate care should be taken to assure the well-being of the child participant.

Two former University of Maryland doctoral students, Robert G. Davis and Larry D. Issacs (1992) have devised the following set of guidelines for those responsible for conducting children's athletic programs.

1. Use quality constructed fitting protective gear.
2. Match teams for competition on the basis of physical fitness, skill level and physical maturation (biological age) – not chronological age only.
3. Children should not be forced into athletic participation. Children who do not want to be involved are at high risk for injury.
4. Young participants should be encouraged to play in different athletic activities and experience different positions within a given activity. This practice tends to reduce injuries which may be a result of over-stressing a particular movement pattern.
5. Pay close attention to signs of physical fatigue. Many injuries occur late in a game or practice session when the children are tired. Unfortunately, the image conveyed by some coaches, "be tough," keeps many young athletes from telling the coach of their fatigue.

There are certain conditions traditionally associated with athletics. "Tennis elbow" is a case in point. This is an inflammation of the rounded portion of the bone at the elbow joint. The name is no doubt a misnomer because the majority of these cases are a result of activities other that swinging a tennis racquet.

The same could probably be said of what has become commonly known as "Little League elbow." The technical name for this condition is *osteochondritis capitulum* which like "tennis elbow" is an inflammation of a bone and its cartilage at the elbow joint. It is caused generally by a hard and prolonged act of throwing using the overarm throwing pattern. One would not have to be a "Little Leaguer" to contract this condition. Simply playing catch and throwing hard to a partner for prolonged periods could also bring this about.

One of the most feared injuries in athletics, or any activity for that matter, are those of the eyes. In this regard, Orland (1988) once did an interesting study to determine the severity and frequency of soccer-related eye injuries. The medical charts of 13 soccer players who had sustained blunt trauma to the eye were reviewed. The subjects (five girls, eight boys) ranged in age from 8 to 15 years. The most common injury was *hyphemia* (a hemorrhage in the eyeball). Others included *retinal edema* (excessive accumulation of fluid in the innermost layer of the eye), *secondary glaucoma* (increased pressure within the eyeball), *chorioretinal rupture* (an inflammatory condition in the back of the eye), and *angle recession*. Six injuries were caused by the soccer ball, three by a kick, and one by a head butt. In three cases the cause was unknown. As a result of the study, the author made the following recommendations: (1) education of coaching staff, parents, and officials; (2) protective eye wear; (3) proper conditioning; (4) strictly enforced rules; and (5) an emphasis on having fun to help reduce the number and severity of soccer-related eye injuries.

For several decades some critics have been concerned with possible injuries that children might sustain in *contact* athletics. This concern has centered around the notion that too much pressure would be applied to the *epiphyses*, particularly in such activities as football.

In the long bones there is first a center of ossification for the bone called the *diaphysis*. As each new portion is ossified thin layers of cartilage continue to develop between the diaphysis and epiphysis and during this period of growth, these outstrip ossification. When this ceases the growth of the bone stops. Injury can occur as a result of trauma which could be due to a 'blow' incurred in a contact athletic activity.

If we are to be successful in our efforts to avoid injuries to child athletic participants, more emphasis need to be exerted in the direction of preventative measures. Such measures can be taken by those who have the direct responsibility of working with children in athletic activities. And this is the subject of the ensuing discussion.

## SUPERVISION

In the present context, the term *supervision* is essentially concerned with those persons who *coach* or *manage* children's athletic teams. We are frequently asked by parents about the advisability of their children's participation in athletics. The immediate response is to "check out" the qualifications and objectives of those persons who will assume the responsibility for coaching.

At one time this was a much more serious matter because many coaches have little experience, especially in how to deal with growing children in competitive situations.

At the present time, however, this situation has been alleviated somewhat, mainly because of such organizations as the *National Youth Sports Coaches Association* (NYSCA). This organization is a nonprofit association that has proven to be a frontrunner in the development of a national training system for volunteer youth sports coaches.

One of our former students, Fred Engh, is the Association's President/CEO and he has provided us with materials, some of which we would like to pass on to the reader.

About one-half million coaches have undertaken the NYSCA's three-year, three-level program to qualify for membership and certification. This certification program focuses on helping volunteer coaches understand the physiological, physical, and emotional impact they have on children age 6 to 12. The criteria for NYSCA certification and membership are reviewed by the NYSCA National Executive Board which is comprised of representatives from the fields of education, recreation and sports law.

One of the important aspects of the NYSCA is the following "Coaches' Code of Ethics."

- I hereby pledge to live up to my certification as a NYSCA Coach by following the NYSCA Code of Ethics.
- I will place the emotional and physical well-being of my players ahead of any personal desire to win.
- I will remember to treat each player as an individual remembering the large spread of emotional and physical development for the same age group.
- I will do my very best to provide a safe play situation for my players.
- I promise to review and practice the necessary first aid principles needed to treat injuries of my players.
- I will do my best to organize practices that are fun and challenging for all my players.
- I will lead, by example, in demonstrating fair play and sportsmanship to all my players.
- I will insure that I am knowledgeable in the rules of each sport that I coach, and that I will teach these rules to my players.
- I will use those coaching techniques appropriate for each of the skills that I teach.

One would hope that those coaches who supervise children's athletics would have as their goal the best interest of the child.

In this regard, our extensive surveys of children's athletic participants on this subject have yielded some interesting results.

On a scale with 4.0 being the highest, boys rated their coaches at 3.4 and girls gave their coaches a 3.3 rating.

In answer to the question, "what do you like *best* about your coach?" boys gave the following most prominent answers.

The coach:

- is nice (34 %)
- is fair (26 %)
- teaches us good things (26 %)
- is funny (7 %)
- says it is all right if we lose (7 %)

Girls gave the following answers to this question.
The coach:

- is nice (42 %)
- is funny (28 %)
- is fair (14 %)
- helps us to play better (10 %)
- is young (6 %)

In answer to the question: What do you like *least* about your coach?" boys answered as follows.
The coach:

- gets mad and yells at us (64 %)
- works us too hard (22 %)
- doesn't let me play enough (8 %)
- is not a good teacher (3 %)
- doesn't praise us enough (3 %)

Girls answered this question as follows.
The coach:

- gets mad and yells at us (57 %)
- doesn't teach us much (19 %)
- works us too hard (14 %)
- doesn't praise us enough (5 %)
- seems unhappy (5 %)

In attempting to verbalize all of these data, one could come up with several possibilities of how children characterize their coach. Here is one such possibility. *The coach is usually a nice person with a sense of humor who is generally fair, but at the same time one who is likely to get mad and yell at the players.*

There is no question about it, the quality level of supervision is an important factor in children's athletics. In the final analysis the success or failure of any program will ultimately depend upon its contribution to the total development of the child.

## THE NEGATIVE ASPECT OF CHILDREN'S ATHLETICS

The negative dimension of children's athletics is seen in such recent headlines as:

Coach Breaks Child's Arm
Child's Play – and Adult Rage

The previously-mentioned Fred Engh once reported that he had witnessed much "ugliness in children's athletics." He attributed this to vicarious parents who will stop at nothing to push their child unmercifully to be a star athlete and will cheat, bend the rules and even risk the safety of children. He maintained that this condition exists because some leagues are operated by parents who (1) have no official standards to allow equal play opportunity for children; (2) have no requirements that make it mandatory that coaches are trained and monitored for their behavior; (3) have no guidelines to prevent injuries and first aid procedures should injuries occur; and (4) have no policy that states that adult volunteers are drug, alcohol and tobacco free at youth athletic activities. To this end Engh's *National Youth Sports Coaches Association* has developed the following "Parents' Code of Ethics."

- I hereby pledge to provide positive support, care and encouragement for my child participating in youth sports by following this Code of Ethics.
- I will encourage good sportsmanship by demonstrating positive support for all players, coaches, and officials at every age, at practice or other youth sports events.

- I will place the emotional and physical well-being of my child ahead of any personal desire to win.
- I will insist that my child plays in a safe and healthy environment.
- I will provide support for coaches and officials working with my child to provide a positive, enjoyable experience for all.
- I will demand a drug-, alcohol- and tobacco-free sports environment for my child and agree to assist by refraining from their use at all youth sports events.
- I will remember that the game is for the children and not for adults.
- I will do my very best to make youth sports fun for my child.
- I will ask my child to treat other players, coaches, fans and officials with respect regardless of race, sex, creed, or ability.
- I will promise to help my child enjoy the youth sports experience within my personal constraints by assisting with coaching, being a respectful fan, providing transportation or whatever I am capable of doing.
- I will require that my child's coach be trained in the responsibilities of being a youth sports coach and that the coach agree to the youth sports Coaches' Code of Ethics.
- I will read the NYSCA National Standards for Youth Sports and do everything in my power to assist all youth sports organizations and enforce them.


_____        _____        _____
Parent Signature        Parent Signature        Date

In closing, we are pleased to report on an interesting study by Horschhorn and Loughead (2000) that is very pertinent to this discussion. They examined the two main approaches that parents take in dealing with their child's participation in athletics – "supportive and non-interfering" and "overbearing and stress causing."

Supportive and Non-interfering Parents tended to follow these principles.

- Define winning by the level of effort, not the score of the game.
- Maintain open communication with the child throughout the sport experience.
- Establish ground rules for the child, with appropriate consequences for breaking them.
- Model appropriate behavior for the child.
- Allow the child to experience the dynamics of the sport at his or her own pace.
- Provide unconditional love and support regardless of the child's success or failure in the sport.

Overbearing and Stress Causing Parents tended to follow these principles:

- Try to live out their own athletic dreams through the child.
- Believe their child's success and failure in a sport is a reflection of their parenting ability.
- Send the message to the child that their love, support, and approval is dependent on the child's level of performance on the playing field.
- Are quick to criticize and slow to praise.
- May use age-inappropriate motivational techniques or drills with the child that may lead to overuse injuries or lowered self-esteem.
- Are cold and critical, which leads to detrimental youth sport experience.

Finally, if those parents who are involved in children's athletics expect to be successful in that involvement they will want to consider the positive aspects set forth in this discussion.

# REFERENCES

Davis, Robert G. And Isaacs, Larry D., (1992), *Elementary Physical Education*, Winston-Salem, NC, Hunter Textbooks, Inc.

Hirschhorn, Douglas Kamin and Loughead, Teri Olinsky (2000), Parental Impact on Youth Participation in Sport, *Journal of Physical Education, Recreation and Dance*, November/December, p. 26.

Horney, Karen (1937), *The Neurotic Personality of Our Times*, W. W. Norton and Company, Inc.

Kohn, A., *No Contest: The Case Against Competition*, (1986), Boston, Houghton-Mifflin.

Orland, R. G., (1988), Soccer-Related Eye Injuries in Children and Adolescents, *Physician and Sports Medicine*, November.

Scanlan, Tara K., (1984), Social Psychological Aspects of Competition for Male Youth Participants: Predictors of Competitive Stress, *Journal of Sport Psychology*, 6.

Youth Sports Deaths, (2000), *The AAALF Active Voice, Newsletter of the American Association for Active Lifestyles and Fitness*, Fall, p. 6.

Issues in Contemporary Athletics
Editor: James H. Humphrey, pp. 11-20
ISBN 1-59454-595-2

*Chapter 2*

# CONDUCTING THE ATHLETIC LEARNING EXPERIENCE WITH CHILDREN

## *Deborah A. Yow and James H. Humphrey*
University of Maryland, College Park, Maryland, USA

## ABSTRACT

An important factor in the success of any children's athletic program is the ability of those in charge to provide desirable and worthwhile athletic learning experiences. Taken into account here are the principles of learning applied to athletics, along with a detailed discussion of the various phases of the teaching-learning situation in athletics.

It should be obvious that the success of athletic learning will depend in a large degree upon how well the experiences are presented. Some athletic programs for children are destined to failure because those in charge do not have the knowledge and training to provide desirable and worthwhile athletic learning experiences for children. This discussion is intended to provide a more or less scientific approach to the conducting of such experiences.

The term teacher in the present discussion refers to any adult (usually the coach) who will assume the responsibility for conducting athletic learning experiences.

The teacher should be aware that every child is highly unique and that he or she approaches all learning tasks with his or her own level of motivation, capacity, experience and vitality. Moreover the teacher must by a combination of emotional and logical appeal, help each individual find his or her own way through the experience and at his or her own rate. The teacher must also help the individual understand the meaning of the experience and help meaningfully to incorporate it and its use into the child's own life.

The teacher's role should be that of a guide who supervises and directs desirable and worthwhile learning experiences. In providing such experiences, the teacher should constantly keep in mind how an athletic experience can contribute to the physical, social, emotional and intellectual development of the child. This implies that the teacher should develop an understanding of the principles of learning and apply these principles properly in presenting athletic learning experiences to children.

## SOME PRINCIPLES OF LEARNING APPLIED TO ATHLETICS

There are various facts about the nature of human beings of which modern educators are more aware than educators of the past. Essentially these facts involve some of the fundamental aspects of the learning process which all good teaching should take into account. Older ideas of teaching methods were based on the notion that the teacher was the sole authority in terms of what was best for children, and that children were expected to learn regardless of the conditions surrounding the learning situation. For the most part, modern teaching replaces the older concept with methods that are based on certain beliefs of educational psychology. Outgrowths of these beliefs emerge in the form of *principles of learning*. The following principles should provide important guidelines for adults for arranging learning expeiences for children and they suggest how desirable learning can take place when the principles are satisfactorily applied to learning through athletics.

*The child's own purposeful goals should guide learning.* For a desirable learning situation to prevail, adults should consider certain features about purposeful goals that guide learning activities. Of utmost importance is that the goal must seem worthwhile to the child. This will involve such factors as interest, attention and motivation. Fortunately, in athletics, interests, attention and motivation are often 'built in' qualities. Thus, the adult does not necessarily need to "arouse" the child with various kinds of extrinsic motivating techniques.

*The child should be given sufficient freedom to create his or her own responses in the situation faced.* This principle indicates that *problem solving* is a very important way of human learning and that the child will learn mainly through experience, either direct or indirect. This implies that an adult should provide every opportunity for the child to use judgment in the various situations that arise in the athletic experience.

*The child agrees to and acts upon the learning that he or she considers of most value.* Children accept as most valuable those things that are of greatest interest to them. This principle implies, in part, that there should be a satisfactory balance between *needs* and *interests* of children in their athletic experiences. Although it is of extreme importance to consider the needs of children in developing experiences, an adult should keep in mind that their interest is needed if the most desirable learning is to take place.

The child should be given the opportunity to share cooperatively in learning experiences with others under the guidance but not the control of the adult. This principle is concerned with those athletic experiences that involve several players. The point that should be emphasized here is that although learning is an individual matter, it can take place well in a group. This is to say that children learn individually but that socialization should be retained. This can be achieved even if there are only two members participating.

*The adult should act as a guide who understands the child as a growing organism.* This principle indicates that the adult should consider learning as an evolving process and not just instant behavior. If an adult is to regard his or her efforts in terms of guidance and direction of behavior that results in learning, then wisdom must be displayed as to when to "step in and teach" and when to step aside and watch for further opportunities to guide and direct behavior. The application of this principle precludes an approach that is adult dominated. In this regard the adult could be guided by the old saying "children should learn by monkeying and not by aping.

It is quite likely that adults will have good success with athletic learning experiences if they apply the above principles. The main reason for this is that their efforts in helping children learn about athletics will be in line with those conditions under which learning takes place most effectively.

# CHARACTERISTICS OF GOOD TEACHERS

Over the years there have been numerous attempts to identify objectively those characteristics of good teachers that set them apart from average or poor teachers. Obviously, this is a difficult matter because of the countless variables involved.

We should keep in mind here that effective coaches are almost always also good teachers. For that reason, coaches should understand the basic principles of effective teaching.

It is entirely possible for two teachers to have the same degree of intelligence and understanding of what they are teaching. Yet, it is also possible that one of these teachers will consistently achieve good results with children, while the other will not have nearly as much success. Perhaps a good part of the reason for this difference in success lies in those individual differences of teachers that relate to certain personality factors and how they deal and interact with children. Based upon the available research and numerous interviews with both teachers and children, we have found the following characteristics tend to emerge most often among good teachers.

1. Good teachers possess those characteristics that in one way or another have a humanizing effect on children. An important factor about good teachers that appeals to most children is a sense of humor.
2. In all cases, good teachers are fair and democratic in their dealings with children and tend to maintain the same positive feelings toward the so-called "problem" child as they do with other children.
3. Good teachers are able to relate easily to children. They have the ability and sensitivity to "listen through children's ears and see through children's eyes."
4. Good teachers are flexible. They know that different approaches need to be used with different groups of children as well as individual children. In addition, good teachers can adjust easily to changing situations.
5. Good teachers have control. Different teachers exercise control in different ways, but good teachers tend to have a minimum of control problems because they provide a leaning environment where control becomes less of a problem.

In addition to these factors, the pedagogical strategies (teaching methods or practices) that the teacher uses do significantly influence the scope and quality of learning on children.

# TEACHING AND LEARNING IN ATHLETICS

The teaching-learning process is complicated and complex. For this reason it is important that a teachers have as full an understanding as possible of the role of teaching and learning in athletics. The following discussion considers this issue.

# BASIC CONSIDERATIONS

The concepts of learning that a teacher subscribes to are directly related to the kind and variety of athletic learning activities and experiences that he or she will provide for children. Thus, it is important for teachers to explore some of the factors that make for the most desirable and worthwhile learning. Among the factors that should help to orient the reader with regard to some basic understandings in the teaching of athletic activities are (1) an understanding of the meaning of certain terms, (2) an understanding of the derivation of teaching methods, and (3) an understanding of the various learning outcomes in athletics.

## MEANING OF TERMS

Due to the fact that certain terms, because of their multiple use, do not actually have a universal definition, an attempt will not be made here to *define* terms. On the other hand, it will be the purpose to *describe* certain terms rather than attempt to define them. The reader should view descriptions of terms that follow with this general idea in mind.

## Learning

Most of the descriptions of learning are characterized by the idea that learning involves some sort of change in the individual. This means that when an individual has learned, behavior is modified in one or more ways. Thus, a valid criterion for learning would be that after having an experience, a person could behave or perform in a way in which he or she could not have behaved or performed before having the experience.

## Teaching

Several years ago the first author was addressing a group of teachers on the subject of teaching and learning. Introducing the subject in somewhat abstract terms, he asked, "What is teaching?" After a short period of embarrassing deliberation, one member of the group offered the following answer with some degree of uncertainty: "Is it imparting information?" This kind of thinking is characteristic of the traditional meaning of the term teaching. A more acceptable description would be to think of it in terms of guidance, direction and supervision of behavior that results in desirable and worthwhile learning. This is to say that it is the job of the teacher to guide the child's learning rather than to impart to him or her what could be conceived as a series of unrelated and sometimes meaningless facts. This concept of teaching as guidance, direction and supervision is particularly useful when considering teaching in the dimension of athletics.

## Method

The term method might be considered as an orderly and systematic means of achieving an objective. In other words, method is concerned with "how to do" something in order to achieve desired results. If best results are to obtained for children in their athletic experiences, it becomes necessary that the most desirable athletic learning experiences be provided. Consequently, it becomes essential that teachers use all the ingenuity and resourcefulness at their command in the proper direction and guidance of these learning experiences. The procedures that teachers use are known as teaching methods and in the case of coaching, coaching methods. It is estimated, based on our surveys, that only about 10% of coaches involved in the guidance of children's teams have any significant training in teaching methods and that this is a serious issue in this field of endeavor.

## DERIVATION FOR TEACHING METHODS

Beginning teachers often ask, "Where do we get our ideas for teaching methods?" For the most part this question should be considered in general terms. Although there are a variety of acceptable teaching procedures, all of these are likely to be derived from two somewhat broad sources.

The first of these involves an accumulation of knowledge of educational psychology and what is known about the learning process in providing for athletic learning experiences. The other is the practice of successful teachers.

In most instances, professional preparation of prospective teachers includes at least some study of educational psychology as it applies to the learning process and certain accepted principles of learning. With this basic information it is expected that beginning teachers have sufficient knowledge to make application of it in the practical situation.

It has been our observation over a period of years that many beginning teachers tend to rely too much upon the practices of successful teachers as a source of teaching methods. The validity of this procedure is based on the assumption that such successful practices are likely to have as their bases the application of fundamental psychological principles of learning. While there is certainly value in observing and/or studying the practices of successful teachers, it should be the responsibility of every teacher or coach to become familiar with the basic psychological principles of learning and to attempt to apply these in the best possible way when providing the most desirable and worthwhile learning experiences for children.

## LEARNING PRODUCTS IN ATHLETICS

In general, three learning outcomes (products) can be identified that accrue from participation in athletic activities, namely, *direct, incidental*, and *indirect*. In a well-planned teaching/coaching program, these learning outcomes should develop satisfactorily through athletic activities.

Direct learning products are those that are the direct object of teaching. For instance, running, dribbling, passing, catching and shooting are some of the important skills necessary for reasonable degrees of proficiency in the game of basketball. Through the learning of skills, more enjoyment is derived from participating in an activity than just the practice of the skills. For this reason the learning of skills is one of the primary direct objects of teaching. However, it should be understood that certain incidental and indirect learning products can result from direct teaching in athletics. The zeal of a participant to become a more proficient performer gives rise to certain incidental learning products. These may be inherent in the realization and acceptance of practices of healthful living, which make the individual a more skilled performer in the activity.

Attitudes have often been considered with direct learning products. This type of learning product involves such qualities as sportsmanship, appreciation of certain aspects of the activity and other factors that involve the adjustment and modification of the individual's reaction to others.

Adults who have the responsibility for providing athletic programs for children should give a great deal of consideration to these various kinds of learning products. This is particularly important if children are to receive the full benefit of athletic learning experiences that are provided for them.

# PHASES OF THE TEACHING - LEARNING SITUATION

There are certain fundamental phases involved in almost every athletic teaching-learning situation. These are (1) auditory input, (2) visual input, (3) participation and (4) evaluation. Although these four phases are likely to be weighted in various degrees, they will occur in the teaching of practically every athletic situation regardless of the type of activity that is being taught. While the application of the various phases may be of a general nature, they nevertheless should be utilized in such a way that they become specific in a particular situation. Depending upon the type of activity, the use and application of the various phases should always include flexibility and awareness of the objectives of the specific teaching/coaching situation.

## Auditory-Input Phase

The term *auditory* may be described as stimulation occurring through the organs of hearing. The term *input* is concerned with the use of as many media as are deemed necessary for a particular teaching-learning situation. The term *output* is concerned with behaviors or reactions of the learning resulting from the various forms of input. Auditory input involves the various learning media that are directed to the auditory sense. This should not be interpreted to mean that the auditor-input phase is a one-way process. Although much of such input may originate with the teacher, consideration should also be given to the verbal interaction among children and between children and the teacher.

Athletics provide a most desirable opportunity for learning through direct, purposeful experience. In other words, the athletic learning situation is largely "learning by doing," or learning through pleasurable, and sometimes demanding, physical activity. Although verbalization might well be kept to a minimum, a certain amount of auditory input, which provides for auditory association, appears to be essential for a satisfactory teaching-learning situation. The quality of "kinesthetic feel" may be described as the process of changing ideas into muscular action and is of primary importance in the proper acquisition of athletic skills. It might be said that the auditory-input phase helps set the stage for a kinesthetic concept (muscular action) of the particular activity being taught.

Great care should be taken with the auditory-input phases in athletic teaching-learning situations. The ensuing discussions are intended to suggest to the reader ways in which the greatest benefits can accrue when using this particular learning medium.

### Preparing Children for Listening

Since it is likely that the initial part of the auditory-input phase will originate with the teacher, care should be taken to prepare children for listening. The teacher may set the scene for listening by relating the activity to the interests of children. In addition, the teacher should be on the alert to help children develop their own purposes for listening. These methodologies are particularly useful in children's athletics.

In preparing children to listen, the teacher should be aware that it is of importance that the comfort of children be taken into consideration and that attempts should be made for removing any possible attention-distracting factors. Although evidence concerning the effect of environmental distractions on listening effectiveness is not in great abundance, there is reason to believe that distraction does interfere with listening comprehension. Moreover, it is well known that being able to see as well as hear the speaker is an important factor in listening distraction.

These factors have a variety of implications for the auditory-input phase. For example, consideration should be given to the placement of children when an athletic activity requires auditory input by the teacher. This means, for instance, that if the teacher is providing auditory input from a circle formation, the teacher should take a position as a part of the circle instead of speaking from the center of the circle. Also, it might be well for teachers to consider that an object, such as a ball, can become an attention-distracting factor when an activity is being discussed. The attention of the children is sometimes focused on the ball, and they may not listen to what is being said. The teacher might wish to place such an object out of the line of vision until time for its use is most appropriate.

## Teacher-Child and Child-Child Interaction

It was mentioned previously that the auditory-input phase is a two-way process. As such, it is important to take into account certain factors involving verbal interaction of children with children, and teacher with children.

By "democracy some people seem to mean everyone doing or saying whatever happens to cross his or her mind at the moment. This raises the question of control, and it should be emphasized that group discussions, if they are to be democratic, must be in control. This is to say that if a group discussion is to succeed it must be under control, so let us emphasize that democracy implies discipline and control.

Group discussion is a kind of sociointellectual exercise (which can involve numerous bodily movements, of course) just as an athletic activity is a kind of sociointellectual exercise (which can involve higher mental functioning). Both imply individual discipline to keep play moving within bounds, and both require moderators (officials) overseeing, though not participating in, the play in the manner that is objective and transcendent from the heat of competition. In brief, disciplined, controlled group discussion can be a training ground for living in a society in which both individual and group interests are profoundly respected – just as athletics can serve a comparable function.

Another important function in teacher-child interaction is with the time given to questions after the teacher has provided auditory-input. The teacher should give time for questions, but should be very skillful in the use of questions. It must be determined immediately whether or not a question is a legitimate one. This implies that the type of questions asked can help serve as criteria for the teacher to evaluate the auditory-input phase. For example, if numerous questions are asked, it is apparent that either the auditory-input from the teacher was unsatisfactory, or the children were not paying attention.

## Directionality of Sound

Summarizing recent findings concerned with the directionality of sound, a number of interesting factors important to the auditory-input phase have emerged. For example, individuals tend to initiate movements toward the direction from which the sound emanates. That is, if a verbal clue is given that instructs the individual to more a body segment or segments to the left, but the verbal clue emanates from the right side of the individual, the initial motor response is to the right, followed by a reverse response to the left. It is recommended that when working on direction of motor responses with children, one should make certain that the sound clues come from the direction in which the motor response is made. The point is that children have enough difficulty in discriminating left from right without confusing them further.

## Visual-Input Phase

Various estimates indicate that the visual sense brings us approximately three-fourths of our knowledge. If this postulation can be used as a valid criterion, the merits of the visual-input phase in teaching about athletics are readily discernible. In many cases, visual input, which should provide for visual-motor association, serves as a effective and functional medium between verbal symbols and direct participation in helping teachers further prepare children for the kinesthetic feel mentioned previously.

In general, there are two types of visual input that can be used satisfactorily in teaching about athletics. These are visual symbols and human demonstration (live performance).

### *Visual Symbols*

Included among the visual symbols used in athletics are motion pictures and various kinds of flat or still pictures. One of the disadvantages of the latter centers around the difficulty of portraying movement with a two-dimensional, still figure. Although movement is obtained with a motion picture, it is not depicted in third dimension, which causes some degree of ineffectiveness when this medium is used. One valuable use of visual symbols is that of employing diagrams to show the dimension of activity areas. Computer screens can of course also depict movement with effective motion, color and in some cases a sense of dimension.

### *Human Demonstration*

Some of the guides to action in the use of demonstration follow:

1.  If the teacher plans to demonstrate, this should be included in the preparation by practicing and rehearsing the demonstration.
2.  The teacher does not need to do all of the demonstrating; in fact, in some cases it may be much more effective to have one or more children demonstrate. Since the teacher might be expected to be a skilled performer, a demonstration by a child will oftentimes serve to show other children that one of their peers can perform the activity and that they should be able to do it also.
3.  A demonstration should be based on the skill and ability of a given group of children. If it appears to be more difficult for them, they might not want to attempt the activity.
4.  When at all possible, a demonstration should parallel the timing and the conditions under which it will be put to practical application. However, if the situation is one in which the movements are complex or done with great speed, it might be well to have the demonstration conducted at a slower rate than that involved in the actual performance situation.
5.  If there is a group, the children should be arranged so that everyone is in a favorable position to see the demonstration. Moreover, the children should be able to view the

demonstration from a position where it takes place. For example, if the activity is to be performed in a lateral plane, children should be placed so that they can see it from this position.

6. Although auditory input and human demonstration can be satisfactorily combined in many situations, care should be taken that the auditory input is not lost, because the visual sense offsets the auditory sense. That is, one should not become an attention-distracting factor for the other. It will be up to the teacher to determine the amount of verbalization that should accompany the demonstration.

7. After the demonstration has been presented it might be a good practice to demonstrate again and have the children go through the movements with the demonstrator. This provides for the use of the kinesthetic sense together with the visual sense that makes for close integration of the two sensory stimuli.

## Participation Phase

The following considerations should be kept in mind in connection with the participation phase of teaching.

1. The practice session should be planned so that the greatest possible amount of time is given to participation.

2. If the activity does not progress as expected in the participation phase, perhaps the fault may lie in the procedures used in the auditory-input phases. Participation then becomes a criterion for the evaluation of former phases.

3. The teacher should take into account the fact that the original attempts in learning an activity should meet with a reasonable degree of success.

4. The teacher should constantly be aware of the possibility of fatigue on children during participation and should understand that individual differences of children create a variation with regard to how rapidly fatigue takes place.

5. Participation should be worthwhile for every child and all children should have the opportunity to achieve.

6. During the participation phase the teacher should constantly analyze the performance of children in order to determine those who need improvement in skills. Behaviorisms of children should be observed while they are engaging in the athletic activity. For example, various types of emotional behavior might be noted in athletic situations that might not be indicated in most other experiences.

7. Problems involved during the participation should be kept in mind for subsequent evaluation with the children.

## Evaluation Phase

Evaluation is a very important phase of the athletic teaching-learning situation, and yet, perhaps one of the most neglected aspects of it. For instance, it is not uncommon to have a practice session end without an evaluation of the results of the session.

Children should be given the opportunity to discuss the session and suggest ways in which improvement might be effected. When this procedure is followed, children are placed in a problem-solving situation and desirable learning is more likely, with the teacher guiding learning rather than dominating the situation in a direction-giving type of procedure. Also, more and better continuity is likely to be provided from one session to another when time is taken for evaluation. Furthermore, children are much more likely to develop a clearer understanding of the purpose of athletics if they are given an opportunity to discuss the procedures involved.

Ordinarily, the evaluation phase should take place at the end of the session. Experience has shown that a satisfactory evaluation procedure can be effected in five to six minutes, depending upon the nature of the activity and what actually occurred during the session. Under certain circumstances if an activity is not proceeding well in the participation phase, it may be desirable to stop and carry out what is known as a "spot" evaluation this does not mean that the teacher should stop an activity every time the situation is not developing according to plan. A suggestion or hint to children who are having difficulty with performance can perhaps preclude the need for having all of the children cease participation. On the other hand, if the situation is such that the needs of the group will best be met by a discussion concerning the solution of a problem, the teacher is indeed justified in stopping the activity and conducting an evaluation "on the spot.

In conclusion, let us say that if the teacher is to provide athletic learning experiences that contribute to total development of children there must be a clear perspective of the total learning that is expected from the area of athletics. This implies that in order to provide for progression in athletic learning there must be some means of preserving continuity from one session to another. Consequently, each individual session becomes a link in the chain of athletic learnings that contribute to the total development of the child. Experience has shown that the implementation of this theory into reality can be most successfully accomplished by the wise and careful planning of every session. Finally, this planning will more likely produce enhanced learning and participant performance when it is done in concert with the principals of conducting the athletic learning experience with children that are discussed in this paper.

Issues in Contemporary Athletics
Editor: James H. Humphrey, pp. 21-29

ISBN 1-59454-595-2

*Chapter 3*

# SOCIAL DEVELOPMENT OF CHILDREN THROUGH ATHLETICS

## *James H. Humphrey*

University of Maryland, College Park, Maryland, USA

## ABSTRACT

Proponents of children's athletics are high in their praise of how social development can be accomplished through this medium. This is a valid assumption provided programs are conducted in a satisfactory manner. Guidelines for social development of children through athletics are provided along with various possibilities for such development. Also, methods of evaluating how athletics can contribute to social development are considered.

Supporters of children's athletics seem firm in their belief that this experience is an outstanding medium for contributing to social development of children. This was shown in an analysis that I made of more than 50 books that dealt in some way with children's physical activity programs, including athletics.

The purpose of this analysis was to identify declarative statements that proclaimed positive contributions of the various forms of development – physical, social, emotional, and intellectual. Forty-five percent of the total number of statements indicated contributions to social development, followed by physical development with 29 percent, emotional development with 17 percent and intellectual development with 9 percent.

Although the above attests to the subjective pronouncements of the social values of children's physical activity programs and athletics, at the same time it is interesting to note that little research has been conducted to build an objective foundation under this long-held theoretical postulation. In order to examine this more thoroughly, I made a documentary analysis of children's physical activity programs and athletic research reported in the *Research Quarterly for Exercise and Sport* over a 20-year period (80 issues). Seven percent of all the studies reported met the criterion that was established to determine if a study was concerned with children in the 6-12 year age range. Sixty-seven percent of this number dealt with whole or part of the physical aspect. This compared with 12 percent with the emotional aspect, 11 percent with the intellectual aspect and 10 percent with the social aspect.

Moreover, in a very small percentage of the cases it was demonstrated that physical activity and athletic programs made significant contributions to social development.

Most of the research that has been done in this general area has been devoted to relationships between social and physical factors. The majority of these findings generally show that the most popular children are those who are most adept in the performance of physical skills required in athletics. In this regard it is interesting to note that some studies of boys and girls reveal that both sexes express a preference for good school marks over excelling in sports and being popular. It has also been reported that many children selected as outstanding academically and athletically were listed as popular more often than children not in these categories. When outstanding students, athletes and student-athletes (outstanding academically *and* athletically) are compared as to popularity, it is generally found that among boys, athletes are somewhat more popular while among girls, student-athletes seemed to be slightly more popular.

It is interesting to note that some studies have yielded slightly different results. For example, in studying the role of sports as a social status determinant for children, Chase and Dummer (1992) had a total of 227 boys and 251 girls in Grades 4, 5, and 6 complete a questionnaire to determine which criteria were most important in determining personal, female, and male popularity. Personal popularity was answered by the girls and boys according to "what would make you well liked by your classmates." Female and male popularity was determined by asking both boys and girls to decide "what would make (girls, for female subjects, and boys, for male subjects) well liked by your classmates." For boys, it was revealed that sports have become more important and academic achievement less important in determining personal popularity. Boys reported sports to be the most important determinant of personal and male popularity and appearance as the most important determinant of female popularity. Sports and appearance became more important for boys with each higher grade level. Girls reported appearance to be the most important determinant of personal, male, and female popularity. For girls, appearance became more important with each higher grade level.

Admittedly, the whole area and sociality and children's athletics is difficult to study objectively, and this may be a part of the reason why so little research has been undertaken.

The above should not be interpreted to mean that athletic experiences have little to contribute to social development of children. On the contrary, the *potential* values of athletics in making positive contributions to social development are tremendous. Let us examine the premise.

## SOME GUIDELINES FOR SOCIAL DEVELOPMENT OF CHILDREN THROUGH ATHLETICS

It is important to set forth some guidelines for social development if we are to meet with any degree of success in our attempts to provide social development of children through athletics. The reason for this is to assure, at least to some extent, that our efforts in attaining optimum social development through athletics will be based upon a scientific approach. These guidelines might well take the form of valid *concepts of social development*. When we have some basis for social behavior of children as they grow and develop we are then in a better position to select and conduct athletic activities that are likely to be compatible with social development. The following list of concepts of social development with implications for children's athletics is submitted with this general idea in mind.

1. *Interpersonal Relationships Are Based on Social Needs.* All children should be given an equal opportunity in athletic participation. Moreover, the coach should impress upon children their importance to the team. This can be done in connection with the team or group effort, which is so essential to successful participation. It is encouraging that some baseball leagues have a rule that every child must play and that every player must play in the infield at least part of the time.

2. *A Child Can Develop His or Her Self-Concept Through Undertaking Roles.* A child is more likely to be aware of his or her particular abilities if given the opportunity to play different positions on a team. Rotation of such responsibilities as team captains tends to provide opportunity for self-expression of children through role playing.

3. *There are Various Degrees of Interaction Between Individuals and Groups.* The athletic experience should provide an outstanding for the child to develop interpersonal interaction. The coach has the opportunity to observe children in action rather than in only sedentary situations. Consequently, the coach is in a good position to guide integrative experiences by helping children to see the importance or satisfactorily interrelationships in athletic group situations.

4. *Choosing and Being Chosen – An expression of a Basic Need – is a Foundation of Interpersonal Relationships.* As often as possible, children should be given the opportunity for choosing teammates, partners and the like. However, great caution should be taken by the coach to see that this is carried out in an equitable way. At practice sessions the coach should devise ways of choice so that certain children are not always selected last or left out entirely.

5. *Language is a Basic Means and Essential Accompaniment of Socialization.* Children can be taught the language of the body through using the names of its parts as they participate in athletics. For example, "Good arm, Jane," or "Put some foot into it Joe." This is an important dimension in the development of body awareness. Athletic experiences should be such that there is opportunity for oral expression among and between children. For example, in the *evaluation phase* of an athletic learning situation, children have a fine opportunity for meaningful expression if the evaluation is skillfully guided by the coach.

6. *Learning to Play Roles is a Process of Social Development.* A child may be given the opportunity to play as many roles as possible in the athletic experience. This could be involved in the organization and administration of athletic activities such as selection of activities, making rules of play, and helping other with skills. Doing a physical skill is in itself the playing of a role, such as being a better thrower, catcher, and the like. Thus, the very medium of athletic activities is the process of social adjustment.

7. *Integrative Interaction Tends to Promote Social Development.* The key word in this process to promote social development is *action*, which is the basis for athletic participation. Athletic participation is unique in its potential to accomplish integrative interaction, and thus promote social development. Spontaneity can be considered as one of the desired outcomes of integrative experiences, which means the opportunity for actions and feelings expressed by the child as he or she really is. Active play is perhaps the most important aspect of life for children, and thus, spontaneous actions and feelings are best expressed through physical activity.

8. *Resistance to Domination is an Active Attempt to Maintain One's Integrity.* The coach migh well consider child resistance as a possible indicator of coach domination. If this occurs, the coach might look into his or her actions, which may

be dominating the athletic teaching-learning situation. Child resistance should be interpreted as a sign of a healthful personality, and a wise coach will likely be able to direct the energy into constructive channels to promote social development. A very natural outlet for this frustrated energy is found in desirable activities presented in an athletic program.

9.  *Interpersonal Interaction Between Children is a Basis for Choice.* If children are left out by other children, this symptom should be studied with care to see if this is an indication of poor interpersonal relationships with other children. Very interesting aspects of interpersonal relationships can be observed by the wise coach. Children may realize the value of a child to a specific activity and accept such a child accordingly. On the other hand, they may be likely to accept their friends regardless of ability in athletic skills.

10. *A Child, in and as a result of Belonging to a Group, Develops Differently Than He or She Can as an Individual Alone.* Most athletic activities provide for an outstanding opportunity for children to engage actively in group experiences. Merely being a member of a team can be a most rewarding experience for a child. If properly conducted, athletic activities should provide an optimal situation for desirable social development because children focus their greatest personal interest in active play.

## SOCIAL POSSIBILITIES FOR SOCIAL DEVELOPMENT OF CHILDREN THROUGH ATHLETICS

It has already been suggested that the "athletic laboratory" should present near-ideal surroundings and environment for the social development of children. It has also been indicated that coaches are convinced that his area provides some of the best means for teaching vital social skills. In fact, the American Sports Education Program has proclaimed that participation in sports "develops social skills with other children and adults such as taking turns and sharing playing time" (1994).

There are numerous athletic situations through which children may gain a better understanding of the importance of cooperation. By their very nature, many games depend upon the cooperation of group membership in achieving a common goal. In skills such as throwing and catching there must be a coordinated action of the thrower and catcher. In certain kinds of gymnastic activities, children participate and learn together in groups of three – two children assisting the performer and the other taking turns in performing. In these and countless other situations the importance of cooperating together for the benefit of the individual and group is readily discerned.

In this general regard, the following study conducted by Berlage (1981) is of interest. The researcher studied the similarities between children's competitive team sports and the typical corporate ro business environment. Two research questions were posed: (1) Does the structural organization of children's soccer and ice hockey organizations resemble that of American corporations? and (2) Are the values of children's competitive sports similar to corporate values? Questionnaires were distributed to 222 Connecticut and New York fathers of 11- or 12-year-old sons on soccer and ice hockey teams. Through observations and interviews, it was found that the structural organization of the children's ice hockey and soccer programs clearly resembled that of corporations. An organizational chart illustrated the hierarchies and divisions in a youth soccer program, and it was also found that the values in competitive sports are similar to corporate values. The fathers selected teamwork (cooperation) as the most important sports attribute that would contribute to success in business. The importance of learning to be part of a team was a constant theme in the father's responses. Although some fathers expressed misgivings about the amount of politics in the team selection process and the inconveniences of complying with practice and travel schedules, mots fathers had positive attitudes toward competitive youth sports. It was concluded that those who have participated in competitive sports have an advantage over others who have not socialized in these values, skills, and attitudes.

Issues that come up as a result of certain misunderstandings in athletic activities give rise to the exercise of wholesome social controls. The relationship of these controls in athletic experiences to those in community living might possibly be understood in varying degrees by children at the different age levels. In these situations, outstanding settings are provided for the development of problem-solving technique in which children are placed to make value judgments.

Some coaches have observed that although athletics provide opportunities to encourage interpersonal communication and understanding among children, at the same time these opportunities are occasionally manifested in the form of minor conflicts. A procedure used by some coaches to solve such minor conflicts is the "talking bench" where two children sit until they have agreed upon the origin of their conflict and resolved it to the satisfaction of both.

The above discussion included but a few of the numerous possiblities for social control, social interaction, and thus social development, that are likely to be inherent in the athletic experience. Admittedly, this does not accrue automatically, and any degree of success in social development through athletics rests heavily upon the coach and parents as well.

## IMPLICATIONS OF RESEARCH IN SOCIAL BEHAVIOR OF CHILDREN

As has been mentioned previously, not a great deal of research has been undertaken in the field of athletics in relation to social development of children. This being the case, we should consider the psychological research that has been conducted in social development so that we can draw some implications for athletics. This is to say the in utilizing such findings, we will be better able to conduct athletic experiences that are more likely to result in positive social development. A report by the National Institute of Educaiton provides some information that might be useful.

The purpose of this report was to provide elementary school teachers with a summary of psychological research concerned with social development of young children. In submitting the report, it was noted that caution should prevail with reference to basic research and practical implications. In this regard, the following suggestions are submitted.

1. What seems to be "true" at one point in time often becomes "false" when new information becomes available or when new theories change the interpretation of old findings.
2. Substantial problems arise in any attempt to formulate practical suggestions for professionals in one discipline based on research findings from another discipline.
3. Throughout the report, recommendations for teachers (coaches) have been derived from logical extensions of experimental findings and classroom (athletic fields) adaptations of experimental procedures.

4. Some of the proposed procedures may prove unworkable in the classroom (on the athletic field) even though they may make sense from a psychological perspective.

5. When evaluating potential applications of psychological findings it is important to remember that psychological research is usually designed to derive probability statements about the behavior of groups of people.

6. Individual teachers (coaches) may work better with a procedure that is on the average, less effective.

The following list of generalizations, which have been derived from the findings are accompanied by possible general implications for children's athletics. In considering these implications, the above cautions should be kept in mind. Moreover, each individual coach or parents will no doubt be able to draw his or her own implications and make practical applications that apply to particular situations.

1. *Reasoning with an Emphasis on Consequences for Other People is Associated with the Development of a Humanistic Concern for Others.* Coaches might give consideration to encouragement of social behavior in the athletic experience by discussing the implications of children's and coaches' actions for the feelings of others; poor performers should be encouraged rather than ridiculed.

2. *Children Tend to Show Empathy Toward Individuals Similar to Themselves.* In the athletic experience it is important to emphasize the likenesses of people; although all children may differ in one or more characteristics they are stlil more alike than they are different.

3. *Children May Learn Techniques for Positive Social Interaction by Observing Who Are Behaving Cooperatively.* In team games, particularly, cooperation of each individual is very important to the success of the team; the coach can suggest ways children can cooperate and reinforce children when these suggestions are followed.

4. *The More Children Voluntarily Practice Social Skills, the More Likely They are to Use These Skills in Less Structured Situations.* In the athletic situation, children can be assigned certain responsiblities that require the practice of social skills. The coach can coordinate the experience with the parent, and each can determine the results of the other's efforts.

5. *Children are Likely to use Behaviors for Which They Have Been Reinforced.* The coach can focus his or her attention on children who are cooperating, sharing, and helping the coach and other children in the athletic situation.

6. *Children are Likely to Imitate Behaviors for Which They See Other Children Being Reinforced.* The coach can compliment those children who are saying cooperative, helpful things to each other, particularly in team games. At the same time, the coach should consider simultaneously ignoring negative social interactions of children.

7. *Children are Likely to Help and Share When They Have Seen Someone Else do it, Particularly if They Know and Like the Model.* The coach and parents can take the lead by providing examples of sharing, helping, and cooperating.

8. *Ignored Behavior May Increase at First, but Eventually it is Likely to Decrease if the Child Does not Receive Reinforcement from Other Sources.* The coach may wish to pointedly ignore misbehavior whenever possible by turning away from a misbehaving child and attending to a child who is behaving appropriately. Obviously, all misbehavior cannot be ignored because in some instances such

behavior might be concerned with safety factors in the athletic experience. Thus, it is sometimes appropriate for the coach to act expediently.

9. *Consistent, Immediate Punishment May Tend to Discourage the Behavior it Follows.* When this is necessary, the coach might consider choosing mild punishment related to the activity, which can follow misbehavior immediately. For example, if a child is misusing a piece of material such as a ball, it can be removed, at least temporily.

10. *Reasoning can Increase Children's Awareness of the Needs of Others, and it (Reasoning) is a Form of Attention That Should be Limited to Occasions When Children are Behaving Appropriately.* In many athletic teaching-learning situations there is a need for certain rules and regulations. It might be well to discuss the reasoning behind rules when children are following the rules and *not* when the rules are being disobeyed. However, this does not necessarily preclude a negative approach if a given situation warrants it.

## EVALUATING CONTRIBUTIONS OF ATHLETICS TO SOCIAL DEVELOPMENT

It has already been mentioned that coaches place great store in the contributions of athletics to social development of children. It has also been suggested that little solid scientific evidence is available to support this belief. This makes it all the more important that coaches and parents as well examine critically those athletic experiences that are being provided for children.

## PROCESSES FOR EVALUATING SOCIAL GROWTH IN ATHLETICS

In the past, most of what has been done in this area has been of a subjective nature. The process of "observation" has been considered satisfactory because it has been felt that for the most part we can merely watch children to see the kinds of relationships that exist between them.

In more recent years, I have approached this problem from a more scientific standpoint, using certain *sociometric techniques* with varying degrees of success. Included among such techniques are (1) sociograms, (2) sociographs, and (3) social distance scales.

### Sociograms

In this technique, a child is usually asked to name in order of preference those persons liked best on a team. In the athletic situation, a child may be asked to name those he/she would like to be with or play with most. After the choices are made, the results are plotted on a sociogram.

If two children choose each other, they are known as "mutual choices of pairs." Those not selected by anyone in the group and who do not choose anyone are called "isolates." "Islands" is the name given to pairs or small groups of mutual choices not selected by any in the large group. Although the sociogram is a worthwhile device for identifying certain aspects of interpersonal relationships, it is a time-consuming procedure and for this reason it is not one of the more popular methods used.

## Sociographs

The sociograph is a more expedient and practical way of tabulating and interpreting data. Instead of plotting as in a sociogram, choces are recorded in tabular form opposite the names of children. This readily shows the number of rejections, mutual choices, choices received, and choices given.

## Social Distance Scales

This sociometric technique has been used in research in social psychology for many years. In this procedure, each member of a group is asked to check the other members according to certain degrees of social intimacy such as:

1. Would like to have him/her as one of my friends.
2. Would like to have him/her on my team, but not as a close friend.
3. Would like to be with him/her once a while, but not often or for very long
4. Would like to be with him/her being on the team, but I do not want anything to do with him/her.
5. Wish he/she were not on team.

This procedure can be used as an athletic experience social distance scale to attempt to determine the general social tone of a team. Team social distance scores on each individual child can be obtained be arbitrarily weighting the items listed above. For exapmle, if a child checked two times for item number one (2 x 1 = 2); six times for item two (6 x 2 = 12); eight times for item three (8 x 3 = 24); three times for item four (3 x 4 = 12); and one time for item five (1 x 5 = 5) the total score would be 55. (The lower the score the greater the acceptance by the group and the less the social distance).

These data can be used to determine with some degree of objectively, the extent to which the athletic experience has contributed to social relationships; that is, a coach can compare scores before and after a group of children have been involved in a particular athletic experience. This can be done on an individual game basis when a team has won or when it has lost. Also, it can be done at the beginning and at the end of an entire season to measure whatever social growth may have taken place among the participants.

Over a period of years, I have used all of the above sociometric techniques when I have been asked to make an assessement of a certain children's athletic program. In some instances, the results have provided guidance in efforts to obtain a better understanding of social relationships and thus contribute to social development. It is recognized that most all coaches are aware of those obvious factors concerned with group social structure. However, the many aspects of interpersonal relationships that are not so obvious can be difficult to discern. It is the purpose of sociometric techniques to assist in the emergence of these relationships.

# REFERENCES

American Sports Education, *Sport Parent*, Champaign, IL, Human Kinetics Publishers, Inc., 1994, p. 142.

Berlage, G. Are Children's Competitive Team Sports Socializing Agents for Corporate America, Paper presented at the *North American Society for Sociology of Sport*, Fort Worth, TX, November 12-15, 1981.

Chase, Melissa A. and Dummer, Gail M., The Role of Sports as a Social Determinant for Children, *Research Quarterly for Exercise and Sport,* December 1992.

Issues in Contemporary Athletics
Editor: James H. Humphrey, pp. 31-42
ISBN 1-59454-595-2

*Chapter 4*

# DEVELOPING A PHILOSOPHY AND OBJECTIVES OF INTERSCHOLASTIC ATHLETICS

### *James H. Humphrey*
University of Maryland, College Park, Maryland, USA

## ABSTRACT

The first step in developing a successful program of interscholastic athletics should be in the direction of a sound philosophy and valid objectives of the program. Considered here are suggestions for such development that are compatible with principles of total development of the student athletes who participate.

Having started my career as a public school director of physical education and athletics, I still maintain a strong interest in interscholastic athletics as an important dimension of the total educational program. In fact, on occasion I am called upon to consult with school administrators in the evaluation and development of these programs. The first step is the consideration of a sound philosophy and valid objectives.

Whether they are aware of it or not, all individuals have developed some sort of philosophy of life. They may not have put it into so many words, but their philosophy is manifested in their daily actions. Regardless of the professional endeavor in which one chooses to engage, he or she will have some sort of philosophy about it. Thus, those persons who are involved in interscholastic athletics maintain a philosophy about the field. The development of such a philosophy should begin soon after one begins to prepare for a career in athletics. One's philosophy need not necessarily remain static and may be subject to change as the needs of society change.

In line with developing a philosophy one needs to give very serious consideration to the objectives of interscholastic athletics. This is to say that it is necessary to have an understanding of the potential contributions athletics can make to participants and to proceed in a manner whereby these contributions might be realized.

## MEANING OF TERMS

A standard dictionary definition of the term *philosophy* usually refers to it as a pursuit of wisdom or enlightenment. Another generalized description of the term is that it concerns our fundamental beliefs or practicing those things in which we believe. More specifically, a philosophy of interscholastic athletics is concerned with a careful systematic intellectual endeavor in which we attempt to see athletics as a whole and at the same time as an integral part of the culture of man.

The term *objective* appears to have been adopted by education from the military. The latter uses it to identify an area to be assaulted and/or captured in some way. The *Dictionary of Education* gives the following definition of the term: "Aim, end in view, or purpose of a course of action or a belief; that which is anticipated as desirable in the early phases of an activity and serves to select, regulate, and direct later aspects of the activity so that the total process is designed and integrated."

It is noted that various other terms are used to convey the same meaning. Some of these include *aim, goal,* and *purpose.* Regardless of the particular terms used, we might well consider it with regard to a very simple meaning; that is, where are we trying to go or what are we trying to accomplish through the medium of interscholastic athletics?

## DEVELOPING A PHILOSOPHY AND FORMULATING OBJECTIVES

Until about the twelfth century, few European sailors were willing to sail far beyond the sight of land because on the open seas they had no reliable way of knowing whether they were on course. Then the compass became known in Europe. From that time on seamen had something to sail by and thus could travel in all kinds of weather with considerable confidence that they were moving in the direction they wished. The compass made possible the explorations of such people as Columbus and Magellan, who first sailed around the world.

Those in the field of interscholastic athletics also need something to guide their efforts, a guiding philosophy so to speak. Otherwise they are like sailors of long ago who sailed about aimlessly when away from land, now moving this way, that way – but without any real confidence that they were "on course" and moving as they should. At times they need to be able to "check the course" by referring to a compass in their own minds so as to know if they are moving in the proper direction. In order to do this they must have a magnetic north composed of clearly defined, desirable and worthwhile objectives. If they have their objectives in mind as they make decisions about their programs, they will not be sailing blind. If they do not, they will have no basis for knowing whether or not they are doing the right thing and making wise decisions.

This problem of philosophy and objectives applies to living in general. Many people are unhappy and feel their lives are empty simply because they have never thought out for themselves what is important to them and what they really wish to achieve in life. Without a philosophy to guide their thinking and actions they are like sea voyagers without a compass so of course they feel lost. Similarly, in those situations where athletic experiences are not very effective, there is a good chance that the people in charge are confused about the purpose of their work and are failing to operate in terms of desirable and worthwhile objectives.

Above all, objectives should always be in the best interest of the individual. This precludes the practice of some coaches using an injured player simply because their philosophy is concerned only with winning.

The approach taken here is that athletics should be looked upon as a means of providing experiences which benefit the *whole* person; that is, athletics has objectives which apply to the *total personality* of those who participate in them.

# A CONCEPT OF TOTAL PERSONALITY DEVELOPMENT

A great deal of clinical and experimental evidence indicates that a human being must be considered as a whole and not a collection of parts. Some terms used to describe this situation are *whole child*, *unified individual*, and *total personality*. The latter term is commonly used in the fields of mental health and psychology and is gaining more usage in the field of education. Moreover, when we consider it from a point of view of one existing as a person, it is interesting to note that "existence as a person" is one rather common definition of personality.

What then comprises the total personality? Anyone who has difficulty in formulating views with regard to what the human personality actually consists of can take courage in the knowledge that many experts who spend their time studying it are not always in complete agreement as to what it is or how it operates. Indeed, one of the greatest mysteries which confronts man in modern society is man himself. If one were to analyze the literature on the subject it would be found generally that the total personality consists of the sum of all the *physical, social, emotional*, and *intellectual* aspects of any individual. The total personality is *one* thing comprising these various major aspects. All of these components are highly interrelated and interdependent. All are of importance to the balance and health of the personality because only in terms of their health can the personality as a whole maintain a completely healthy state. The condition of any one aspect affects each other aspect to a degree and hence the personality as a whole.

When a nervous person stutters or becomes nauseated, a mental state is *not* causing a physical symptom. On the contrary, a pressure imposed upon the organism causes a series of reactions which include thought, verbalization, digestive processes, and muscular function. Mind does not cause the body to become upset; the *total* organism is upset by a situation and reflects its in several ways, including disturbance in thought, feeling, and bodily processes. The whole individual responds in interaction with the social and physical environment. As the individual is affected by the environment, he or she in turn has an effect upon it.

However, because of a long tradition during which physical development *or* intellectual development, rather than physical *and* intellectual development, has been glorified, we often times are still accustomed to dividing the two in our thinking. The result may be that we are sometimes pulling human beings apart with this kind of thinking. Traditional attitudes which separate mind and body tend to lead to unbalanced development of an individual with respect to mind and body and/or social adjustment.

The foregoing statements have attempted to point out rather forcefully that the identified components of the total personality – physical, social, emotional, and intellectual – characterize the totality of being. It should be obvious that each of these aspects warrants a separate discussion. This appears to be extremely important if one is to understand fully the place of each aspect as an integral part of the whole personality. The following discussions of the physical, social, emotional, and intellectual aspects of personality as they relate to interscholastic athletics should be viewed in this general frame of reference.

As these aspects of total personality are discussed, there will emerge objectives of interscholastic athletics as they relate to the various aspects. There will emerge a *physical objective* of athletics, a *social objective* of athletics, an *emotional objective* of athletics and an *intellectual objective* of athletics. The reason for this approach to the formulating of objectives of interscholastic athletics lies in the fact that in order to make a valid exploration of the area of athletics in the school program, it becomes necessary to consider the guiding philosophy and purpose of education as a whole. The necessity of this consideration becomes most important when one takes into account that the basic philosophy which guides the entire educational program should also apply to athletics.

If one were to analyze to various statements of purpose of the whole of education which have been made by responsible educational groups through the years, it would be a relatively easy matter to identify a constantly emerging pattern. These statements have gradually evolved into a more or less general agreement among present-day educational leaders that the general goal of education is to stimulate and guide the growth of an individual so that he or she will function in life activities involving vocation, citizenship, and enriched leisure; and further stimulate the individual so that he or she will possess as high a level of physical, social, emotional, and intellectual development as the individual capacity will permit. If it is a valid assumption that the purpose of education is to attempt to insure development of the total personality, then it is incumbent upon those in interscholastic athletic to explore these developmental processes as they relate to athletics.

In this regard, a recent study by Yin and Ryska (1999) is of interest. They attempted to determine the relationship between participation in interscholastic athletics and various academic and psychological indices among middle and high school students. They found that self-esteem and grade point average were significantly higher in student athletes than student non-athletes. In addition, the risk for school dropout rate was significantly lower for student athletes. They concluded that these findings may provide new insight into the ongoing debate about the role of school athletic programs as well as the relative impact of such programs on secondary school students.

## THE PHYSICAL ASPECT OF PERSONALITY

One point of departure in discussing the physical aspect of personality could be to state that "everybody has a body." Some are short, some are tall, some are lean, and some are fat. People come in different sizes but all of them have a certain innate capacity which is influenced by the environment.

As far as any individual is concerned, it might be said that he or she *is* his or she body. It is the base of operation – what can be referred to as the "physical base." The other components of the total personality – social, emotional, and intellectual – are somewhat vague as far as some individuals are concerned. Although these are manifested in various ways, a person does not necessarily see them as he or she does the physical aspect. Consequently it becomes all important that one be helped early in life to gain control over the physical aspect, to develop what is known as basic body control. The ability to do this, of course, will vary from one person to another. It will depend upon the status of physical fitness of the individual. The broad area of physical fitness can be broken down into certain components, and it is important that individuals achieve to the best of their natural ability as far as these components are concerned. There is not complete agreement as far as identification of the components of physical fitness is concerned. However, the following information provided by the President's Council on Physical Fitness and Sports considers certain components to be basic as follows:

1. *Muscular strength*. This refers to the contraction power of the muscles. The strength of muscles is usually measured by dynamometers or tensiometers which record the amount of force particular muscle groups can apply in a single maximum effort. Man's existence and effectiveness depend upon the muscles. All movements of the body or any of is parts are impossible without action by muscles attached to the skeleton. Muscles perform vital functions of the body as well. The heart is a muscle; death occurs when it ceases to contract. Breathing, digestion, and elimination are impossible without muscular contractions. These vital muscular functions are influenced by exercising the skeletal muscles; the heart beats faster, the blood circulates through the body at a greater rate, breathing becomes deep and rapid, and perspiration breaks out on the surface of the skin.

2. *Muscular endurance*. Muscular endurance is the ability of the muscles to perform work. Two variations of muscular endurance are recognized: *isometric* whereby a maximum static muscular contraction is held and *isotonic* whereby the muscles continue to raise and lower a sub-maximal load as in weight training or performing push-ups. In the isometric form, they alternately shorten and lengthen. Muscular endurance must assume some muscular strength. However, there are distinctions between the two: muscle groups of the same strength may possess different degrees of endurance.

3. *Circulatory-respiratory endurance*. Circulatory-respiratory endurance is characterized by moderate contractions of large muscle groups for relatively long periods of time during which maximal adjustments for the circulatory-respiratory system to the activity are necessary, as in distance running and swimming. Obviously, strong and enduring muscles are needed. However, by themselves they are not enough; they do not guarantee well-developed circulatory-respiratory functions.

In addition to the basic three above, there are other components of physical fitness to be considered:

1. *Muscular power*. Ability to release maximum muscular force in the shortest time. Example: standing long jump.

2. *Agility*. Speed in changing body position or in changing direction. Example: dodging run.

3. *Speed*. Rapidity with which successive movements of the same kind can be performed. Example: 50-yard dash.

4. *Flexibility*. Range of movements in a joint or a sequence of joints. Example: Touch fingers to floor without bending knees.

5. *Balance*. Ability to maintain position and equilibrium both in movement (dynamic balance) and while stationary (static balance). Example: Walking on a line or balance team (dynamic); standing on one foot (static).

6. *Coordination*. Working together of the muscles and organs of the human body in the performance of a specific task. Example: throwing or catching an object.

The components of physical fitness and hence the physical aspect of personality can be measured with calibrated instruments, as in the case of measuring muscle strength mentioned above. Moreover, we can tell how tall or how heavy one is at any stage of development. We can derive other accurate data with measurements of blood pressure, blood counts, urinalyses, and the like.

# PHYSICAL OBJECTIVES

It may be generally stated that a good program of interscholastic athletics is considered a stimulant to physical growth. Moreover, the general consensus indicates that participation in a well-balanced athletic program is an important way of maintaining optimum health.

Two major objectives emerge as far as the physical aspect of personality is concerned. The first of these takes into account *maintaining a suitable level of physical fitness*. Second, there is the consideration of the *development of skill and ability.*

## Maintaining a Suitable Level of Physical Fitness

Physical fitness presupposes an adequate intake of good food and an adequate amount of rest and sleep, but beyond these things activity involving all the big muscles of the body is essential. Just how high a level of physical fitness should be maintained is difficult to determine because we must raise the question: "Fitness for what?" Obviously, the young varsity athlete needs to think of a level of fitness far above that which will concern the average middle-age individual.

Physical fitness has been describe in different ways by different people; however, when all of these descriptions are put together it is likely that they will be characterized more by their similarities than their differences. For purposes here I will think of physical fitness as the level of ability of the human organism to perform certain physical tasks or, put another way, the fitness to perform various specified tasks requiring muscular effort.

## Development of Skill and Ability

The second major physical objective of athletics has to do with disciplined body movement. The physically educated individual, commensurate with his or her capacity and within his or her own limitations, is adept in a variety of athletic activities. We enjoy those activities in which we are reasonably proficient. We are dealing with an important principle related to our athletic objectives; that is, if people are to enjoy participating in an activity, they need to be reasonably competent in the skills involved in the activity. Consequently, there must be objectives both in terms of the *number* of skills to which student athletes are introduced and the level of competence to be achieved so that they will associate a pleasurable experience with participation.

We must reckon with another matter that is closely related to competence in a wide variety of skills. Some physical education teachers have stressed the very strenuous team sports in their programs and others have placed emphasis on what have been called "life-time sports" which may be used later on in life. A sensible point of view on this subject would appear to be that we should develop competence in a variety of skills for use *now and in the future*. Stated more specifically, as an objective of athletics it could be said that all individuals should be prepared by their athletic experience to participate in suitable and satisfying activities for use now and in the future.

# THE SOCIAL ASPECT OF PERSONALITY

Human beings are social beings. They work together for the benefit of society. They have fought together in time of national emergencies in order to preserve the kind of society in which they believe, and they play together. Although all this may be true, the social aspect of personality still is quite vague and confusing as far as some individuals are concerned.

It was a relatively easy matter to identify certain components of physical fitness such as strength and endurance. However, this does not necessarily hold true for components of social fitness. The components for physical fitness are the same for children as adults. On the other hand, the components of social fitness for children may be different from the components of social fitness for adults. By some adult standards children and particularly teenagers, might be considered social misfits because some of their behaviors might not be socially acceptable to some adults.

To the chagrin of some adults, parents as well as teachers, children and teenagers are likely to be inhibited as far as the social aspect of personality is concerned. In this regard we need to be concerned with maturity as it pertains to the growing and ever changing individual. This is to say that we need to give consideration to certain characteristics of social maturity and how well they are dealt with at the different stages of growth and development of children and youth.

Perhaps we need to ask ourselves such questions as: Are we helping children and youth to become self-reliant by giving them independence at the proper time? Are we helping them to be outgoing and interested in others as well as themselves? Are we helping them to know how to satisfy their own needs in a socially desirable way? Are we helping them to develop a wholesome attitude toward themselves and others?

Social maturity and hence social fitness might well be expressed in terms of fulfillment of certain social needs. In other words, if certain social needs are being adequately met, children and youth should be in a better position to realize social fitness. Among the needs we must give consideration to are (1) the *need for affection* which involves acceptance and approval by persons, (2) the *need for belonging* which involves acceptance and approval of the group, and (3) the *need for mutuality* which involves cooperation, mutual helpfulness, and group loyalty.

When it comes to evaluating the social aspect of personality we do not have the same kind of objective and calibrated instruments that are available in assessing the physical aspect of personality. Mainly for diagnostic purposes in their dealings with students some teachers have successfully used some of the sociometric techniques. At best, however, the social aspect of personality is difficult to appraise objectively because of its somewhat nebulous nature.

# SOCIAL OBJECTIVES

The school athletic "laboratory" (areas where activities take place) should present near ideal surroundings and environment for the social development of young people. Why are people in the field of athletics convinced that this area of the school program provides some of the very best means for teaching vital social skills? By their very nature athletic activities are essentially socially oriented. The team sports are obviously so, but so too are activities like gymnastics, swimming, tennis and golf. It is important to note that when students engage in athletics, they will be participating actually in social experiences. If any type of play is to be successful and satisfying, the people involved must possess or acquire considerable skill in dealing with one another. They must learn to work together in the interest of the team. They must learn to accept and respect the rules of the games that they play. They must learn that sometimes it is necessary to place the welfare of the team ahead of their own personal desires. They must respect the rights of others. They must be loyal to their group. They must think and plan with the group and for the group. They must learn to win and lose gracefully.

In looking back over this list of social skills that are "musts" in athletic activities, it should be discerned that it is just such social skills that are necessary for happy and successful social living everywhere. A certain level of social skills on the part of each performer is absolutely essential if play is to be successful. Everyone knows, for example, what the effects of a "poor sport" are upon a friendly game. A qualified coach finds numerous opportunities to develop skills of interpersonal relationships which far exceed the basic essentials for successful play. Indeed, men and women coaches should consider the development of increased social awareness and social skills as important objectives of their programs, and they should make specific plans to reach these objectives. They should recognize that athletic activities can have a profoundly humanizing effect upon people, in that participants quickly learn to evaluate their teammates and opponents on the basis of what they can do and what kinds of persons they are rather than on the basis of their looks, race, religion, or their economic status.

## THE EMOTIONAL ASPECT OF PERSONALITY

In introducing the subject of emotion we are confronted with the fact that for many years it has been a difficult concept to define and in addition there have been many changing ideas and theories as far as the study of emotion is concerned.

Obviously, it is not the purpose of this discussions to attempt to go into any great depth on a subject that has been one of the most intricate undertakings of psychology for many years. A few general statements relative to the nature of emotion do appear to be in order if we are to understand more clearly this aspect of personality as it concerns athletics.

Emotion may be described as a response a person makes to a stimulus for which he or she is not prepared or which suggests a possible source of gain or loss. For example, if an individual is confronted with a situation and does not have a satisfactory response, the emotional pattern of fear may result; if a person is in a position where desires are frustrated, the emotional pattern of anger may occur.

This line of thought suggests that emotions might be classified in two different ways – those which are *pleasant* and those which are *unpleasant*. For example, *joy* could be considered a pleasant emotional experience while *fear* would be an unpleasant one. It is interesting to note that a good proportion of the literature is devoted to emotions that are unpleasant. I have found that in psychology textbooks much more space is given to such emotional patterns as fear and hate, than to such pleasant emotions as love, sympathy, and contentment.

Generally speaking, the pleasantness or unpleasantness or an emotion seems to be determined by its strength or intensity, by the nature of the situation arousing it, and by the way an individual perceives or interprets the situation. A far as young people are concerned, their emotions tend to be more intense than those of adults. If an adult is not aware of this aspect of child behavior, he or she will not likely understand why a child may react rather violently to a situation that to an adult seems somewhat insignificant. The fact that different individuals will react differently to the same type of situation also should be taken into account: for example, something that might anger one person might have a rather passive influence on another individual. In this regard, it is interesting to observe the effect that winning or losing a game has on certain individuals.

When we attempt to evaluate the emotional aspect of personality, we tend to encounter much the same situation as when we attempt to evaluate the social aspect; perhaps the emotional aspect is even more difficult to evaluate than the social aspect. Included among some of the methods used for attempting to measure emotional responses are the following:

1. *Blood pressure.* It rises when one is under some sort of emotional stress.
2. *Blood sugar analysis.* Under stressful conditions more sugar enters the blood stream.
3. *Pulse rate.* Emotional stress causes it to elevate.
4. *Galvanic skin response.* Similar to the lie detector technique and measurements recorded in terms of perspiration on the palms of hands.

These as well as others have been used by investigators of human emotion and they have various and perhaps limited degrees of validity. In attempting to assess emotional reactivity we often encounter the problem of the extent to which we are dealing with a purely physiological response or a purely emotional response. For example, one's pulse rate could be elevated by engaging in some sort of physical exercise. It could likewise be elevated if a person were the object of an embarrassing remark by another. Thus, in this illustration the elevation of pulse could be caused for different reasons, the first being physiological and the second being emotional. Then too, the type of emotional pattern is not identified by the measuring device. A joy response and an anger response could show the same or nearly the same rise in pulse rate. These are some of the reasons why it is most difficult to arrive at a high degree of objectivity in studying the emotional aspect of personality.

## EMOTIONAL OBJECTIVES

Most everyone recognizes that athletic contests are highly emotionalized situations for both participants and spectators. For the participant, there is the excitement before a contest. When play is in progress there is the thrill of making skillful moves and plays, and the disappointments at being frustrated or bested by an opponent. Finally, the after-play emotions determined to some extent by how well the participant performed in relation to how well he or she thinks they can perform, but in almost all instances the pleasurable emotions caused by the good feeling that the time has been well spent. As for the spectator, he or she is likely to be swept by powerful feelings of excitement, joy, anger, and disappointments from the start to the finish of a good contest. Many sociologists are tending to believe that spectators find in their favorite athletic event some of the thrills, excitements, triumphs that are missing from the rest of their lives, and thus athletics are of great importance to them.

From the point of view of athletic objectives there is at least one very important thing that might well be accomplished as far as the emotional aspect of personality is concerned. That is, to develop in students an increased capacity to control their emotions, *both as participant and as spectators*, and thus contributing to the development of emotional maturity.

## Emotional Control

It could be said that the major difference between you and some criminals confined to prison is that you have the ability to control you emotional impulses to a greater degree than they. Perhaps all of us at one time or another have experienced the same kinds of emotions that have led the abnormal individual to commit violence, but we have been able to hold our powerful and violent emotions in check. This may be an extreme example but it should suggest something of the importance of emotional control in modern society.

It would appear that a reasonable and natural objective of athletics should be to help participants increase their capacity to handle and control their emotions. The thoughtful coach is aware of educational opportunities offered in athletic situations for people, both participants and spectators, to learn to deal with their emotional arousals in *socially acceptable ways*. He or she can try to guide students in such a way that they learn to take pride in their ability to restrain themselves when necessary in order to abide by the rules of fair play and to behave like reasonable and decent human beings. The coach has real emotionally charged situations with which to work in order to teach young people to deal with strong emotions. Unfortunately, it cannot be said unequivocally that all coaches are taking very great advantage of an excellent opportunity. For example, one of my studies concerning spectator problems in high schools indicated that the behavior of the coach during games is one of the main things that determines how spectators behave.

Another aspect of controlling the emotions is becoming able to function effectively and intelligently in an emotionally charged situation. Athletic success hinges upon this ability as does success in many other life situations. Extremes of emotional upset must be avoided if the individual is to be able to think and act effectively. In athletic situations young people should learn that if they immediately put their minds to work on other things, such as team strategy, they can then control their emotions.

It is sometimes helpful to visualize your emotions as being forces within you which are in a struggle for power with your mind as to which is to control you, your reason or your emotions. Often times our basic emotions are blind and unconcerned with the welfare of other people or sometimes even with our own welfare. Emotional maturity has to do with gaining increased mastery over our emotions – not, of course, eliminating them – so that we may behave as intelligent and civilized human beings rather than as savages or children in temper tantrums.

In summarizing emotional objectives of athletics, it could be said that these objectives should imply that sympathetic guidance should be provided in meeting anxieties, joys, and sorrows, and help given in developing aspirations, affections, and security.

## THE INTELLECTUAL ASPECT OF PERSONALITY

The word intelligence is derived from the Latin word *intellectus* which literally means the "power of knowing." One general description of its is the capacity to learn or understand.

Individuals possess varying degrees of intelligence, with most people falling within a range of what is called "normal" intelligence. In dealing with this aspect of personality we should perhaps give attention to what might be considered as some components of *intellectual fitness*. However, this is difficult to do. Because of the somewhat vague nature of intelligence, it is practically impossible to identify specific components of it: hence, we need to view intellectual fitness in a somewhat different manner.

For purposes of this discussion, I will consider intellectual fitness from two different, but closely related points of view. First, from a standpoint of intellectual *needs* and second, from a standpoint of how certain things *influence* intelligence. It might be said that if a person's intellectual needs are being met, then he or she is intellectually fit. From the second point of view, if we know how certain things *influence* intelligence then we might understand better how to contribute to intellectual fitness by improving upon some of these factors.

There appears to be some rather general agreement with regard to the intellectual needs of human beings. Among others, these needs include (1) a need for challenging experiences at the individual's level of ability, (2) a need for intellectually successful and satisfying experiences, (3) a need for the opportunity to solve problems, and (4) a need for the opportunity to participate in creative experiences instead of always having to conform.

Some of those factors which tend to influence intelligence are (1) health and physical condition, (2) emotional disturbance, and (3) certain social and economic factors.

When coaches have a realization of intellectual needs and factors influencing intelligence, perhaps then they can deal satisfactorily with student athletes in helping them in their intellectual pursuits.

## INTELLECTUAL OBJECTIVES

Of the contributions that athletics might make to the development of total personality, the one concerned with intellectual development has been subjected to a certain degree of criticism by some general educators. Close scrutiny of the possibilities of intellectual development through athletics reveals, however, that a very desirable contribution can be made through this medium. This belief is substantiated in part by the affirmations of such prominent philosophers as Plato, Locke, Rousseau, Pestalozzi, and numerous others. Plato's postulation that learning could take place better through play, Locke's thoughts of a sound mind and sound body, Rousseau's belief that everyone should receive plenty of wholesome physical activity early in life, and Pestalozzi's observations that students approach their studies with a greater amount of interest after engaging in enjoyable physical activity, have all contributed to the modern idea that athletics and intellectual development might well be closely associated.

In a well-coached athletic activity there are numerous opportunities to exercise judgment and resort to reflective thinking in the solution of various kinds of problems. In addition, individuals might acquire a knowledge of certain rules and regulations in various kinds of games. It is also essential for effective participation that individuals gain an understanding of the various fundamentals and strategy involved in the performance of athletic activities. Perhaps of more importance is the fact that all of the systems of perception are inherent in most athletic experiences. This means that these experiences provide for the improvement upon such perceptual-motor qualities as auditory and visual perception skills and kinesthetic and tactile perception skills.

In summary, there is no question that the development of a sound philosophy and the formulation of valid objectives is perhaps the most important aspect of a successful interscholastic athletic program.

# REFERENCE

Yin, Zemong and Ryska, Todd A., (1999), Reexamining the Roles of Interscholastic Sports Participation in Education, *Research Quarterly for Exercise and Sport,* March Supplement, p. A131.

Issues in Contemporary Athletics
Editor: James H. Humphrey, pp. 43-52

ISBN 1-59454-595-2
© 2007 Nova Science Publishers, Inc.

*Chapter 5*

# STRESS AMONG WOMEN COLLEGE COACHES AND THEIR ATHLETES

## *William W. Bowden\* and Deborah A. Yow\*\**

\*Strategic Management Associates, USA
\*\*University of Maryland, College Park, Maryland, USA

## ABSTRACT

The unprecedented popularity of women's athletics has been accompanied by the many problems associated with athletic programs. Not the least of these problems is the stress imposed upon women coaches and the athletes they coach. This paper takes into account the many stress-inducing factors in women's athletics including causes of such stress, the affect it has on coaches and athletes, as well as how they attempt to cope with this stress.

Stress is a highly individualized and often subjective perception and therefore raises at least two obvious questions with regard to stress in the female population. First, "Is there a commonality of stressors to which women are uniquely susceptible?" To this, the consensus is affirmative, as is the judgment that such stressors have multiplied in recent decades at a rate in excess of those of their male counterparts. This is attributed in large measure to pronounced changes in societal norms which have attended women's suffrage, the feminist movement, dramatic rates of divorce, increased geographical mobility, discontinuity in extended family relationships, and a steady influx of women into occupations and professions, previously the proprietary interest of males.

Second, "Do these stressors carry a price that is nondiscriminatory?" Among the negative consequences of such emphatic cultural transformations in the role of women have been disturbing qualitative and quantitative changes in illness patterns and increased incidence of life-threatening diseases. In fact, some recent evidence suggests that there are at least as many over-stressed women as men, and that women are beginning to suffer from a variety of traditionally male-related, stress-related disorders.

Without question, as the era of changing sex roles progresses, perceptions of stress responsiveness are changing as well. Since cultural factors do indeed influence perceptions of responsiveness, there seems to be little doubt that there would be a more homogeneous perception of stress reactions among males and females.

It is interesting to ponder the implications of this for women college coaches, and the athletes they coach, particularly if women use as a model men's athletic programs that have had intermingled degrees of success and failure over the years.

# STRESS AMONG WOMEN COLLEGE COACHES

In our quest for information, two of the populations that we studied in some detail were that of women college coaches and their athletes. We were able to obtain and assess firsthand information about women college coaches and their athletes regarding the factors (causes) that induce the most stress, its effect upon them, and how coaches and athletes attempt to cope with stress.

## Causes of Stress among Women Coaches

The causes of stress (stressors) identified by the women coaches were classifies as follows: (1) players, (2) coaching performance, (3) outside influences, (4) time, (5) associates, (6) public relations, and (7) finances.

### *Players*

Participants on athletic teams are the most important asset. Without the proper *material* (adequate player personnel), coaches would not be able to consistently produce competitively successful teams. But, many coaches are in the profession because of the personal satisfaction they derive from interacting with the young women with whom they are associated.

It is not uncommon for coaches to refer to team members and others closely associated with them as a "family." And, even though in most families the members love and respect one another, at the same time they can be stressful to one another. Players are frequently a significant stress inducing factor for coaches. In this classification (players) 86 percent of the coaches reported sources of stress. These stressors are identified in the following list of sub-classifications, with the descriptors paraphrased in the words of the coaches.

### Player Behavior and Attitude

This was a serious stressor for coaches as was evidenced by 40 percent of the player stressors in this category. The most stressful items for coaches were apathy and indifference; social problems, such as the need for drug testing; insubordination; dissension; selfishness; team conflict; not accepting responsibility for their own actions; lack of maturity; and players who do not have the best interest of the team.

### Recruiting

It is not surprising that 30 percent of player stressors are found in this category. Coaches were not only stressed by the general aspect of recruiting, but specific aspects were stated as failing to sign top athletes, not getting their quota of recruits, the last two days of recruiting, and rejecting people who expected to be recruited.

### Academic Performance of Players

This accounted for 15 percent of the player stressors. It is well known that numerous troubling and even scandalous incidents in college athletics have been related to academic issues. Among the stressors for coaches were players not interested in graduating; and cheating on examinations or otherwise receiving fraudulent grades.

## Player Performance

Fourteen percent of the stressors were in this category. Among the most important were players not performing to their potential; not getting the best effort or attitude from players; difficulty in motivating players to perform; excuses of players for not performing well; and the lack of dedication and commitment of players.

## Injuries

Coaches worry about injuries to players both in regard to the success of the team and their feelings and concern for their players. Six percent of the stressors were in this category.

Finally, it should be mentioned that the player-coach stress factor is a natural phenomenon. In most instances, the same sort of relationship prevails among most caretakers or custodians with persons who are in their charge.

## Coaching Performance

This category of stressors pertains to the performance of the coach. In this area, a notable 89 percent of the coaches reported sources of stress. This classification overlaps to some extent with performance of players, but for the most part involved coaches' feelings about their ability and performance. Coaches stated these examples of performance-related stressors: inability to produce consistently winning teams; frustration of not having practices which prepare for games; game-day performance; losing games that should have been won; not winning the big game; and losing games on chance factors beyond the coach's control.

## Outside Influences

Included here is any individual outside the immediate group of team members, coaches, and others who have a close-working relationship with the team (i.e., trainers, managers, and team physicians). A remarkable 50 percent of the coaches reported stressors in this classification. Included also were reactions of alumni/other fans; not being able to please administrators; officiating; hate mail; NCAA rules/policies; dealing with unqualified people; things controlled by others; unwarranted criticism; outside influences on athletes such as drugs and alcohol; and faculty members who do not accept the value of athletics in the total university program.

## Time

In most studies of occupational stress, well over one-fourth of the respondents cite factors related to time as serious causes of stress. Half of this number say that there is not enough time for planning and about one-third say that there is not enough time in the day to perform the job expected of them. Notably, 49 percent of the coaches reported stressors in this classification.

Such stressors included not having enough time for family; time to get everything done for players' needs; time and priority allocations; abundance of time-consuming travel required; and meeting deadlines.

## Associates

Success in any endeavor, coaching included, depends upon the cooperation of group members. In the present context, associates are identified as assistants to head coaches. It was surprising to find that 21 percent of the coaches reported this classification as a cause of stress.

Most coaches maintain firm control and good relationships in dealing with staff members, but according to our findings, this is clearly not always the case. In fact, one coach made this statement, "Much stress is created by groups within the staff itself." Selfishness is a key to stressful situations. The less selfishness within the staff, the less stressful situations are seen. The following were stated as most stressful in this category: getting personalities in the program to work together; unpleasant interpersonal staff relationships; treating conflicts among staff members; lack of communication with staff; staff placing recruits ahead of needs of the team; motives of associates; motivating staff; and hiring and maintaining a stable staff.

## Public Relations

Six percent of the coaches reported some aspect of public relations as being stressful. These stressors were misunderstanding by the media and public; lack of media understanding and printing of the truth; media innuendo; dealing with time demands of the media; being in public after losing a game; and boosters, alumni and fans who do not have a clue. Women coaches felt that generally they did not have enough media attention for their teams and this created stress for some.

## Finances

A majority of coaches feel that the financing of athletic programs is primarily the responsibility of others and only 10 percent of them reported this classification as a source of stress. A few coaches indicated they felt stress due to the lack of program funding.

## EFFECTS OF STRESS ON WOMEN COACHES

The effect that stress has on coaches can be classified into the following two major areas: (1) impact on physical health and (2) impact on mental/emotional health.

Forty five percent of the coaches perceived an impact on their physical health while more than half said stress impacted their mental/emotional health.

Physically, coaches experienced loss of sleep; influences on eating resulting in an upset stomach.

Regarding the effect on mental/emotional health, comments included, "Sometimes I have an emotional outburst against the team and I hate myself for it after it is over;" "I get terribly frustrated when I lose and it takes me too long to get over it;" and "It causes me to get angry with no really good reason for it."

Only about 10 percent of the coaches said stress did not bother them. They made such comments as, "Stress in coaching can be handled with a daily routine of spiritual nourishment;" "If you're organized and have a plan you should not be stressed;" and "I never feel any stress in coaching; however, maybe I experience it but don't know that I am experiencing it."

## COPING WITH STRESS

Stress-coping methods fall into coping behaviors and coping techniques.

## Coping Behaviors

We considered coping behaviors in terms of the extent to which coaches practiced certain *principles of living*. Regarding the coping behaviors inherent in the basic principles of living, the following results were apparent, showing percent of coaches practicing each principle.

*Principle*: *Practicing good personal health habits* – 45 percent.
*Comment*: The imposing workload of coaches may cause them to neglect the basic requirements that are essential to maintain an adequate functional health level. With 45 percent of the coaches abiding by this principle, this means that over half of them are neglectful of some aspect of their personal health.

*Principle*: *Learn to take one thing at a time – 67 percent.*
*Comment*: Some coaches are likely to put things off, especially if it is unpleasant, and as a consequence frustrations can build. An important solution to this for coaches is the practice of taking one problem at a time. Everyone is familiar with coaches who talk about "taking one game at a time." Budgeting time can also help eliminate serious worries related to time urgency and the feeling of "too much to do in too short a time."

*Principle*: *Learn to take things less seriously – 45 percent.*
*Comment*: Often a coach will take the loss of a game too seriously. It is important to remember this simple truism: A game that has been lost can never be won no matter how much a coach may fret or agonize over it. Those coaches who are able to keep the challenges of their profession and specific losses in perspective and to see the humorous side of various situations tend to look at a potentially stressful situation more objectively. This can assist in keeping stress levels lower.

*Principle*: *Do things for others – 42 percent.*
*Comment*: It can be stated that most coaches try to do a considerable amount on behalf of their players. That in itself, as well as other acts of assisting individuals in some way, can help to relieve coaches from stress. Generally, this is a principle of human nature.

*Principle: Talk things over with others – 78 percent.*

*Comment*: One coach commented it could be a good idea for coaches to get together in order to have a dialogue about the stressful conditions of the profession. It is important to keep in mind such discussions should be positive and objective. However, there is value in simply venting frustrations or fears regarding challenges, problems and issues with family members or close friends in whom they have confidence.

## Coping Techniques

Coaches were asked to identify those techniques they used in attempting to deal with stress. Three techniques that are specifically used for inducing the relaxation response are *muscle relaxation* - 18 percent; *meditation* - two percent; and *biofeedback* – less than one percent. They also used the techniques of *physical exercise, recreational activities, turning to divine guidance*, and *consumption of alcoholic beverages*.

Ninety one percent of the coaches engaged in physical exercise; however, the majority said it was done sporadically. Thirty six percent of the respondents said they engaged in recreational activities, including reading, card games, and listening to music. Slightly more than half of the coaches turned to divine guidance. Eight percent of the coaches said they used alcohol with some regularity in an attempt to cope with stress.

Simply stated, individuals dealing with the problems of stress differ, techniques for dealing with stress differ and what might be successful for one person might not be necessarily so for another.

We have presented in some depth the stressors that challenge women college coaches, the results or effects of these stressing factors and the ways in which women college coaches attempt to cope with stress in their professional experience. The findings are interesting and compelling – and indicate the prevalence of mild to serious stress among women who coach college athletic teams.

## STRESS AMONG FEMALE COLLEGE ATHLETES

As the era of changing sex roles progresses, perceptions of stress responsiveness are changing as well. As stated earlier, since cultural factors do indeed influence perceptions of responsiveness, there seems to be little doubt that there would be a more homogeneous perception of stress reactions among young men and women. It is interesting to ponder the implications of this for female college athletes.

## Causes of Stress among Female College Athletes

Factors that induce stress are likely to be both general and specific in nature. This means that certain major life events can be stress inducing. Also, in our day-to-day environments (daily hassles), many specific concerns can elevate undesirable stress levels. In addition, causes of stress may be peculiar to certain populations – in this case female college athletes.

Our responses to causes of stress from female college athletes were classified as: (1) academic problems, (2) athletic demands, (3) time, (4) relationships with others, and (5) finances.

In the area of *academic problems*, 86 percent of the female athletes were stressed by such factors as tests and examinations, preparing papers for classes, missing classes because of travel to athletic events, and making up missed assignments. One of the foremost stressors in this classification was the tests that students are required to take in the various subject areas – specifically, the preparation for those tests in the context of their physically and emotionally demanding sports practices and competitions.

Also test anxiety is a significant factor for all students, including student-athletes. In this regard it is interesting to note that there is now an area of extensive psychological study known as *test anxiety*. Among other things, educators are attempting to determine what the nature and scope of test anxiety implies for educational goals and practice.

For student-athletes, the time and the physical and mental energy needed to prepare for tests as well as other academic requirements were frequently cited as a serious problem for them because of the demands of their sport.

With regard to *athletic demands*, 60 percent of the female athletes reported such demands as stress inducing. By far the greatest stressor for athletes was the pressure for them to win. Other stressors cited were exhausting and stressful practice sessions and distant travel to athletic contests.

Various factors related to *time* were serious causes of stress for well over half of female athletes. Many said they were put under stress because of insufficient time for planning. Most of the respondents felt that there was not enough time to combine academics and athletics and to do their best in both areas.

Seven percent of the female athletes were stressed by *relationships with others*. Included here were negative and unsatisfactory relationships with teachers, coaches and fellow athletes.

Finally, seven percent of female athletes contended that *finances* (or lack thereof) was a stressful concern. Practically all of these respondents were athletes who were not recipients of athletic grants.

## Effects of Stress

It has been clearly established that stress can result in many serious health problems. This is especially true of prolonged and unrelenting stress that becomes chronic. Although not all young female athletes are immediately at risk for serious stress-related conditions, there is some evidence that they could be affected in some way later in life. Also, we are all well aware of some older adults who have vivid memories of a poor athletic performance that they have recalled and which has troubled them for years – and therefore has created stress for them over time.

Based upon the survey results, we have identified effects of stress among female athletes as follows: (1) impact on mental/emotional health, (2) impact on physical health, (3) negative impact on athletic performance, and (4) negative impact on academic performance.

Slightly more than half of the female athletes said that stress affected their *mental/emotional health*. They cited such factors as outbursts of anger, pressure to win, excessive anxiety, frustration, conflict, irritation and fear.

As far as impact on *physical health* was concerned, about one in five of the female athletes mentioned such factors as not enough sleep, continuous tension, fatigue, headaches, and digestive problems.

Five percent of female athletes said that stress negatively influenced *athletic performance*, mainly in terms of tension and being overanxious before and during participation. This was described as being "uptight" or "too tight."

Fourteen percent of female athletes reported that stress was a negative impact on *academic performance*. They identified such factors as lower grades and not acquiring needed information as a result of missing classes because of team travel.

An unexpected, but encouraging finding, was that stress had a positive influence on some of the female athletes. Nine percent of them indicated that they found stress to be a motivational factor. Also, one-fifth of them reported that they felt no ill effects from stress. However, some respondents suggested that a negative effect might have been present, but that they might not have been aware of it.

## Coping with Stress

As in the case of women coaches, we divided coping procedures into the two major areas of coping behaviors and coping techniques.

### Coping Behaviors

As mentioned previously, we considered behavior as anything that the human body does as a result of some sort of stimulus. We asked college female athletes to respond to the same principles of living as the women coaches. The percent of female athletes who reported that they engaged in these behaviors is shown following each principle.

*Principle*: *Practice good health habits* – 60 percent.
*Comment*: This is an easy principle to accept, but sometimes it is difficult to implement. This should not be difficult for female athletes, at least in season, since they are expected to "keep in training" with regard to healthful nutrition, sleep habits, conditioning, and other factors. However, off-season behavior could differ markedly. A significant percentage of female athletes indicated that this principle of practicing good health habits was an important way in which they coped with stress.

*Principle*: *Learn to recognize your own accomplishments* – 33 percent.
*Comment*: The college female athletes in the survey indicated that this life principle was helpful in managing stress when used sensibly.

*Principle*: *Learn to take one thing at a time* – 72 percent.
*Comment*: As previously stated, the time factor can be stress inducing for student-athletes. Tasks need to be sorted out in order of importance and attacked one at a time.

*Principle*: *Learn to take things less seriously* – 44 percent.
*Comment*: The female athletes did not mean that schoolwork and athletics should not be taken seriously. They clearly understood that a fine line exists between what we sometimes deem to be serious or preeminently important, but may not be so. Sometimes when people look back at an event, they may wonder how they could have become so concerned about it. Many female athletes indicated that they were attempting to keep these issues in balanced perspective in order to cope with stress.

*Principle*: *Do things for others* – 49 percent.

*Comment*: A significant number of female athletes indicated that they found this to be a healthy principle in dealing with stress.

*Principle*: *Talk things over with others* – 58 percent.

*Comment*: Many of the athletes found that discussing their problems with teammates and others helped them cope with their own problems.

## Coping Techniques

Surveys of various populations show that people use a variety of techniques to cope with stress. This was also true of the female college athletes in our survey, as follows.

Three-fourths of the female athletes engaged in *physical exercise* as a means of coping. This included exercise activities other than those required in athletic participation.

*Recreational activities* were used as coping techniques, with 63 percent of the female athletes engaging in such activities as reading, card playing, table games, video games, and other similar activities.

For several years the technique of *muscle relaxation* has been one of the most important stress reducers. Indeed, about one-fourth of the female athletes practiced this procedure.

About 15 percent of female athletes engaged in *meditation* while less than two percent used *biofeedback*. The latter technique has met with a great deal of success in reducing many stressful conditions. Perhaps its lack of use among college female athletes is due to their unfamiliarity with this technique.

About 14 percent of the athletes indicated a personal faith and the belief in some form of *divine guidance*. This included prayer as well as reading various forms of religious literature such as the Bible, Talmud, or Koran for peace of mind and stress management.

Finally, a very disturbing finding was revealed in the use of *alcoholic beverages* as a means of coping with stress. More than one-third of the female athletes engaged in this practice regularly.

In this regard, recent studies show that drinking among college athletes as well as the general student population has increased dramatically in recent years. In fact, it has become one of the most challenging situations for college officials who try to deal with this increasing problem. One relevant question is: "Does regular drinking of alcoholic beverages *reduce* or *induce* stress?" Some studies suggest that acute or chronic exposure to low doses of alcohol actually induce the stress response by stimulating hormones released by the hypothalamus, pituitary, and adrenal glands. In addition to the hormone stress response, chronic exposure to alcohol also results in an increased adrenaline release into the circulatory system along with other mood-altering and physiological results. The regular or chronic use of alcohol by young adults has serious negative implications for the individual practicing this technique.

In conclusion, we have profiled the causes, effects, and coping strategies of women college coaches as well as the female college athletes, related to stress in their athletic experience. We repeat that the findings are interesting and compelling and include the fact that there is a prevalence of mild to serious stress among women college coaches and those they coach.

Issues in Contemporary Athletics
Editor: James H. Humphrey, pp. 53-72

ISBN 1-59454-595-2

*Chapter 6*

# IMPACTING ATHLETIC DEPARTMENT EFFECTIVENESS THROUGH HUMAN RESOURCE MANAGEMENT: A MULTI-LEVEL MODEL AND REVIEW OF PRACTICES

*Marlene A. Dixon\*, Raymond Noe\*\* and Donna L. Pastore\*\**

\*Rice University, Houston, Texas, USA
\*\*The Ohio State University, Athens, Ohio, USA

## ABSTRACT

As restraints are imposed, administrators within non-profit organizations, including universities and their individual departments, must make the most efficient and effective use of the resources at their disposal. The effective management of human resources, in particular, consistently has been linked to the performance and even survival of organizations in a variety of industries including banking, manufacturing, and industrial products. The purpose of this paper is first, to review previous models of the relationship between HRM and OE and second, to propose a measurement model that overcomes noted limitations of the previous models. The third purpose is to review and provide a rationale for best human resource practices that should be included in research regarding non-profit sport settings. Finally, directions for future research, extensions of the model, and practical implications are discussed.

## IMPACTING ATHLETIC DEPARTMENT EFFECTIVENESS THROUGH HUMAN RESOURCE MANAGEMENT: A MULTI-LEVEL MODEL

Non-profit organizations are increasingly concerned with the performance and effectiveness of their organizations (Bozzo, 2000; Fine, Thayer and Coghlan, 2000). Universities, operating as non-profit institutions, share this concern (Millet, 1998). They are asked by the public, their governing boards, students, parents, and/or faculty to demonstrate the effectiveness not only of their academic programs but also their extra-curricular activities including athletics (Trail and Chelladurai, 2000). Furthermore, economic constraints and concern with the rising costs of education force administrators to tightly control their operating budgets. As limits are imposed, administrators must make the most efficient and effective use of the resources at their disposal.

Individual departments, such as athletics, must also be concerned with producing quality outputs. This concern reaches beyond individual coach and team performance to the overall effectiveness of the athletic department—including fiscal responsibility, conference, and national competitiveness, and academic progress (Wolfe, Hill, and Babiak, 2000). However, athletic departments, like the universities in which they are housed, do not have unlimited resources at their disposal in order to produce these outcomes. They must make the most efficient use of the resources available to them. This argument is particularly valid at the National Collegiate Athletic Association (NCAA) Division III level, where departments do not have access to the financial revenues from television, athletic companies, or extensive ticket sales that are available to professional sports or NCAA Division I schools. Thus, at a very broad level, the problem faced by athletic directors at this level is: given limited resources, how can those resources best be managed to achieve optimal organizational effectiveness?

The effective management of human resources, in particular, consistently has been linked to the performance and even survival of organizations in a variety of industries including banking, manufacturing, and industrial products (Arthur, 1994; Becker and Gerhart, 1996; Becker and Huselid, 1998; Delaney, 1996; Delaney, Lewin, and Ichniowski, 1989; Doherty, 1998; Gerhart, 1999; Huselid, 1995; Huselid et al., 1997; Ichniowski, Shaw, and Prennushi, 1997; MacDuffie, 1995; Thompson, 1967; Welbourne and Andrews, 1996). For example, firms have increased employee satisfaction, decreased turnover, and improved productivity with the implementation of high performance human resource management (HRM) practices and systems. In the realm of athletic administration, Doherty (1998) conducted a review of the literature regarding organizational behavior and HRM. She reported that human resource practices such as job design, staffing, personnel evaluation, leader behavior, power, and conflict resolution have been linked to both affective (satisfaction, commitment, and motivation) and behavioral (turnover and productivity) outcomes in sport settings.

Although some work related to sport and athletics has been conducted in this area, Doherty (1998) maintained that much work remains. She commented,

> It would seem that we know relatively little about organizational effectiveness (OE), including the contribution of human resources. The importance of human resources to OE is implied by a few studies that found little or no effect of leader behaviour on OE, without taking into account the intervening attitudes and behaviours of individuals and groups" (Doherty, 1998, p.18).

In particular, she suggested three important limitations. First, the athletic administration literature has been limited in the number of human resource practices that have been investigated (e.g., job design, leader behavior). Little is known about other important human resource functions such as training and development, compensation, rewards, and performance evaluations. Furthermore, the studies that have been conducted have focused on one or two HRM practices within an athletic organization, ignoring the systems perspective of HRM. That is, studying individual HRM practices in isolation ignores the relationship between practices such as compensation and performance management (Huselid, 1985). Second, more work should be conducted at different levels of analyses. For example, most of the studies regarding job satisfaction have focused on athletic directors at the exclusion of coaches or other departmental staff. Third, more work is necessary at the outcome level. We know relatively little about *how* HRM systems affect outcomes (Ferris et al., 1998). In other words, the link between intermediate and organizational outcomes must be more clearly explored (Kozlowski and Klein, 2000). Managers of non-profit sport related organizations would benefit from research regarding the potential performance gains associated with more sophisticated HRM systems, and explanations of the potential relationships between individual and organizational level outcomes.

While much research exists concerning the conceptual and empirical relationship of various human resource management practices to individual and organizational level outcomes (e.g., Becker and Gerhart, 1996; Becker and Huselid, 1998; Gerhart, Wright, McMahan, and Snell, 2000; Huselid, 1995; Huselid and Becker, 2000; Snell, Youndt and Wright, 1996; Wright and McMahan, 1992), the need for a comprehensive framework integrating the multiple levels and perspectives is certainly evident. This paper has three purposes. The first purpose is to review previous models of the relationship between HRM and OE. Second, the paper proposes a measurement model that overcomes the limitations of previous models. The proposed model takes into account the findings from athletic administration and industrial and organizational psychology, and integrates them into a usable measurement model for a non-profit sport/athletic context. Third, the paper provides a rationale for best in class human resource practices that should be included in future research in non-profit sport settings. Finally, implications and directions for further research are discussed.

## PREVIOUS MODELS OF THE HRM-OE RELATIONSHIP

### Doherty's Model of HRM in Sport

Doherty (1998) proposed a model for HRM in sport organizations (see Figure 1). The author argued that the organization's goals, structure, resources, and culture affect and determine the organizational processes (e.g., internal services, day-to-day operations). These processes interact with individual attributes (values, needs, personality) and group attributes (composition, norms) to form the internal work environment. This internal environment is important to human resource managers because the management practices utilized within this environment influence how individuals and groups interact to create critical work outcomes. For example, Li (1993) found that job influence, incentive system, and leader behavior were significant predictors of job satisfaction and job performance of volunteer coaches. Another study found compensation and job position to be related to job satisfaction in collegiate sport marketers (Barr, McDonald, and Sutton, 2000). Further, leader behavior and job design may influence group composition and productivity (Doherty, 1998).

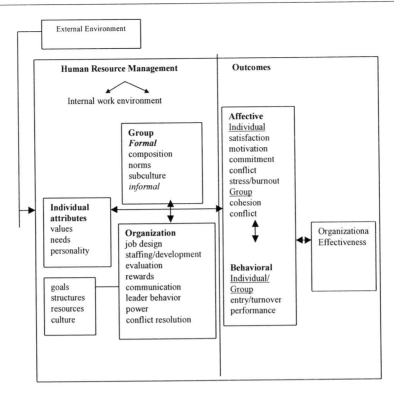

Figure 1: Doherty's (1998) Model of Managing Human Resources in Sport Organizations

At the outcome level, Doherty (1998) suggested that individual outcomes include attitudes and behaviors such as job satisfaction, motivation, commitment, turnover, and performance. Group outcomes include cohesion, conflict, turnover, and performance. Both individual and group level outcomes mediate the relationship between the internal work environment and organizational effectiveness. Doherty (1998) suggests that, HRM practices work to shape individual and group attitudes such that they contribute to organizational effectiveness. While she maintained that the individual and group processes interact, she did not specify how they are distinguished from each other, or whether individual processes or group processes contributed more to organizational effectiveness. Further, she did not include a direct relationship between HRM practices and organizational effectiveness; all organizational level outcomes are mediated by individual attitudes and behaviors. The lack of a direct relationship is consistent with findings in sport settings that enhanced processes affect individual but not organizational outcomes (Chelladurai and Haggerty, 1991). It is also consistent with previous conceptualizations of organizational effectiveness in sport where satisfaction and performance of individuals were considered indicators of organizational effectiveness (Li, 1993).

Doherty's (1998) model and review of the literature are certainly comprehensive and contribute to our understanding of the HRM—OE relationship. There are several notable strengths to the model. First, it demonstrates that in sport management research the relationship between HRM and individual outcomes is fairly well established (e.g., Cleave, 1993; Koehler, 1988; Li, 1993; Wallace and Weese, 1995). Second, it includes several processes and interactions, thereby acknowledging the complexity of the HRM—OE relationship. Third, it accounts for individual level and group outcomes as mediators of the HRM—OE relationship. Fourth, it accounts for the organizational context as a potential influence on the internal work environment.

Despite these attributes, there are several potential limitations of the model. First, it does not seem to distinguish between HRM practices and systems. The implication of the model is that the emphasis is on practices, although neither position is necessarily advocated. Second, the model contains many interactions, which make the model difficult to test in its present form. Third, the model has not yet been tested empirically.

While Doherty's model represents a solid starting point for understanding human resource management in athletic organizations, the literature in this area remains incomplete. Specifically, there is a dearth of empirical support for the relationship between: a) individual level and organizational level outcomes (e.g., Chelladurai and Haggerty, 1991), and b) HRM and organizational level outcomes that are measured at the organizational level (e.g., Li, 1993). Below, the authors propose a multi-level model for the HRM-OE relationship in sports organization based on sports and athletic administration research as well as studies conducted in management and industrial/organizational psychology.

## PROPOSED MODEL: A MULTI-LEVEL MODEL FOR THE HRM-OE RELATIONSHIP IN SPORT ORGANIZATIONS

Within the Industrial and Organizational Psychology literature, Ostroff and Bowen (2000) have provided an example of a multi-level model that includes specific pathways for individual, group, and direct level effects on organizational behavior that supplements some of the weaknesses found in the sport and physical activity literature. The following section contains a review of Ostroff and Bowen's (2000) model with a comparison to Doherty's (1998) model, and presents a conceptual multi-level model for sport/athletic organizations based on the integration of the two models (see Figure 2).

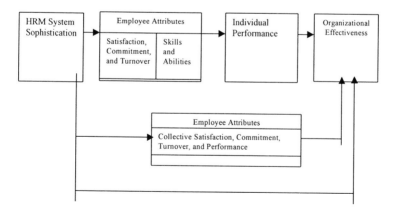

Figure 2: A Multilevel Model of HRM Systems and Organizational Effectiveness in Non-Profit Sport Organizations

Briefly, Ostroff and Bowen (2000) argue that at the individual level HRM systems work to change individual attitudes and behaviors such as satisfaction, commitment, turnover, and performance. These behaviors then lead to increased individual performance, which contributes to the overall performance of the organization. At the group level, HRM systems create a collective atmosphere whereby individuals working under the same system will display similar attitudes and values. These collective attitudes and behaviors influence performance of the firm. At the organizational level, HRM systems create process efficiencies and operational structures that directly enhance organizational effectiveness.

## Systems vs. Individual Practices

One major difference between the two HRM models is the emphasis on individual HRM practices versus HRM systems. Doherty (1998) implied an emphasis on individual practices, while Ostroff and Bowen (2000) embraced a systems perspective. In the HRM literature, there is considerable debate regarding whether individual practices (Delery and Doty, 1996) or overall systems (Arthur, 1994; Becker and Huselid, 1998; Huselid, 1995; Ichniowski et al., 1997; MacDuffie, 1995) contribute more to organizational effectiveness. Becker and Huselid (1998) provide an excellent overview of this problem. They contend that while assessing the effects of individual practices adds some insight, testing these individual effects apart from the entire system may lead to erroneous conclusions for two reasons. First, focusing on a single practice may overestimate its impact on the outcomes (Huselid, 1995). Second, the entire system of practices would be a stronger indicator of an investment in human capital. This overall investment would more likely be a source of competitive advantage for firms than would use of any individual practice. They explained,

> The overwhelming preference in this literature has been for a unitary index that contains a set (though not always the same set) of theoretically appropriate HRM practices derived from prior work. . . . While not without its limitations, we agree with the extant practice in the empirical literature that an index derived from the prior empirical work is the more appropriate measure of the HRM system. First, a single index reflects the notion of a single HRM system as a strategic asset. Second, since the typical index is a summation of individual element of the HRM system, it implies that within the broad middle range of the index there are multiple ways to increase its value (Becker and Huselid, 1998, p. 63).

In other words, practitioners can still focus on adding or improving individual HRM practices within the index, but the research does not purport to suggest which items would add the most value. While practitioners may be interested in what specific practices would enhance performance the most, it is inappropriate to suggest effects that are overestimated due to measurement error.

Instead, Becker and Huselid (1998) argued for an additive or "sophistication" approach, whereby performance could be predicted on the basis of how many practices were used and how broadly they were implemented. More sophisticated systems are those where more high performance work practices are utilized or the practices are implemented across a greater percentage of the workforce. More sophisticated systems lead to better performance (Delaney et al., 1989). The proposed multi-level model for sport organizations in the current study also adopts this perspective whereby HRM practices are not viewed as separable, but as part of a complete HRM framework. The practices work in concert to add to the sophistication level of the entire system, thereby enhancing performance. The more HR practices implemented, the higher the sophistication level and the better the performance, regardless of HRM system type (and regardless of external fit).

## Organizational Context: Universalistic vs. Fit approaches

Another issue that is addressed in both the business and sport models is that of organizational context. Both the Ostroff and Brown and Doherty models proposed that the context is necessary for understanding the HRM—OE relationship. In the industrial and organizational psychology literature, three main theoretical perspectives (i.e., contingency, configurational, and universalistic) have been proposed to explain differences in HRM and performance. The first is a contingency, or external fit approach. This approach suggests that firms will achieve higher performance gains if they match their HRM practices with their overall strategy (Delery and Doty, 1996). Some, albeit limited, support has been demonstrated for this perspective (Wright and Sherman, 1999). For example, Delery and Doty (1996) found that participation, results-oriented appraisals, and internal career opportunities all explain significant variation in performance when matched with organizational strategy. Huselid (1995) found some significant gains when strategies and practices were matched. However, these gains showed no incremental validity over the basic use of high performance work practices.

In other words, different firms may adopt different practices according to their strategy. A firm focused on growth may rely heavily on high performance staffing practices, whereas a firm focused on stability may rely heavily on performance incentives and voice mechanisms (which enhance retention). Both firms, while adopting different practices and strategies, could have equally sophisticated HRM systems, and could be performing equally well. Thus, as suggested by Huselid (1995), matching practices and strategy may be valuable in a prescriptive sense (i.e., informing managers as to which high performance practices they may want to consider adding in their specific organizational context to enhance performance). From an HRM system standpoint, however, it is not specific practices and/or strategy, but an overall sophisticated system (regardless of strategy) that leads to high performance.

The second approach is a configurational, or internal fit approach. This approach suggests that firms whose HRM practices fit together into appropriate bundles or systems will achieve higher performance gains (Delery and Doty, 1996). For example, Huselid (1995) found a link between systems of thirteen practices and organizational performance, including financial performance, in a wide variety of industries. Delery and Doty (1996) however, found that individual practices explained more variance in outcomes than either system utilized in their study. Becker and Gerhart (1996) suggested that firms may first need to adopt and develop some best practices, then they can combine practices into systems to achieve additional performance gains or competitive advantage. Becker and Huselid (1998), while finding considerable support for an overall systems approach, were unable to find "bundles" or individual configurations of practices that predicted performance better than others.

Configurational systems can also be extended to the strategic level where the entire system of HRM practices must fit with the organizational strategy to achieve desired performance gains. This perspective initially received considerable attention and support. For example, Arthur (1994) found that firms with commitment systems had higher performance than those with control systems. MacDuffie (1995) also found that flexible, "high commitment" systems showed greater performance than more rigid, control systems. Most studies, however, (e.g., Becker and Huselid, 1998; Delery and Doty, 1996; Huselid, 1995) have failed to confirm the link between matching the HR system with overall organizational strategy, leading most reviewers (Becker and Gerhart, 1996; Becker and Huselid, 1998; McMahan, Virick, and Wright, 1999; Wright and McMahan, 1992; Wright and Sherman, 1999) to argue that support for the configurational approach matching HR practices to the firm's strategy is weak.

The third approach is the universalistic or best practices approach. This approach suggests that certain HRM practices should be designated as best practices and will improve organizational performance regardless of the firm's strategy or other HR practices (Delery and Doty, 1996). This approach has consistently received the most support (Delery and Doty, 1996; Huselid, 1995; Pfeffer, 1994). For example, certain best staffing practices (Terpstra and

Rozell, 1993) and compensation policies (Gerhart and Milkovich, 1990) repeatedly have been linked to financial performance. Huselid (1995) and Becker and Huselid (1996, 1998) through numerous studies on a variety of industries found that the utilization of high performance practices explained more variance than fitting those practices externally or internally.

Because of the strong, consistent support for the universalistic/best practices approach, the proposed model for sport/athletic organizations also adopts that perspective. Following the universalistic/best practices approach and the concept of HRM sophistication, the proposed model does not include strategy or HRM strength as moderators of the HRM—OE relationship. While acknowledging that different firms will adopt different configurations of practices according to such factors as their size, strategy, or life cycle, the proposed model emphasizes only the overall sophistication of the HRM system. In contrast to both of the previous models, the proposed model is only concerned with how many practices are utilized, not configurations of practices or the fit of the practices with organizational strategy.

## Three Potential Pathways

Another critical area of difference between the Ostoff and Brown (2000) and Doherty (1998) models relates to the path between HRM and OE. That is, does the process work at the individual, group, or organizational level, or can it work at multiple levels? Doherty's (1998) model suggests that satisfaction, commitment, motivation, conflict, and burnout exist at the individual level and that cohesion and conflict exist at the group level. However, turnover and performance both can be conceptualized as either individual or group level outcomes (Ostroff and Bowen, 2000). Furthermore, Doherty (1998) maintained a fully mediated model whereby there is no direct relationship between HRM practices and organizational effectiveness, except through individual and/or group behavior (Baron and Kenney, 1986). This fully mediated model eliminates the possibility for enhanced process effectiveness, which could directly relate to organizational effectiveness. Ostroff and Bowen (2000), however, suggested that both a mediated relationship and a direct HRM—OE relationship exists through the enhancement of internal processes and work structures.

The proposed multi-level model for the HRM-OE relationship in sport organizations (see Figure 2) incorporates the multi-level perspective proposed by Ostroff and Bowen (2000). In the proposed multi-level athletic model, HRM systems operate on three levels to increase department effectiveness. In the first level, HRM systems influence individual attitudes and behaviors, such that individuals exposed to a more sophisticated HRM system will reflect more productive attitudes (such as satisfaction and commitment). Positive attitudes among coaches and administrators will translate into increased performance of these individuals. Increased individual performance will contribute to departmental effectiveness. In the second level or group pathway, HRM systems create collective organizational climates, whereby patterns of group-level outcomes can be identified between organizations with different HRM systems. In general, organizations with more sophisticated HRM systems will show superior group level attitudes and behaviors (such as increased satisfaction and commitment, and lower group turnover), which will lead to increased organizational effectiveness. For example, coaches who are evaluated and/or rewarded as a group, may feel a sense of solidarity that may lead to a greater commitment in the group and more cooperative behaviors. Finally, in the third level or pathway, HRM systems create efficient internal processes such that departments with more sophisticated HRM systems will be more effective than those with less sophisticated systems, regardless of individual or group level outcomes.

For example, quality selection systems may increase efficiency of the hiring process, such that less time is spent away from everyday administrative tasks, making the department or organization function more productively.

## Summary

A substantial body of evidence exists which suggests that HRM systems can affect not only individual performance (which leads to increased organizational effectiveness), but also group climate (such that individuals operating under one HRM system will feel and act differently than individuals operating under a different HRM system) and important task processes (such that departments who operate more efficiently will be more effective). The proposed conceptual model for HRM systems in sport settings (see Figure 2) includes the three pathways from Ostroff and Bowen (2000), yet eliminates strategy and context, which were included in both of the reviewed models.

# MEASUREMENT: BEST HUMAN RESOURCE MANAGEMENT PRACTICES

In order to move the proposed model from its theoretical to practical uses, appropriate HRM practices must be specified. The following section proposes these, with regard to the unique nature of athletic departments at the Division III level (although applications of the model need not be limited to this specific setting). Again, these organizations are selected since the focus of this model is on the relationship of HRM to OE in the non-profit sector. Even though much emphasis is placed on professional and Division I level athletics in the media and in sport management literature, nearly twice as many schools compete at the Division III level (compared to Division I), which indicates a need for investigation there, not simply the elite levels of sport. Further, these departments more closely match the resource structure of other non-profit organizations such as high school athletics, kinesiology departments, and participant sport organizations, thus making possible much broader applications of the model.

## HRM System

Schuler and Jackson (1987) suggested that the critical areas of HRM are 1) planning, 2) staffing, 3) training and development, 4) compensation, and 5) evaluation. In addition, a number of researchers (Osterman; 1994; Pfeffer, 1994; Welbourne and Andrews, 1996) have suggested that the overall philosophy is important to firm performance. Appendix A lists the HRM practices utilized in ten key studies over the past seven years. The table provides an overview of the various operationalizations of each practice and gives examples of HR practices that fall under each of the categories suggested by Schuler and Jackson (1987) and Osterman (1994). More specifically, Becker and Huselid (1998) developed a 24-item index of HRM sophistication. Their index was derived from previous work and has shown considerable reliability (Cronbach's $\alpha = .75$) and predictive validity for firm performance across a number of industries. Using the categorization suggested by Schuler and Jackson (1987) and the specific index created by Becker and Huselid (1998), the following section describes each practice and reviews previous research that may add insight as to why it is related to organizational effectiveness.

## Overall Philosophy

Becker and Huselid (1998) included five items that could be regarded as overall HRM philosophy. These are: 1) the proportion of the workforce that is promoted due to merit versus seniority, 2) the number of jobs filled internally, 3) the proportion of the workforce included in information sharing, 4) the proportion of the workforce included in quality of life circles, and 5) the proportion who has access to formal grievance procedures. Virtually every study (in Appendix A) also examined these practices. Although their use may vary, these practices, with the exception of quality circles, are certainly applicable in athletic departments.

The overall HR philosophy relates to the idea that higher commitment from the employer will lead to higher commitment from the employee (Arthur, 1994; MacDuffie, 1995; Mowday, 1998). Because they are committed to the organization, the employees, in turn, are trusted to use their knowledge, skills, and abilities to achieve organizational goals. Further, higher commitment is often related to reduced turnover and the presence of extra-role behaviors that may enhance employee performance. Thus, practices that demonstrate the organization has a high commitment to human resources will be related to both individual and firm level outcomes (Arthur, 1994; Delery and Doty, 1996; MacDuffie, 1995).

## Planning

The two items contained in Becker and Huselid (1998) related to planning are: 1) the proportion of the workforce included in a formal written plan, and 2) the proportion of jobs that have been subjected to a formal job analysis. A job analysis, the gathering of information about a specific job, is critically important to effective HR functioning because it informs every other process what is required for that job (Noe et al., 2003). For example, the job analysis identifies the critical competencies needed for the job, and provides information regarding the level at which the competencies must be performed. This type of information is needed for both employee selection and performance management. While research has not specifically measured the impact of job analysis on performance of the firm, it is considered absolutely essential to effective development of human resource management practices.

A written plan specifies what employees are needed, what skills those employees will need, and how the human resources fit with the overall firm strategy. For example, coaches who implement recruiting plans that match the skills of the athletes to their preferred strategy, have demonstrated higher effectiveness than coaches who do not match the skills (Wright et al., 1995). Often, organizations will also utilize succession planning, targeting individuals to fill key roles pending the departure of current key employees. Considering the frequent movement of coaches from one organization to another, the importance of succession planning is apparent.

## Staffing

The items related to staffing on the HRM index are: 1) selection ratios, and 2) the use of validated selection tests (Becker and Huselid, 1998). Huselid (1995) argued that "recruiting procedures that provide a large pool of qualified applicants, paired with a reliable and valid selection regimen, will have a substantial influence over the quality and type of skills new employees possess" (p. 637). This proposition has received support in the literature regarding firm-level outcomes. Terpstra and Rozell (1993) found that the use of five staffing practices was related to annual profit and profit growth across a number of industries. Specifically, the staffing practices were the use of: 1) follow-up studies of recruiting practices, 2) validation studies for selection tools, 3) structured, standardized interviews, 4) cognitive aptitude and ability tests, and 5) weighted application blanks or biographical information blanks. Interestingly, they found the strongest relationship between staffing practices and organizational performance in the service industry. This finding has direct relevance to the current study since athletic departments are definitely a part of that industry.

## Training and Development

Three items on the Becker and Huselid (1998) instrument directly relate to training and development: 1) hours of training for a first year employee, 2) hours of training for an experienced employee, and 3) the proportion of the workforce capable of performing more than one job. The role of training and development in organizational effectiveness is two-fold. First, training programs enhance employee skills and abilities such that they become more productive workers and the firm, in turn becomes more productive (Goldstein, 1990). For example, Bartel (1994) demonstrated that the implementation of formal training programs increased labor productivity in a variety of industries. Training and development also serve a latent function of communicating to employees (especially new ones) that they are valuable to the organization (Moreland and Levine, 2001). These employees, in turn, show a greater commitment to the organization. Participation in required training and development programs has been empirically linked to higher job satisfaction and organizational commitment (Birdi, Allan, and Warr, 1997).

The impact of training and development in athletic departments has yet to be investigated. However, based on the rationale in other organizations, it follows that training and development of coaches would enhance both their coaching skills (e.g., tactical, technical, recruiting) and their commitment to the organization.

## Compensation

Eight items on the Becker and Huselid (1998) scale fall under the category of compensation: 1) percentile comparison of salary levels, 2) the total compensation that is cash and bonuses, 3) the proportion eligible for cash incentive plans, 4) the proportion eligible for deferred incentive plans, 5) the proportion who would lose incentives based on company performance, 6) the proportion who would gain incentives based on company performance, 7) the percentage of a merit increase or decrease an employee could receive as a result of their performance review, and 8) the proportion who owns company stock shares.

Performance-based compensation has been linked to firm performance in a variety of industries (Banker, Lee, Potter and Srinivasan, 1996; Gerhart and Milkovich, 1990). Because athletic departments operate as non-profit entities, some of these practices are not applicable. Employees of non-profit organizations would not be eligible for gain-sharing plans, and universities do not offer stock. However, there are some athletic department employees who receive cash incentives based on winning their conference or post-season play. Furthermore, some employees receive compensation in the form of cars or country club memberships. Thus, while the items may be relevant, some would need to be reworded or deleted to be applicable in a non-profit setting.

## Evaluation/ Appraisal

Evaluation and appraisal can take place at both the individual and the departmental level. Three items relate to individual performance evaluation: 1) the proportion of the workforce that receives a regular formal performance appraisal, 2) the proportion that has merit or pay increases tied to their performance appraisals, and 3) if the basis for the performance appraisal is an objective measure. One additional item relates to departmental evaluation: the proportion of the workforce who regularly receives attitude surveys.

Delery and Doty (1996) demonstrated that results-oriented appraisals were positively related to firm performance. While no other studies have confirmed these specific results, work in the area of performance management has confirmed that the introduction of feedback systems (appraisals from multiple sources, or upward feedback from subordinates) is related to enhanced individual performance (e.g., Johnson and Ferstl, 1999; Smither et al., 1995; Walker and Smither, 1999) especially by those who were initially the lowest performers. Thus, the basic use of performance evaluations may enhance individual and overall firm performance and should be included in an HRM system.

Second, performance appraisals that include a voice mechanism for the person being rated may enhance perceptions of trust in the organization (Cropanzano and Greenberg, 1997; Greenberg, 1982), which may enhance satisfaction and commitment. Voice mechanisms may also serve to reduce negative employee behaviors such as absenteeism, theft, and turnover.

The use of performance appraisals works on two levels. They enhance employee productivity by holding employees accountable for their performance (Walker and Smither, 1999). They aid employees in seeing where their performance can be enhanced (Kluger and DeNisi, 1996; Walker and Smither, 1999), and they provide employees with a voice such that they feel more valued and appreciated in the organization. Little research has investigated the effects of performance appraisals that are used for development versus those used for administrative decisions (e.g., compensation). Therefore, an evaluation of the HRM system should contain both a general assessment of performance appraisal use, and an evaluation of its use for compensation decisions.

## CONCLUSION AND DIRECTIONS FOR FUTURE RESEARCH

The obvious next step in the research process is to test the model. The relationships described have been aimed at the Division III college level, although they certainly could be slightly altered for other contexts. The model could be utilized to answer research questions such as:

- Do HRM systems relate to individual satisfaction, commitment, tenure, and performance?
- Do HRM systems relate to group satisfaction, commitment, tenure, and performance?
- Do HRM systems relate to academic achievement?
- Do HRM systems relate to athletic achievement?
- Do individual and/or group level outcomes mediate the relationship between HRM systems and organizational effectiveness?

HRM sophistication has been consistently linked to enhanced organizational performance particularly in for-profit firms. This relationship is also expected to hold in non-profit organizations, especially those that rely heavily on human resources for their success and even survival. The proposed model shows how the HRM systems enhance organizational effectiveness.

While no definition or measurement of organizational effectiveness is universally adopted by organizational researchers (Forbes, 1998; Miles, 1980), researchers have maintained that it is the "ultimate dependent variable in organizational analysis" (Chelladurai, 2001, p.351) and that its difficulties did not diminish the usefulness or centrality of the concept in the study of organizational behavior. Others have suggested that effectiveness does not exist apart from the context of the organization, therefore, it should be defined and measured contextually not universally, even if doing so limits comparisons between studies (Becker and Gerhart, 1996; Ferris et al., 1998; Rogers and Wright, 1998). In other words, effectiveness measures need to fit the organizational purpose and the needs of important stakeholders (Ferris et al., 1998; Rogers and Wright, 1998). While no specific organizational effectiveness measures are offered in this review, researchers are encouraged to identify specific indicators that would be appropriate for their given context (see Trail and Chelladurai, 2000 for a review of organizational goals as they relate to specific organizational stakeholders).

For athletic directors, the study has practical implications regarding enhanced academic and athletic performance. An HRM index (such as Becker and Huselid, 1998) provides a useful tool for athletic directors to assess the sophistication level of their HRM system. If their sophistication level is low, they can address areas within the index that will improve their departmental performance. The HRM index does not imply what specific practices should be improved, but shows athletic directors a number of areas they can choose from to enhance performance.

If the model holds for athletic departments, further testing could demonstrate its usefulness in other sport and non-profit organizations. As a sport organization, Division III athletic departments operate similarly to other non-profit sport organizations such as the YMCA, recreation centers, the Special Olympics, and/or community youth sport programs. Given the appropriate measures of organizational effectiveness, the model could be applied quite broadly to a number of non-profit organizations, including universities and individual departments therein. Humans comprise an invaluable resource to service-oriented organizations. The effective systematic management of this resource can become a critical asset to enhanced performance not only in for-profit, but in non-profit organizations as well.

# REFERENCES

Arthur, J.B. (1994). Effects of human resource systems on manufacturing performance and turnover. *Academy of Management Journal, 37* (3), 670-687.

Banker, R.D., Lee, S., Potter, G., and Srinivasan, D. (1996). Contextual analysis of performance impact of outcome-based incentive compensation. *Academy of Management Journal, 39* (4), 920-948.

Baron, R.M., and Kenny, D.A. (1986). The moderator-mediator variable distinction in social psychological research: Conceptual, strategic, and statistical considerations. *Journal of Personality and Social Psychology, 51* (6), 1173-1182.

Barr, C.A., McDonald, M.A., and Sutton, W. A. (2000). Collegiate sport marketers: Job responsibilities and compensation structure. *International Sports Journal, 4*, 64-77.

Bartel, A.P. (1994). Productivity gains for the implementation of employee training programs. *Industrial Relations, 33* (4), 411-425.

Becker, B., and Gerhart, B. (1996). The impact of human resource management on organizational performance: Progress and prospects. *Academy of Management Journal, 39* (4), 779-801.

Becker, B. and Huselid, M.A. (1998). High performance work systems and firm performance: A synthesis of research and managerial implications. *Research in Personnel and Human Resources Management, 16*, 53-101.

Birdi, K., Allan, C., and Warr, P. (1997). Correlates and perceived outcomes of four types of employee development activity. *Journal of Applied Psychology, 82* (8), 845-857.

Bozzo, S.L. (2000). Evaluation resources for nonprofit organizations: Usefulness and Applicability. *Nonprofit Management and Leadership, 10*, 463-472.

Cameron, K. (1978). Measuring organizational effectiveness in institutions of higher education. *Administrative Science Quarterly, 33*, 604-623.

Cameron, K. (1981). Domains of organizational effectiveness in colleges and universities. *Academy of Management Journal, 24* (1), 25-47.

Chelladurai, P. (1985). *Sport Management: Macro Perspectives.* London, Ontario: Sports Dynamics.

Chelladurai, P. (1987). Multidimensionality and multiple perspectives of organizational effectiveness. *Journal of Sport Management, 1*, 37-47.

Chelladurai, P. (2001). *Managing Organizations for Sport and Physical Activity: A Systems Perspective.* Scottsdale, AZ: Holcomb and Hathaway.

Chelladurai, P. and Haggerty, T.R. (1991). Measures of organizational effectiveness of Canadian national sport organizations. *Canadian Journal of Sport Sciences, 16*, 126-133.

Chelladurai, P. Inglis, S., and Danylchuk, K.E. (1984). Priorities in intercollegiate athletics: Development of a scale. *Research Quarterly for Exercise and Sport, 55* (1), 74-79.

Cleave, S. (1993). A Test of the job characteristics model with administrative positions in physical education and sport. *Journal of Sport Management, 7*, 228-242.

Connolly, T., Conlon, E.J., and Deutsch, S.J. (1984). Organizational effectiveness: A multiple-constituency model. *Academy of Management Review, 5* (2), 211-217.

Cropanzano, R., and Greenberg, J. (1997). Progress in organizational justice: Tunneling through the maze. In C.L. Cooper and I.T. Robertson (Eds.), *International Review of Industrial and Organizational Psychology (Vol. 12, pp. 317-372).* London: John Wiley and Sons.

Delaney, J.T. (1996). Unions, human resource innovations, and organizational outcomes. *Advances in Industrial and Labor Relations, 7*, 207-245.

Delaney, J. T., Lewin, D., and Ichniowski, C. (1989). *Human Resource Policies and Practices in American Firms.* Washington, DC: U.S. Department of Labor; U.S. Government Printing Office.

Delery, J.E., and Doty, D.H. (1996). Modes of theorizing in strategic human resource management: Tests of universalistic, contingency, and configurational performance predictions. *Academy of Management Journal, 39* (4), 802-835.

Doherty, A.J. (1998). Managing our human resources: A Review of organizational behaviour in sport. *Sport Management Review, 1,* 1-24.

Etzioni, A. (1964). *Modern Organizations.* Englewood Cliffs, NJ: Prentice Hall.

Ferris, G.R., Arthur, M.M., Berkson, H.M., Kaplan, D.M., Harrell-Cook, G., and Frink, D.D. (1998). Toward a social context theory of the human resource management-organizational effectiveness relationship. *Human Resource Management Review, 8* (3), 235-264.

Fine, A.H., Thayer, C.E., and Coghlan, A.T. (2000). Program evaluation practice in the nonprofit sector. *Nonprofit Management and Leadership, 10,* 331-339.

Forbes, D.P. (1998). Measuring the unmeasurable: Empirical studies of nonprofit organizational effectiveness from 1977-1997. *Nonprofit and Voluntary Sector Quarterly, 27* (2), 183-202.

Gerhart, B. (1999). Human resource management and firm performance: Measurement issue and their effect on causal and policy inferences. *Research in Personnel and Human Resources Management, Supplement, 4,* 31-51.

Gerhart, B. and Milkovich, G.T. (1990). Organizational differences in managerial compensation and financial performance. *Academy of Management Journal, 33,* 663-691.

Gerhart, B. Wright, P.M., and McMahan, G.C. (2000). Measurement error in research on the human resources and firm performance relationship: Further evidence and analysis. *Personnel Psychology, 53,* 855-872.

Goldstein, I.L. (1990). Training in work organizations. In M.D. Dunnutte and L.M. Hough (Eds.), *Handbook of Industrial and Organizational Psychology,* (pp. 507-619). Palo Alto, CA: Consulting Psychologists Press.

Greenberg, J. (1982). Approaching equity and avoiding inequity in groups and organizations. In J. Greenberg and R.L. Cohen (Eds.), *Equity and Justice in Social Behavior (pp. 389-426).* New York: Academic Press.

Hall, R.H. (1996). *Organizations: Structures, Processes, and Outcomes.* Englewood Cliffs, NJ: Prentice Hall.

Herman, R.D., and Renz, D.O. (1997). Multiple constituencies and the social construction of nonprofit organizational effectiveness. *Nonprofit and Voluntary Sector Quarterly, 26* (2), 185-206.

Herman, R.D., and Renz, D.O. (1998). Nonprofit organizational effectiveness: Contrasts between especially effective and less effective organizations. *Nonprofit Management and Leadership, 9,* 23-38.

Herman, R.D., and Renz, D.O. (1999). Theses on nonprofit organizational effectiveness. *Nonprofit and Voluntary Sector Quarterly, 28* (2), 107-126.

Huselid, M. (1995). The impact of human resource management practice on turnover, productivity, and corporate financial performance. *Academy of Management Journal, 38,* 635-672.

Huselid, M., and Becker, B. E. (2000). Comment on "Measurement Error in Research on Human Resources and Firm Performance: How Much Error is There and How Does it

Infleuce Effect Size Estimates?" by Gerhart, Wright, McMahan, and Snell. *Personnel Psychology, 53,* 835-854.

Huselid, M., Jackson, S.E., and Schuler, R.S. (1997). Technical and strategic human resource management effectiveness as determinants of firm performance. *Academy of Management Journal, 40* (1), 171-188.

Ichniowski, C., Shaw, K., and Prennushi, G. (1997). The effects of human resource management practices on Productivity: A study of steel finishing lines. *American Economic Review,* 87, 291-313.

Johnson, J.W., and Ferstl, K.L. (1999). The effects of interrater and self-other agreement on performance improvement following upward feedback. *Personnel Psychology, 52,* 271-303.

Kluger, A.N., and DeNisi, A. (1996). The effects of feedback interventions on performance: A historical review, a meta-analysis, and a preliminary feedback intervention theory. *Psychological Bulletin, 119,* 254-284.

Koehler, L.S. (1988). Job satisfaction and corporate fitness manager: An Organizational behavior approach to sport management. *Journal of Sport Management, 2,* 100-105.

Kozlowski, S.W., and Klein, K.J. (2000). A Multilevel approach to theory and research in organizations: Contextual, temporal and emergent processes. In K.J. Klein and S.W. Kozlowski (Eds.), *Multilevel Theory, Research and Methods in Organizations* (pp. 3-90). San Francisco: Jossey-Bass.

Li, M. (1993). Job satisfaction and performance of coaches of the spare-time sports schools in China. *Journal of Sport Management, 7,* 132-140.

MacDuffie, J.P. (1995). Human resource bundles and manufacturing performance: Organizational logic and flexible production systems in the world auto industry. *Industrial and Labor Relations Review, 48* (2), 197-221.

McMahan, G.C., Virick, M., and Wright, P.M. (1999). Alternative theoretical perspective for strategic human resource management revisited: Progress, problems, and prospects. *Research in Personnel and Human Resources Management, Supplement, 4,* 99-122.

Miles, R.H. (1980). *Macro Organizational Behavior.* Santa Monica, CA: Goodyear.

Millet, J.D. (1998). Allocation decisions in higher education. *Report for The Academy for Educational Development.* Washington, DC: Academy for Educational Development, Inc.

Moreland, R.L., and Levine, J.M. (2001). Socialization in organizations and workgroups. In M. Turner (Ed.), *Groups at Work: Theory and Research* (pp.69-112). Mahwah, NJ: Earlbaum.

Mowday, R.T. (1998). Reflections on the study and relevance of organizational commitment. *Human Resource Management Review, 8,* 387-401.

Noe, R., Hollenbeck, J.R., Gerhart, B., and Wright, P.M. (2003). *Human Resource Management: Gaining a Competitive Advantage.* Burr Ridge, IL: Irwin McGraw-Hill. .

Osterman, P. (1994). How common is workplace transformation and who adopts it? *Industrial and Labor Relations Review, 47* (2), 173-188.

Ostroff, C., and Bowen, D.E. (2000). Moving HR to a higher level: HR practices and organizational effectiveness. In K.J. Klein and S.W. Kozlowski (Eds.), *Multilevel Theory, Research and Methods in Organizations* (pp. 211-266). San Francisco: Jossey-Bass.

Pfeffer, J. (1982). *Organizations and Organization Theory.* Boston: Pitman.

Pfeffer, J. (1994). *Competitive Advantage Through People.* Boston: Harvard Business School Press.

Putler, D.S., and Wolfe, R.A. (1999). Perceptions of intercollegiate athletic programs: Priorities and tradeoffs. *Sociology of Sport Journal, 16*, 301-325.

Quinn, R.E., and Rohrbaugh, J. (1983). A spatial model of effectiveness criteria: Toward a competing values perspective. In P.J. Frost, L.F. Moore, M.L. Louis, C.C. Lundberg, and J. Martin (Eds.), *Organizational Culture (pp. 315-334).* Beverly Hills, CA: Sage.

Rogers, E.W., and Wright, P.M. (1998). Measuring organizational performance in strategic human resource management: Problems, prospects, and performance information markets. *Human Resource Management Review, 8* (3), 311-331.

Schuler, R.S., and Jackson, S.E. (1987). Linking competitive strategy and human resource management practices. *Academy of Management Executive, 3,* 207-219.

Seashore, S.E., and Yuchtman, E. (1967). Factorial analysis of organizational performance. *Administrative Science Quarterly, 12,* 377-395.

Smither, J.W., London, M., Vasilopoulos, N.L., Reilly, R.R., Millsap, R.E., and Salvemini, N. (1995). An Examination of the effects of an upward feedback program over time. *Personnel Psychology, 48,* 1-34.

Snell, S. A., Youndt, M.A., and Wright, P.M. (1996). Establishing a framework for research in strategic human resource management: Merging resource theory and organizational learning. *Research in Personnel and Human Resources Management, 14,* 61-90.

Steers, R. M. (1977). *Organizational Effectiveness: A Behavioral View.* Santa Monica: CA. Goodyear.

Terpstra, D.E., and Rozell, E.J. (1993) The relationship of staffing practices to organizational level measures of performance. *Personnel Psychology, 46,* 27-48.

Thompson, J.D. (1967). *Organizations in Action.* New York: McGraw-Hill.

Trail, G. and Chelladurai, P. (2000). Perceptions of goals and processes of intercollegiate athletics: A Case study. *Journal of Sport Management, 14,* 154-178.

Tsui, A.S. (1990). A Multiple constituency model of effectiveness: An empirical examination at the human resource subunit level. *Administrative Science Quarterly, 35,* 458-483.

Walker, A.G., and Smither, J.W. (1999). A Five-year study of upward feedback: What managers do with their results matters. *Personnel Psychology, 52,* 393-423.

Wallace, M., and Weese, W. J. (1995). Leadership, organizational culture and job satisfaction in Canadian YMCA organizations. *Journal of Sport Management, 9,* 182-193.

Welbourne, T.M., and Andrews, A.O. (1996). Predicting the performance of initial public offerings: Should human resource management be in the equation? *Academy of Management Journal, 39* (4), 891-919.

Wolfe, R., Hill, L, and Babiak, K. (2000). *Intercollegiate athletic programs: Determinants of perceptions of success.* Unpublished Manuscript, The University of Michigan.

Wright, P.M., and McMahan, G.C. (1992). Theoretical perspectives for strategic human resource management. *Journal of Management, 18* (2), 295-320.

Wright, P.M., and Sherman, W.S. (1999). Failing to find fit in strategic human resource management: Theoretical and empirical problems. *Research in Personnel and Human Resources Management, Supplement, 4,* 53-74.

Wright, P.M., Smart, D.L., and McMahan, G.C. (1995). Matches between human resources and strategy among NCAA basketball teams. *Academy of Management Journal, 38* (4), 1052-1074.

Yuchtman, E., and Seashore, S.E. (1967). A system resource approach to organizational effectiveness. *American Sociological Review, 32,* 891-903.

Zammuto, R.F. (1984). A Comparison of multiple constituency models of organizational effectiveness. *Academy of Management Review, 9* (4), 606-616.

# APPENDIX

| Delery and Doty, 1996 | Welbourne and Andrews, 1996 | Huselid, Jackson, and Schuler, 1997 | Pfeffer, 1994 | Osterman, 1994 | Arthur, 1994 | Delany, 1996 | Delany, Lewin and Ichniowski, 1989 | Huselid, 1995 | MacDuffie, 1995 |
|---|---|---|---|---|---|---|---|---|---|
| ***Overall Philosophy*** | | | | | | | | | |
| Internal career opportunities | | | promotion from within | senority hiring and promotion | | | | promotion criteria | |
| Employment security | | | employment security | employment security | | | | | |
| voice mechanisms | | participation and empowerment | participation and empowerment | | due process, participation | grievance procedure, employee involvement programs | communication and participation programs | communication and participation programs | employee suggestions made and implemented |
| | | employee and manager communications, employee relations | information sharing | | decentralization | information-sharing procedure | employee relations | employee relations | |
| | full-time employees | HR information systems | overarching philosophy | HRM dept. role | | | | | |
| | climate ratings | | symbolic egalitarianism | | | | | | decentralization of quality tasks |
| ***Planning*** | | | | | | | | | |
| Job definition (tight or narrow) | | teamwork | teams and job re-design | | | flexible job designs | work organization and job design | work organization and job design | work teams, problem solving groups, job rotation |
| | | workforce planning, succession development | long-term perspective | | | | formal, written HR plan | formal, written HR plan | |
| | | | | | | flexible scheduling | | | |

| | Delery and Doty, 1996 | Welbourne and Andrews, 1996 | Huselid, Jackson, and Schuler, 1997 | Pfeffer, 1994 | Osterman, 1994 | Arthur, 1994 | Delany, 1996 | Delany, Lewin and Ichniowski, 1989 | Huselid, 1995 | MacDuffie, 1995 |
|---|---|---|---|---|---|---|---|---|---|---|
| *Staffing* | | | EEO for females, minorities, selection testing | selectivity in recruiting | | skill | | employee selection and staffing, selection ratio | employee selection and staffing (selection ratio) | recruitment and hiring |
| Training and Development | | | | | | | | | | |
| Training systems | | training, including company-specific | management and executive development, employee education and training | training and skill development | off job training | general training | | training and development | training and development, # of training hours/year | training of new employees, training of experienced employees |
| | | | | cross-utilization and cross training | % in cross-training | | | | | |
| Compensation | | | | | | | | | | |
| Profit sharing plans | | | | employee ownership | profit sharing, bonuses, gainsharing | | profit-sharing programs | | | |
| | | | | wage compression | | | | | | |
| | | | compensation | high wages | pay for skill, wage premium | wages | | compensation | compensation | |
| | | rewards programs | | incentive pay | | bonus | | | | contingent compensation |
| | | work-family programs benefits and services, retirement strategies | | | | benefits | -day-care programs -paternity leave programs -employee counseling services | | | |

**APPENDIX (CONTINUED)**

| | Delery and Doty, 1996 | Welbourne and Andrews, 1996 | Huselid, Jackson, and Schuler, 1997 | Pfeffer, 1994 | Osterman, 1994 | Arthur, 1994 | Delany, 1996 | Delany, Lewin and Ichniowski, 1989 | Huselid, 1995 | MacDuffie, 1995 |
|---|---|---|---|---|---|---|---|---|---|---|
| ***Evaluation/Appraising*** | | | | | | | | | | |
| Appraisals (beh. or performance—perf is better) | | | performance appraisals | | | | | performance appraisal | performance appraisal | |
| | | | productivity and quality measures, attitude surveys | measurement of practices | | | attitude surveys | formal evaluation of HR policies | formal evaluation of HR policies | |
| ***Other*** | | | | | | supervisor social | | | | |
| | | | social responsibility programs | | | | | union-management relations | union-management relations | |
| | | | safety and health | | | | | | | |

Issues in Contemporary Athletics
Editor: James H. Humphrey, pp. 73-92

ISBN 1-59454-595-2

*Chapter 7*

# CONSUMER EXPECTATIONS OF MARKET DEMAND VARIABLES OF AN NFL EXPANSION TEAM

*James J. Zhang, Dan P. Connaughton,*
*Matthew H. Ellis, Jessica R. Braunstein,*
*Beth Cianfrone and Carrianne Vaughn*
Department of Exercises and Sport Sciences
University of Florida, Gainesville Florida, USA

## ABSTRACT

The purpose of this study was to assess the importance and relevance of market demand factors to the levels of consumption and identification of potential consumers of an NFL expansion team. Research participants (N=308) were residents of a greater metropolitan area, who were interviewed before the inaugural season of an NFL expansion team. A questionnaire was followed for the interviews, which included eight demographic background variables, 18 market demand variables under four factors (game attractiveness, marketing promotions, economic consideration, and socialization opportunity), and 14 criterion variables under two categories (consumption and identification). One-sample t-tests revealed that the overall mean scores of the market demand and the criterion factors were significantly ($p < .05$) greater than their midpoints, respectively, suggesting that there were high expectations of market demands, high intentions of consumption, and high team identifications by the potential NFL consumers. Multiple regression analyses revealed that the market demand factors were positively ($p < .05$) predictive of consumption and identification, indicating that an NFL expansion team should focus on the market demand variables when developing game products and promotional strategies.

## INTRODUCTION

Since its inception in 1902, the National Football League (NFL) has gone through steady expansions in the number of teams, from the original three teams to today's 32 teams

(National Football League, 2003). Expansion fees usually provide the biggest and quickest revenue injection for the league. The league's decision on which community receives an expansion team often depends upon the economic success and profitability in the local community (Rascher, 2002). Although the NFL has expanded, demand continues to exceed supply. Metropolitan areas are continually competing to attract an expansion or relocation franchise (Rappaport and Wilkerson, 2001). An expansion team is an exciting venture to a metropolitan area, its residents, and the team. Obtaining an expansion team signifies a collaborate success of the community and the team owner(s) (King, 2000).

Over half the U.S. population lives in one of 39 metropolitan areas that host one or more major league sports teams. Welcoming a new professional sport team to the community helps to increase the residents' quality of life and enhances the positive perception of metropolitan attractions. Many sport fans enjoy attending home games of a major league team and follow the team through broadcasting and printed media (Rappaport and Wilkerson, 2001). Hosting a new NFL team also provides residents with civic pride by contributing to a sense that they live in a 'big football' city. As an American tradition, a football game event is often viewed and promoted as a community festivity to build community bond, common interests, and cultural identity (Bowling, 1999; Leone, 1997). Sport fans gradually grow an emotional attachment with a new team, with a sense of empowerment, excitement, familiarity, and passion (Grossberg, 1992; Mitrano, 1999). Many metropolitan areas are willing to significantly increase public outlays for constructing new stadiums to attract a new NFL team and, in the meantime, economic benefits from the arrival of the new team is also anticipated by the community (Rappaport and Wilkerson, 2001; Rosentraub and Swindell, 2002). Zhang, Pease, and Hui (1996) submitted that the potential value to a community with a new professional sport team might fall into eight dimensions: community solidarity, public behavior, pastime ecstasy, excellence pursuit, social equity, health awareness, individual quality, and business opportunity.

However, a new NFL team usually faces great financial and administrative challenges particularly in inaugural seasons. The owner(s) usually has to pay a large sum of expansion fees. For instance, Bob McNair, the owner of newly expanded Houston Texans, paid over $700 million, which did not include $449 million that the owner and the local public spent to build a new retractable-roof stadium (Mullen, 1999; Sport Business Research Network, 1999). About half of the Texas expansion fees were financed (Kaplan, 2002). Under the NFL's revenue sharing system, one-third of a team's gate receipts and club-seat revenue goes to the league, creating pressure among teams to maximize non-shared revenue such as personal seat licenses, stadium naming rights, local media contracts, luxury suites, and in-stadium advertising and sponsorships. Most importantly, sales of game tickets are fundamental to these non-shared revenue sources (Lombardo, 2000).

Winning brings consumers and profits to a professional football team (Sheehan, 1996). However, DeShazier (2002) once stated that "expansionism is tough business on the football field" (p. 5) and it takes time to build a winning team. According to Zwerneman (2002), the most winning expansion team in NFL history was the Carolina Panthers (7-9) in 1995 and the least winning expansion team was the Tampa Bay Buccaneers (0-14) in 1976. King (2000) further explained that the expansion fee that each NFL team receives is balanced by the proportionally reduced broadcasting income. When an expansion team does not obtain wide popularity, the burden to the league would outweigh the benefits from the expansion fees. This in part explains why the NFL is not currently planning to expand in the near future.

Traditionally, studies of professional sport team expansion issues have primarily adopted a macro approach to examine the viability of individual market environments. A macro study usually includes such variables as population size, sport population size (ages 25-54 years), sport tradition, corporate headquarters, income, retail volume, venue issues, community and politics, and market competitions (Rascher, 2002; Sports Business Research Network, 2003). Findings from macro studies usually do not provide detailed information about the anticipations of potential consumers in a new market environment, which is essential for a new team to effectively promote the consumption of its game products. Recently, Kanters and Greenwood (2002) studied consumers of an expansion arena football team and found that team potential success, the players, the coaches, family love of the sport, and game atmosphere were some of the major reasons that affected fan behaviors. Nonetheless, studies on consumer demands for an expansion professional sport team is lacking.

To a great extent, the marketing success of an expansion NFL team depends on its provision of goods and services that meets consumers' needs. An understanding of the market demand trends and on-going analysis of target markets are essential for an effective provision in formulating marketing strategies (Brooks, 1994; Stotlar, 1989; Yiannakis, 1989). As King (2000) and Lombardo (2000) pointed out, obtaining strong community support, achieving wide popularity among potential consumers, and conducting good services of game ticket sales are fundamental to revenue generation for an expansion team. Thus, in order to attract consumers, it is necessary for an expansion NFL team to evaluate those factors that may affect game attendance and other product consumptions. Periodic evaluation should be conducted to determine target markets, analyze market situation and environment, develop marketing objectives and strategies, and provide feedback about the implementation of an overall marketing plan (Brooks, 1994; Callecod and Stotlar, 1990; Stotlar, 1989; Yiannakis, 1989).

## Market Demands

In recent years, there has been an increased interest in studying consumer demands of core products of sport games. Researchers (Greenstein and Marcum, 1981; Hansen and Gauthier, 1989; Schofield, 1983; Zhang, Pease, Hui, and Michaud, 1995) have generally grouped variables affecting game consumption into the following categories: game attractiveness (e.g., athlete skills, team records, league standing, record-breaking performance, closeness of competition, team history in a community, schedule, convenience, and stadium quality); marketing promotions (e.g., publicity, special events, entertainment programs, and giveaways); and economic considerations (e.g., ticket price, substitute forms of entertainment, income, and competition of other sport events). The categories of market demand variables have been validated in numerous studies (e.g., Hansen and Gauthier, 1989; Zhang et al., 1995; Zhang, Lam, and Connaughton, 2003b).

The majority of previous studies have focused on game attractiveness variables, while the other two areas have been studied to a lesser extent (e.g., Baade and Tiehen, 1990; Marcum and Greenstein, 1985; Noll, 1974, 1991; Whitney, 1988; Zak, Huang, and Siegfried, 1979). Game attractiveness and marketing promotion variables have generally been found to be positively related to game consumption (Baade and Tiehen, 1990; Becker and Suls, 1983; Hansen and Gauthier, 1989; Jones, 1984; Marcum and Greenstein, 1985; Noll, 1991;

Whitney, 1988; Zhang et al., 1995). For economic variables, income and ticket discounts have consistently been shown to be positively related to game consumption, while ticket price, substitute forms of entertainment, and competition from other sport events have generally been shown to be negatively related to game consumption (Baade and Tiehen, 1990; Bird, 1982; Hansen and Gauthier, 1989; Noll, 1974; Siegfried and Eisenberg, 1980; Zhang and Smith, 1997; Zhang, Smith, Pease, and Jambor, 1997).

To facilitate research activities and professional practice, researchers have attempted to formulate measurement scales to assess the main areas of market demand variables. For examples, Hansen and Gauthier (1989) intended to develop a scale of 40 items although the factors and items did not converge well enough to be interpretable. Zhang et al. (1995) developed the Spectator Decision-Making Inventory (SDMI) for professional basketball games. The scale includes 15 items under four factors: Game Promotion, Home Team, Opposing Team, and Schedule Convenience. Construct validity of the scale was further assessed and confirmed by Zhang, Lam, Bennett, and Connaughton (2003a). Nevertheless, according to Baumgartner, Jackson, Mahar, and Rowe (2003) and Thomas and Nelson (2001), research findings are population specific. Because the SDMI was developed in a specific sport setting (i.e., professional basketball), it may lack generalizable application in the sport market place. Researchers (Hansen and Gauthier, 1989; Zhang et al., 2003b) have attempted to develop instruments that assess general market demand variables associated with professional sport consumption.

Previous studies examining variables that affect the market demands of sport products have primarily focused on professional baseball (Baade and Tiehen, 1990; Becker and Suls, 1983; Demmert, 1973; Greenstein and Marcum, 1981; Hill, Madura, and Zuber, 1982; Hunt and Lewis, 1976; Lee and Zeiss, 1980; Marcum and Greenstein, 1985; Noll, 1974; Scully, 1974; Siegfried and Hinshaw, 1977; Whitney, 1988) and professional basketball (e.g., Hansen and Gauthier, 1989; Noll, 1974, 1991; Zak et al., 1979; Whitney, 1988; Zhang et al., 1995; 2003a). Other sports have been studied to a much lesser extent. For instance, only a small number of market demand studies were primarily or partially related to professional football (Doyle, Lewis, and Malmisur, 1980; Hansen and Gauthier, 1989; Noll, 1974; Siegfried and Hinshaw, 1977; Whitney, 1988). Experiential studies on market demands of an expansion NFL team have not been found.

Additionally, a number of researchers have pointed out the socialization value of sport events. In particular, as an American tradition, football games offer exciting socializing opportunities and festivities for many people (Coakley, 1998; Gladden and Funk, 2002; Milne and McDonald, 1999; Wann, 1995; Pease and Zhang, 2001). Melnick (1993) and Sloan (1989) submitted the sociability theory of sport spectating and explained that sport consumers generally expect sport marketers to provide a sociable atmosphere at a sport event. Socialization among spectators adds to the entertainment value of spectator sports. Due to social isolation caused by modern urbanization, sporting events provide opportunities for large numbers of spectators to come together to be entertained, enrich their social lives through socialization, experience quasi-intimate relationships, and develop a sense of belonging. Sport arenas and stadia are convenient places that provide an ecological setting and social structure for people to search for and conduct casual socialization. The ever-present noise, hum, and buzz of a crowd create a party-like atmosphere and make spectator interaction probable. Spectators are fully aware of their positions and roles, as well as the types of behaviors expected and permitted at sporting events. Using sports as a media, spectators implicitly understand that their socialization is restricted to the boundaries related to game time and primarily to sport issues. They have a sense of commitment, support, and alliance, as well as shared interests, knowledge, and excitement. Hocking (1982) pointed out that the reactions spectators have to other spectators are a major factor contributing to the excitement of sport spectatorship. In brief, consumer expectations of socialization opportunities in a sport event indicate that socialization through sporting events is another important market demand aspect that previous market demand studies failed to include.

## Criterion Variables

Live and televised football games are the core product function of professional football teams. The relationship between live and televised events is reciprocal. Each has influenced and depended on the other for its popularity and commercial success (Jhally, 1989; Whannel, 1992). Teams also produce revenues through other product extension procedures such as licensed products, parking, concessions, programs, endorsements, uses of team logos, and media productions (Leonard, 1997; Noll, 1991). Consumer attraction and retention to core and extension products are very critical to the financial success of teams. Nevertheless, consumer retention is the most common problem facing the sport industry (Sawyer and Smith, 1999). In order to attract and retain consumers, it is necessary for an NFL expansion team to evaluate those factors that may affect consumer use of core products and product extensions.

Attaining the commitment from the fans is a challenging task, particularly for a recently expanded team that has not established a strong winning record, although a committed fan base is critical to the financial success of the team (Pells, 2002). According to Mullin, Hardy, and Sutton (2000), the affective involvement of consumers is another form of consumption, which positively predicts behavioral commitment. Researchers have proposed various theories in an effort to systematically explain the phenomena of spectator enjoyment of sporting events. For example, the disposition theory of sport spectatorship developed by Zillmann, Bryant, and Sapolsky (1989) suggests that spectators tend to establish implicit alliances and identification with renowned athletes and/or teams. Watching an allied team succeed enhances the affective bond with that team. A positive affect results from past pleasant game attendance experience and the anticipation of future enjoyable spectatorship. Great spectator enjoyment occurs when an allied team defeats a very disliked opponent and vice versa. When an allied team fails, great distress results particularly for those who are highly identified with the team. Thus, variables contributing to game winning of the allied team are enjoyed and applauded by the spectators, apart from an effective play of the allied team or a negative performance by the opponent. Spectator game enjoyment also derives from effective and daring play. Spectator enjoyment reaction is positively related to the perceived riskness, implicit contempt, skill involved, and gusty play that lead to success. Murrell and Dietz (1992), Sloan (1989), and Wann and Branscombe (1990, 1993) have reported the importance of providing cognitive information about the sport and team when attempting to enhance the level of team identification among current and potential consumers. Hansen and Gauthier (1992) indicated that fan image of the team gained through cognitive knowledge would affect game attendance.

Overall, researchers have generally found that the degree of team identification and level of team commitment of the spectators were positively related to game attendance. Fans with higher team identification would have more positive expectations and confidence in team performances and exhibit greater willingness to invest time and money to attend games. Moreover, in order to maintain self-esteem, highly identified fans show a more ego-enhancing pattern of attributions of game results and make greater internal outcome attributions to the team's victory and external outcome attributions to the team's failure (Anderson, 1979; Branscombe and Wann, 1991; Cramer, McMaster, Lutz, and Ford, 1986; Iso-Ahola, 1989; Iso-Ahola and Hatfield, 1986; Lee, 1985; Murrell and Dietz, 1992; Real and Mechikoff, 1992; Smith, 1988; Wann and Branscombe, 1990, 1993). Therefore, when examining the consumption behaviors of NFL expansion team consumers, it is necessary to study their affective involvement levels as well.

The purpose of this study was to assess consumer expectations of market demand and criterion variables (i.e., consumption level and identification) and to examine the predictability of market demand variables to the criterion variables of potential NFL expansion consumers.

# METHOD

## Participants

A total of 308 individuals, who resided in a greater metropolitan city area located in southern United States, voluntarily participated in the interview survey. Only those 18 years and older were interviewed. Youngsters were excluded from this study because many of them were not accompanied by their parents/guardians and the informed consent form could not be signed. The data were collected in two sport bars (N=70), three food courts (N=114), two restaurants (N=37), and one university sport event (N=87).

Descriptive statistics of the sociodemographic variables are presented in Table 1. The characteristics of the respondents were generally consistent with those of NFL consumers (Simmons Market Research Bureau, 2000). When compared to the characteristics of the greater metropolitan population and the U.S. population, certain discrepancies were recognized although consistency still existed in several aspects (U.S. Census Bureau, 2002). About 54% of the subjects were males, which over-represented the male proportions of 49.01-49.76% in the local and national population. The sample also over-represented the younger age groups, with the majority of them (88%) between 18 and 45-year-old. Although the ethnic proportions represented the greater metropolitan population well, with close to 60% being White and 20% being Hispanic, the composition under-represented White by 10% and over-represented Hispanics by 7.5% when compared to the national population. In terms of marital status, the sample over-represented those who were single by 20% but yet under-represented the married by 20%.

Characteristics related to household size were basically consistent with the greater metropolitan and U.S. population. Household sizes with 2 to 4 people were the majority (65%). Annual household income was quite normally distributed with about 80% being between $15,000 and $99,999, and well reflected national norms of income. Close to 50% of the participants had at least one college degree. Professionals, managers, and salespeople accounted for 40% of the sample.

**Table 1. Descriptive Statistics for the Demographic Variables (N=308)**

| Variable | Category | N | % | Cumulative % |
|---|---|---|---|---|
| Gender | Male | 165 | 53.6 | 53.6 |
| | Female | 143 | 46.4 | 100.0 |
| Age | 18-25 | 148 | 48.2 | 48.2 |
| (M=29.9; SD=10.9) | 26-35 | 87 | 28.3 | 76.5 |
| | 36-45 | 35 | 11.5 | 88.0 |
| | 45-55 | 26 | 8.4 | 96.4 |
| | 56 or older | 11 | 3.6 | 100.0 |
| Ethnicity | White | 173 | 56.2 | 56.2 |
| | Hispanic | 60 | 19.6 | 75.8 |
| | African American | 28 | 9.2 | 85.0 |
| | Asian | 25 | 8.2 | 93.2 |
| | Other | 21 | 6.8 | 100.0 |
| Marital Status | Single | 178 | 57.9 | 57.9 |
| | Married | 84 | 27.2 | 85.1 |
| | Divorced | 26 | 8.6 | 93.7 |
| | Widowed | 8 | 2.6 | 96.4 |
| | Other | 11 | 3.6 | 100.0 |
| Household Income | Below $15,000 | 29 | 9.5 | 9.5 |
| | $15,000-$24,999 | 32 | 10.5 | 19.9 |
| | $25,000-$49,999 | 95 | 30.7 | 50.7 |
| | $50,000-$74,999 | 64 | 20.9 | 71.6 |
| | $75,000-$99,999 | 42 | 13.5 | 85.1 |
| | $100,000-$149,999 | 27 | 8.8 | 93.9 |
| | $150,000 or above | 19 | 6.1 | 100.0 |
| Household Size | One | 76 | 24.6 | 24.6 |
| | Two | 79 | 25.6 | 50.2 |
| | Three to Four | 117 | 38.1 | 88.3 |
| | Five to Six | 35 | 11.4 | 99.7 |
| | Seven or more | 1 | 0.3 | 100.0 |
| Education | High School Student | 10 | 3.3 | 3.3 |
| | High School Graduate | 21 | 6.9 | 10.2 |
| | College Student/Associate Degree | 115 | 37.4 | 47.5 |
| | Bachelor's Degree | 110 | 35.7 | 83.2 |
| | Advanced Degree | 43 | 13.8 | 97.0 |
| | Other | 9 | 3.0 | 100.0 |

**Table 1. Descriptive Statistics for the Demographic Variables (N=308)**
**(Continued)**

| Variable | Category | N | % | Cumulative % |
|---|---|---|---|---|
| Occupation | Professional/Management/Sales | 123 | 39.9 | 39.9 |
| | Skilled Worker | 28 | 9.2 | 49.1 |
| | Clerk | 26 | 8.6 | 57.7 |
| | Student | 87 | 28.1 | 85.8 |
| | Housewife/Househusband | 17 | 5.6 | 91.4 |
| | Other | 26 | 8.6 | 100.0 |

## Questionnaire Development

Development of the questionnaire was based upon a review of literature (Greenstein and Marcum, 1981; Hansen and Gauthier, 1989; Hocking; 1982; Melnick, 1993; Pease and Zhang, 2001; Sloan, 1989; Schofield, 1983; Zhang et al., 1995; 2003a, 2003b) and interviewing three administrators of the NFL team located in the greater metropolitan area where this study took place. The questionnaire included eight demographic background variables (gender, age, ethnicity, marital status, household income, household size, education, and occupation); 18 market demand variables under four factors: Game Attractiveness (have been a football player, halftime events, love the NFL, game schedule, and go to see the expansion team), Marketing Promotions (TV publicity, promotional programs for ticket purchase, giveaways, pre-season events, advertising, and radio publicity), Economic Consideration (affordability, ticket discounts/coupons, and ticket price), and Socialization Opportunity (socialize with friends, attend team event with family member(s), family atmosphere, and crowd's enthusiasm); and 14 criterion variables under two categories: consumption (4 items) and identification (10 items). Specifically, the market demand variables were a modified adoption of items suggested by Melnick (1993), Hansen and Gauthier (1989), and Zhang et al. (2003a, 2003b). The consumption variables reflected items suggested by Greenstein and Marcum (1981), Mullin et al. (2000), Schofield (1983), and Zhang et al. (1995). The identification variables were a modified adoption of items suggested by Pease and Zhang (2001) and Sloan (1989). The demographic variables were phrased into multiple-choice questions. The market demand variables were phrased into a Likert 5-point scale statement (5=most important to 1=least important). The criterion variables were phrased into a Likert 5-point scale statements (5=very much to 1=not at all).

Content validity of the questionnaire was attained through a panel of experts including three administrators of the NFL team, three university professors in sport management, and a group of university students (n=12) who were enrolled in sport marketing classes at the graduate and undergraduate levels. The panel members were asked to examine the relevance, clarity, and representativeness of the items in the questionnaire. The questionnaire was approved with minor revisions that were mainly related to formatting and clarity.

## Procedures

Face-to-face interviews took place in two sport bars, three food courts, two restaurants, and one university sport event. For the sport bar, food courts, and restaurants, the interviews were conducted in seating sections. For the sport event, face-to-face interviews were conducted at the entrance areas. Three trained interviewers followed a standard, 10-step procedure during all interviews, which included: (a) approaching all people regardless of gender and race, (b) politely approaching each potential participant, (c) explaining the purpose of this study, (d) explaining that voluntary participation was encouraged and that participation was anonymous, (e) explaining that there was no penalty for not participating or not answering some of the questions, (f) explaining that in order to qualify for the study, an individual had to reside in the greater metropolitan city area at the time of data collection, (g) explaining that a participant had to be 18-years or older, (h) asking the participant to sign the informed consent form for participating in the study, (i) conducting the interview, and (j) thanking the individual for his/her time and support for the study. The average duration of the interviews was about 15-20 minutes. After an individual agreed to participate in the study, he/she usually answered all of the questions with sincerity. Overall, a total of 308 individuals responded to the survey. The entire data collection was completed within two months.

## Data Analyses

The procedures from Version 10.0 of the *SPSS for Windows* (SPSS, 1999) programs were utilized to conduct data analyses. Descriptive statistics were calculated for the demographic variables. Descriptive statistics and one-sample t-tests were conducted for the market demand and the criterion variables. The alpha level of .05 was adjusted using the Bonferroni approach for items within a factor to avoid an inflated type I error in the statistical testing. Stepwise multiple regression analyses were conducted to examine the relationships between market demand and criterion factors.

## RESULTS

The findings are presented in the following two sections: (a) expectations of potential consumers and (b) predictability of market demand to criterion variables.

## Expectations of Potential Consumers

Descriptive statistics and findings from one-sample t-tests for the market demand variables are presented in Table 2. Perceived importance levels of the variables are listed from high to low. The overall mean score of Game Attractiveness was significantly ($p < .05$) greater than the factor midpoint (i.e., 3.0x5=15.0). After adjusting for the alpha level, three items (have been a football player, halftime events, and love the NFL) had a mean score that was significantly ($p < .05$) greater than the item midpoint (i.e., 3.0), and were thus considered to be major contributing variables to the overall importance of Game Attractiveness. The overall mean score of Marketing Promotion was significantly ($p < .05$) greater than the factor midpoint (i.e., 3.0x6=18.0). After adjusting for the alpha level, four items (TV publicity, promotional programs for ticket purchase, giveaways, and pre-season events) had a mean score that was significantly ($p < .05$) greater than the item midpoint (i.e., 3.0), and were thus considered to be major contributing variables to the overall importance of Marketing Promotion. The overall mean score of Economic Consideration was significantly ($p < .05$) greater than the factor midpoint (i.e., 3.0x3=9.0). After adjusting for the alpha level, two items (affordability and ticket discounts/coupons) had a mean score that was significantly ($p < .05$) greater than the item midpoint (i.e., 3.0), and were thus considered to be major contributing variables to the overall importance of Economic Consideration. The overall mean score of Socialization Opportunity was significantly ($p < .05$) greater than the factor midpoint (i.e., 3.0x4=12.0). After adjusting for the alpha level, all four items (socialize with friends, attend team event with family member(s), family atmosphere, and crowd's enthusiasm) had a mean score that was significantly ($p < .05$) greater than the item midpoint (i.e., 3.0), and were thus considered to be major contributing variables to the overall importance of Socialization Opportunity.

**Table 2. Descriptive Statistics and One-Sample T-Tests for the Market Demand Variables**

| Variable | M | SD | t | p |
| --- | --- | --- | --- | --- |
| Game Attractiveness | | | | |
| Have been a football player | 3.64 | 1.23 | 9.166 | .000* |
| Halftime events | 3.44 | 1.30 | 5.976 | .000* |
| Love the NFL | 3.29 | 1.28 | 3.908 | .000* |
| Game schedule | 3.16 | 1.19 | 2.312 | .021 |
| Go to see the expansion team | 3.01 | 1.32 | 0.139 | .889 |
| | | | | |
| Total | 16.54 | 4.13 | 6.523 | .000 |
| | | | | |
| Marketing Promotion | | | | |
| TV publicity | 4.23 | 0.99 | 21.844 | .000* |
| Promotional programs for ticket purchase | 3.92 | 1.14 | 14.058 | .000* |
| Giveaways | 3.82 | 1.23 | 11.716 | .000* |
| Pre-season events | 3.24 | 1.24 | 3.442 | .001* |
| Advertising | 3.13 | 1.32 | 1.689 | .092 |
| Radio publicity | 2.95 | 1.29 | 0.637 | .524 |
| | | | | |
| Total | 21.42 | 4.92 | 12.211 | .000 |
| | | | | |
| Economic Consideration | | | | |
| Affordability | 4.01 | 1.19 | 14.932 | .000* |
| Ticket discounts/coupons | 3.58 | 1.30 | 7.803 | .000* |
| Ticket price | 2.89 | 1.54 | 1.250 | .212 |

**Table 2. Descriptive Statistics and One-Sample T-Tests for the Market Demand Variables (Continued)**

| Variable | M | SD | t | p |
|---|---|---|---|---|
| Total | 10.48 | 2.68 | 9.677 | .000 |
| Socialization Opportunity | | | | |
| Socialize with friends | 4.16 | 0.99 | 20.628 | .000* |
| Attend team event with family member(s) | 3.72 | 1.17 | 10.834 | .000* |
| Family atmosphere | 3.37 | 1.35 | 4.853 | .000* |
| Crowd's enthusiasm | 3.36 | 1.34 | 4.744 | .000* |
| Total | 14.62 | .265 | 17.324 | .000 |

* Significant at .05 level after the alpha level was adjusted

**Table 3. Descriptive Statistics and One-Sample T-Tests for the Criterion Variables**

| Variable | M | SD | t | p |
|---|---|---|---|---|
| Consumption | | | | |
| I will watch the expansion team's games on TV. | 4.01 | 1.10 | 16.160 | .000* |
| I will attend the expansion team's games. | 3.74 | 1.20 | 10.770 | .000* |
| I will listen to the expansion team's games on radio. | 3.64 | 1.30 | 8.629 | .000* |
| I have purchased the expansion team's merchandise. | 2.33 | 1.33 | -8.825 | .000* |
| Total | 13.72 | 3.54 | 8.539 | .000 |
| Identification | | | | |
| I am excited when I see media coverage about the expansion team. | 3.83 | 1.22 | 11.894 | .000* |
| I follow the expansion team in the media closely. | 3.75 | 1.22 | 10.713 | .000* |
| I feel that attending the games of this expansion team is important for me. | 3.55 | 1.22 | 7.957 | .000* |
| I am enthusiastic about the expansion team's first season. | 3.36 | 1.22 | 5.254 | .000* |
| I perceive that the expansion team has established a positive public image. | 3.21 | 1.29 | 2.861 | .005* |
| I am happy to see advertisements of the expansion team. | 3.08 | 1.18 | 1.157 | .248 |
| I believe the expansion team represents the city well | 2.88 | 1.36 | -1.584 | .114 |
| I feel proud that the city has this expansion team. | 2.69 | 1.26 | -4.304 | .000* |
| I know a lot about this expansion team. | 2.63 | 1.36 | -4.815 | .000* |
| I feel thrilled when I see the expansion team's logo. | 2.50 | 1.18 | -7.436 | .000* |
| Total | 31.47 | 7.97 | 3.247 | .001 |

* Significant at .05 level after the alpha level was adjusted

Descriptive statistics and findings from one-sample t-tests for the criterion variables are presented in Table 3. Magnitudes of the variables are listed from high to low. The overall mean score of the Consumption factor was significantly ($p < .05$) greater than the factor midpoint (i.e., 3.0x4=12.0). After adjusting for the alpha level, all four items had a mean score that was significantly ($p < .05$) greater than the item midpoint (i.e., 3.0), and were thus considered to be major contributing variables. The overall mean score of the Identification factor was significantly ($p < .05$) greater than the factor midpoint (i.e., 3.0x10=30.0). After adjusting for the alpha level, five items had a mean score that was significantly ($p < .05$) greater than the item midpoint (i.e., 3.0) and were thus considered to be major contributing variables; whereas, three items had a mean score that was significantly ($p < .05$) lower than the item midpoint (i.e., 3.0) and were thus considered to be adverse contributing variables.

## Predictability of Market Demand to Criterion Variables

Findings from stepwise multiple regression analyses on the relationships between the market demand and the criterion factors are presented in Table 4. Three market demand factors (Economic Consideration, Game Attractiveness, and Game Promotion) were significantly ($p < .05$) predictive of product consumption of the NFL expansion team, with a total of 27.2% variance explained. All four market demand factors were significantly ($p < .05$) predictive of Identification with the expansion team, with a total of 36.2% variance explained. The intercorrelation between the Consumption and the Identification factors was .78, which was statistically significant ($p < .05$). The relationships between market demand and the criterion factors are further depicted in Figure 1.

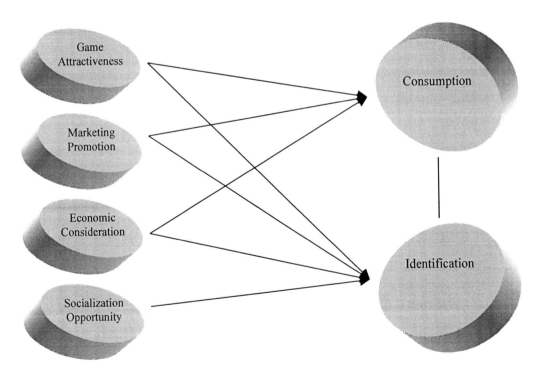

Figure 1. Predictability of Market Demand Factors to Consumption and Identification

**Table 4. Stepwise Multiple Recreation Analyses Examining the Relationships Between Market Demand and Criterion Variables**

| Variable | r | r² | Δr² | b | SE B | ß | t | p |
|---|---|---|---|---|---|---|---|---|
| Criterion Variable – Consumption | | | | | | | | |
| Economic Consideration | .453 | .205 | .205 | 0.599 | 0.067 | 0.453 | 8.891 | .000 |
| Game Attractiveness | .512 | .262 | .057 | 0.263 | 0.054 | 0.252 | 4.860 | .000 |
| Game Promotion | .522 | .272 | .010 | 0.088 | 0.043 | 0.122 | 2.021 | .044 |
| Socializing Opportunities | .527 | .277 | .005 | 0.102 | 0.069 | 0.093 | 1.476 | .141 |
| | | | | | | | | |
| Criterion Variable – Identification | | | | | | | | |
| Game Attractiveness | .503 | .253 | .253 | 1.182 | 0.116 | 0.503 | 10.184 | .000 |
| Economic Consideration | .583 | .340 | .087 | 0.927 | 0.146 | 0.311 | 6.341 | .000 |
| Game Promotion | .595 | .354 | .014 | 0.235 | 0.092 | 0.145 | 2.552 | .011 |
| Socializing Opportunities | .602 | .362 | .008 | 0.282 | 0.146 | 0.114 | 1.932 | .054 |

## DISCUSSION

Effective sport marketing is the performance of activities that direct the flow of goods and services from a sport organization to consumers. For a new sport organization, one critical concern is the formulation of strategies to attract and reach potential consumers, which requires the provision of consumer needs, wants, and expectations in order to efficiently identify contingent variables and accordingly formulate marketing procedures (Gray, 1996; Yiannakis, 1989). Remaining consistent with these indications, this study was designed to examine the expected market demands by potential consumers of an NFL expansion team. The findings of this study revealed that four market demand factors (game attractiveness, marketing promotions, economic consideration, and socialization opportunity) were expected to be important and relevant to the consumption level of the NFL expansion team's products and the level of identification with the team. Generally speaking, findings about the market demand issues in this study were consistent with previous research findings (e.g., Greenstein and Marcum, 1981; Hansen and Gauthier, 1989; Schofield, 1983; Zhang et al., 1995). Nevertheless, to some extent, specific elements of the market demand factors and their marketing implications may vary for an NFL expansion team. An NFL expansion team should pay particular attention to the uniqueness of the market demands when formulating its marketing mix, i.e., product, place, price, and promotion.

To enhance game attractiveness, three areas should be emphasized by the expansion team in order to generate community interests and potential consumption of game products: grassroots promotion, game entertainment value, and NFL branding. Grassroots promotion may be achieved through offering football education and training programs, sponsoring youth, school, and community football programs, cultivating community pride and passion towards football through multimedia sources, and developing sound public and media relations (Irwin, Sutton, and McCarthy, 2002; Pitts and Stotlar, 2002; Zhang et al., 2003).

During a football game, there are designed stoppages. After each play in football, both teams typically huddle before continuing play. Spectators should be consistently attracted to the game environment during those play stoppages. To maximize the entertainment value of a football event, from the moment a spectator enters the stadium till he/she leaves after the game, the individual should experience nonstop entertainment activities such as music, symphony, band, singing, dancing, laser show, magic show, circus, mascot, and/or contests. Inviting reputable individuals or organizations to perform quality amenity activities would enhance spectators' sensational feelings. It is important to keep halftime activities new and original, especially to those potential consumers who intend to frequently attend games. While exhilarating halftime entertainment packages may not be appreciated in the short-term, the results may come in the long-term through the effect of walk-up ticket sales. Through various communication procedures, an expansion team should inform the potential consumers about the maximized entertainment value and nonstop amusement elements of the game (Milne and McDonald, 1999; Mullin et al., 2000; Zhang et al., 2001; 2003). To enhance consumer passion of the NFL as a brand association, the expansion team may educate the community about, and promote the league through, the league's attributes (such as history and tradition, success, star coaches and players, notable managers and management teams, stadiums, and logo designs), benefits (such as identification, pride, nostalgia, entertainment and leisure, and peer acceptance), and attitude (such as social importance, knowledge, and affection) (Gladden and Funk, 2002).

Marketing promotions should begin immediately after the league makes the decision on an expansion team. Promotions may be accomplished through TV, promotional programs for ticket sales, giveaways, and various pre-team and pre-season events. Great free publicities may be obtained in local, regional, and national media through celebration events, press release and conferences, naming contests, logo design contests, stadium bidding, stadium naming, contracts, and other progress reports. Besides season and club-seat ticket sales, a recent trend of ticket promotions focuses on personal seat licenses, luxury suites, and in-stadium advertising and sponsorships (Lombardo, 2000; Mullin et al., 2000). The expansion team should inform the community that the team would often have "giveaway days" to spectators at the games. When the team gives away t-shirts, hats, towels, bags, etc., these giveaways are a reward from the team to fans for attending the game. Spectators are always pleased to receive a giveaway or souvenir from the event they attend. Where possible, giveaways and souvenirs may be available at pre-team and pre-season events, such as the opening ceremonies for introducing the team name and logo (Zhang et al., 2003). The expansion team may seek and also publicize giveaways potentially provided by corporate sponsorships. Today, businesses see professional sports as another vehicle, or medium, to get their message across to their designated target audience. Corporations are looking for more ways to become attached to professional sports than they ever have before (IEG Sponsorship Report, 1999). The affiliation and connection with a favored property (sports franchise) increases among those who recognize that a company is lending financial support (sponsorship) to the property, so too will their willingness be to purchase the sponsor's product (Madrigal, 2000).

Two Economic Consideration items (affordability and ticket discount/coupons) were considered important by the respondents. Although it is a contemporary trend that professional sports are becoming increasingly expensive, an NFL expansion team should focus on providing a quality game package at a reasonable price. Although winning brings consumers and profits for a professional football team (Sheehan, 1996), an expansion team usually does not have a winning season in its inaugural years and it takes time to build a winning team (DeShazier, 2002). Thus, tickets discounts, such as buy one ticket and get the second at half price, may be used when attendance is expected to be low. The same type of promotion may also be used to maintain spectator support, for instance, when the team is not performing well. Upgrading seat sections and/or occasionally providing better seats without additional costs or with low costs are enormous incentives for spectators (Helitzer, 1994; Irwin et al., 2002; Mullin et al., 2000; Pitts and Stotlar, 2002)

An NFL expansion team may formulate promotional themes with promising socializing opportunities. Socialization is an ingredient for human diversion and recreation. To some extent, the findings of this study may have reflected the mutual relationship between socialization and spectatorship: spectators socialize into and through sport spectating. Socialization among friends, family members, or with other spectators adds to the excitement of a sporting event. The reactions spectators have to other spectators are a major factor contributing to the excitement of sport spectatorship (Coakley 1998; Melnick, 1993). The expansion team should make socialization more convenient through promotional programs and game operations such as ticket discounts for a friend, family tickets, group tickets, club seats, replay screen zoomed on spectators, and celebrity appearances. Team cheerleaders may go into the audience to greet spectators. Team management could initiate and coordinate the team fan club(s) for additional social opportunities. A social atmosphere may be emphasized through 'family' and 'friends' theme game days. Developing team rituals, fighting songs, and unique game presentations and routines may help to enhance the crowd's enthusiasm. The band, public address announcer, cheerleaders, and the replay screen may be utilized to coordinate and escalate a party atmosphere.

In addition to the market demand factors, researchers and NFL teams should look for additional methods for increasing fan identification. Highly identified fans may be able to combat some of the more traditional problems of core product consumption. This may be achieved by discovering what creates the most positive experience for fans consuming core products. According to Maslow (1970), human need for accomplishment is generally expressed as a desire for prestige, accomplishment, and overcoming obstacles. Sloan (1989) summarized four tools that sport fans use for identification seeking: (a) selective information processing: attending to success, remembering good events better, taking personal credit for success, and avoiding blame for failure; (b) manipulated appraisals: associating with those who endorse oneself and formulating better belief about those who appraise oneself; (c) selective social comparison: making comparisons to less impressive others, overrating oneself, and degrading opponent; and (d) selective commitment to identity: assigning more importance to positive identity and increasing identification with a successful group for positive esteem. To a great extent, an NFL expansion team may adopt these principles in their core product design, event operation, and community outreach procedures in an effort to nurture, channel, direct, and control the achievement seeking processes of spectators. Furthermore, in this study, fan identification was regarded as a criterion variable. However, according to previous researchers (e.g., Gladden and Funk, 2002; Milne and McDonald, 1999; Wann, 1995; Pease and Zhang, 2001), fan identification may have a direct relationship with game consumption. Findings of this study strongly supported this speculation. Future studies may consider examining the mediating effect of fan identification on the relationships between market demand factors and game consumption.

This study was limited to a sample of residents in a major southern U.S. metropolitan area, where a new NFL expansion team was recently granted. Although market similarities exist among expansion teams of different regions or climates, differences may exist. When possible, similar studies should be conducted in the market environments of other expansion teams in order to extend the generalizability of the findings of this study. Future studies should examine other factors that affect the marketing success of an NFL expansion team and how they function together to increase consumption level. Finally, the findings of this study should be utilized in the setting of an NFL team. Further validations are necessary when the findings are used in other competition levels of football and/or other sports.

## REFERENCES

Anderson, D. F. (1979). Sport spectatorship: Appropriation of an identity or appraisal of self. *Review of Sport and Leisure, 4*(2), 115-127.

Baade, R. A., and Tiehen, L. J. (1990). An analysis of major league baseball attendance, 1969 - 1987. *Journal of Sport and Social Issues, 14*(1), 14-32.

Baumgartner, T.A., Jackson, A.S, Mahar, M.T., and Rowe, D.A. (2003). *Measurement and evaluation in physical education and exercise science* (7th ed.). Boston, MA: McGraw-Hill.

Becker, M. A., and Suls, J. (1983). Take me out to the ball game: The effect of objective, social, and temporal performance information on attendance at major league baseball games. *Journal of Sport Psychology, 5,* 302-313.

Bird, P. J. (1982). The demand for league football. *Applied Economics, 14*(6), 637-649.

Bowling, R. T. (1999). Sports aggravated: The fan's guide to the franchise relocation problem in professional sports. *Stetson Law Review, 28*(3), 645-683.

Branscombe, N. R., and Wann, D. L. (1991). The positive social and self-concept consequences of sports team identification. *Journal of Sport and Social Issues, 15*(2), 115-127.

Brooks, C. M. (1994). *Sport marketing: Competitive business strategies for sport.* Englewood Cliffs, NJ: Prentice-Hall.

Callecod, R. L., and Stotlar, D. K. (1990). Sport marketing. In J. B. Parks, and B. R. K. Zanger (Eds.), *Sport and fitness management: Career strategies and professional content* (pp. 73-84). Champaign, IL: Human Kinetics.

Coakley, J. J. (1998). *Sport in society: Issues and controversies* (6th ed.). Boston: McGraw-Hill.

Cramer, R. E., McMaster, M. R., Lutz, D. J., and Ford, J. G. (1986). Sport fan generosity: A test of mood similarity, and equity hypotheses. *Journal of Sport Behavior, 9*(1), 31-37

Demmert, H. G. (1973). *The economics of professional team sport.* Lexington, MA: D. C. Heath.

DeShazier, J. (2002, September 26). Texas, Wells build foundation for future. *The Times-Picayune (New Orleans), 5.*

Doyle, R. C., Lewis, J. M., and Malmisur, M. (1980). A sociological application of Rooney's fan region theory. *Journal of Sport Behavior, 3*(2), 51-60.

Gladden, J. M., And Funk, D. C. (2002). Developing An Understanding Of Brand Associations In Team Sport: Empirical Evidence From Consumers Of Professional Sport. *Journal Of Sport Management, 16,* 54-81.

Gray, D. P. (1996). Sport Marketing: A Strategic Approach. In B. L. Parkhouse (Ed.), *The Management Of Sport: Its Foundation And Application* (2nd Ed.) (Pp. 249-289). St. Louis, MO: Mosby.

Greenstein, T. N., Marcum, J. P. (1981). Factors Affecting Attendance Of Major League Baseball: I. Team Performance. *Review Of Sport And Leisure, 6*(2), 21-34.

Grossberg, L. (1992). Is There A Fan In The House? The Attractive Sensibility Of Fandom. In L. A. Lewis (Ed.), *Adoring Audience: Fan Culture And Popular Media* (Pp. 208-236). New York: Routledge.

Hansen, H., And Gauthier, R. (1989). Factors Affecting Attendance At Professional Sport Events. *Journal Of Sport Management, 3,* 15-32.

Hansen, H., And Gauthier, R. (1992). Marketing Objectives Of Professional And University Sport Organizations. *Journal Of Sport Management, 6,* 27-37.

Helitzer, M. (1994). *The Dream Job: Sport Publicity, Promotion, And Public Relations.* Athens, OH: University Sports.

Hill, J. R., Madura, J., And Zuber, R. A. (1982). The Short Gun Demand For Major League Baseball. *Atlantic Economic Journal, 10*(2), 31-35.

Hocking, J. E. (1982). Sports And Spectators: Intra-Audience Effects. *Journal Of Communication, 32,* 100-108.

Hunt, J. W., And Lewis, K. A. (1976). Dominance, Recontracting, And The Reverse Clause: Major League Baseball. *The American Economic Review, 66,* 936-943.

IEG Sponsorship Report. (1999, December 20). No Bugs Here: Big Jump In Sponsorship Spending Projected For 2000. *IEG Sponsorship Report 18*(24), 1, 4-5.

Irwin, R. L., Sutton, W. A., And Mccarthy, L. M. (2002). *Sports Promotion And Sales Management.* Champaign, IL: Human Kinetics.

Iso-Ahola, S. E. (1989). Attributional determinants of decisions to attend football games. *Scandinavian Journal of Sports Science, 2*(2), 39-46.

Iso-Ahola, S. E., and Hatfield, B. (1986). *Psychology of sports: A social psychological approach.* Dubuque, IA: Wm. C. Brown.

Jhally, S. (1989). Cultural studies and the sports/media complex. In L. A. Wenner (Ed.), *Media, sports, and society* (pp. 70-93). Newbury Park, CA: Sage.

Jones, J. C. H. (1984). Winners, losers and hosers: Demand and survival in the National Hockey League. *Atlantic Economic Journal, 12*(3), 54-63.

Kanters, M. A., and Greenwood, P. B. (2002). Sport team identification in a professional sport expansion setting. Paper presented at the 17th North American Society for Sport Management, Canmore, Canada.

Kaplan, D. (2002). Texans borrow $100m for next NFL payment. *Street and Smith's Sport Business Journal, 5*(30), 4.

King, W. (2000). Sun sets on expansion era. *Street and Smith's Sport Business Journal, 2*(45), 1.

Lee, M. J. (1985). Self-esteem and social identity in basketball fans: A closer look at basking-in-reflected glory. *Journal of Sport Behavior, 8*(4), 210-223.

Lee, B. A., and Zeiss, C. A. (1980). Behavioral commitment to the role of sport consumer: An exploratory analysis. *Sociology and Social Research, 64*(3), 405-419.

Leonard, W. M. (1997). Some economic considerations of professional sports. *Journal of Sport Behavior, 20,* 338-346.

Leone, K. C. (1997). No team, no peace: franchise free agency in the National Football League. *Columbia Law Review, 97*(2), 472-523.

Lombardo, J. (2000). NFL Texans' revenue to top Skins'. *Street and Smith's Sport Business Journal, 3*(22), 1and59.

Madrigal, R. (2000). The influence of social alliances with sports teams on intentions to purchase corporate sponsors' products. *Journal of Advertising, 29*(4), 13-24.

Marcum, J. P., and Greenstein, T. N. (1985). Factors affecting attendance of major league baseball: II. Within-season analysis. *Sociology of Sport Journal, 2,* 314-322.

Maslow, A. (1970). *Motivation and personality.* New York: Harper and Row.

Melnick, M. J. (1993). Searching for sociability in the stands: A theory of sports spectating. *Journal of Sport Management, 7,* 44-60.

Milne, G. R., and McDonald, M. A. (1999). *Sport marketing: Managing the exchange process.* Sudbury, MA: Jones and Bartlett.

Mitrano, J. (1999). The sudden death of jockey in Hartford: Sports fans and franchise relocation. *Sociology of Sport Journal, 16,* 134-155.

Mullen, L. (1999). Houston's $700m ups ante. *Street and Smith's Sport Business Journal, 2*(25), 1.

Mullin, B.J., Hardy, S. and Sutton, W. A. (2000). *Sport Marketing* (2nd ed.). Champaign, IL: Human Kinetics.

Murrell, A. J., and Dietz, B. (1992). Fan support of sport teams: The effect of a common group identity. *Journal of Sport and Exercise Psychology, 14,* 28-39.

Noll, R. G. (1974). Attendance and price setting. In R. G. Noll (Ed.), *Government and the sports business* (pp. 115-157). Washington, DC: The Brookings Institute.

Noll, R. G. (1991). Professional basketball: Economic and business perspectives. In P. D. Staudohar and J. A. Mangan (1989), *The business of professional sports* (pp.18-47). Urbana, IL: University of Illinois.

National Football League. (2003). *NFL football history.* On-line: *http://www.nfl-football-tickets.net/nfl_history.htm* (retrieved on March 13, 2003).

Pease, D. G., and Zhang, J. J. (2001). Socio-motivational factors affecting spectator attendance at professional basketball games. *International Journal of Sport Management, 2,* 31-59.

Pells, E. (2002, August 29). *NFL '02: Jaguars offer blueprint for good and bad in expansion.* On-line: *http://web.lexis-nexis.com/universe/document* (retrieved on February 21, 2003).

Pitts, B. G., and Stotlar, D. K. (2002). *Fundamentals of sport marketing* (2nd ed.). Morgantown, WV: Fitness Information Technology.

Rappaport, J., and Wilkerson, C. (2001). What are the benefits of hosting a major league sports franchise? *Economic Review, 86,* 18-35.

Rascher, D. A. (2002). *A strategic analysis of team relocation or league expansion.* Paper presented at the 17th North American Society for Sport Management, Canmore, Canada.

Real, M. R., and Mechikoff, R. A. (1992). Deep fan: Mythic identification, technology, and advertising in spectator sports. *Sociology of Sport Journal, 9,* 323-339.

Rosentraub, M., and Swindell, D. (2002). Negotiating games: Cities, sports, and winner's curse. *Journal of Sport Management, 16,* 18-35.

Sawyer, T. H., and Smith, O. (1999). *The management of clubs, recreation and sport: Concepts and applications.* Champaign, IL: Sagamore.

Schofield, J. A. (1983). Performance and attendance at professional team sports. *Journal of Sport Behavior, 6*(4), 196-206.

Scully, G. W. (1974). Pay and performance in Major League Baseball. *The American Economic Review, 64,* 915-930.

Sheehan, R. (1996). *Keeping score: The economics of big-time sports.* South Bend, IN: Diamond Communications.

Siegfried, J. J., and Eisenberg, J. D. (1980). The demand for minor league baseball. *Atlantic Economic Journal, 8*(1), 59-71.

Siegfried, J. J., and Hinshaw, C. E. (1977). Professional football and the anti-blackout law. *Journal of Communication, 17,* 169-174.

Simmons Market Research Bureau. (2000). *Study of media and markets: Sports and leisure.* New York: Simmons.

Sloan, L. R. (1989). The motives of sports fans. In J. H. Goldstein (Ed.), *Sports, games, and play: Social and psychological viewpoints* (2nd ed.) (pp. 175-240). Hillsdale, NJ: Lawrence Erlbaum.

Smith, G. J. (1988). The noble sports fan. *Journal of Sport and Social Issues, 12*(1), 54-65.

Sports Business Research Network. (1999). *NFL selects Houston over Los Angels with $700 million bid.* On-line: *http://www.SBRnet.com* (retrieved on February 21, 2003).

Sports Business Research Network. (2003). *Football: Consumer expenditures.* On-line: *http://www.SBRnet.com* (retrieved on April 18, 2003).

SPSS. (1999). *SPSS 10.0: Guide to data analysis.* Upper Saddle River, NY: Prentice Hall.

Stotlar, D. K. (1989). *Successful sport marketing.* Dubuque, IA: W.C. Brown.

Thomas, J. R., and Nelson, J. K. (2001). *Research methods in physical activity* (4th ed.). Champaign, IL: Human Kinetics.

U.S. Census Bureau. (2002). *U.S. Census Bureau.* On-line: *http://www.census.gov* (retrieved on April 18, 2003).

Wann, D. L. (1995). Preliminary validation of the Sport Fan Motivation Scale. *Journal of Sport and Social Issues, 19,* 377-396.

Wann, D. L., and Branscombe, N. R. (1990). Die-hard and fair-weather fans: Effects of identification on BIRGing and CORFing tendencies. *Journal of Sport and Social Issues, 14,* 103-117.

Wann, D. L., and Branscombe, N. R. (1993). Sports fans: Measuring degree of identification with their team. *Journal of Sport and Social Issues, 14*(2), 103-117.

Whannel, G. (1992). *Fields in vision: Television sport and cultural transformation.* London, England: Routledge.

Whitney, J. D. (1988). Winning games versus winning championships: The economics of fan interest and team performance. *Economic Inquiry, 26,* 703-724.

Yiannakis, A. (1989). Some contributions of sport sociology to the marketing of sport and leisure organizations. *Journal of Sport Management, 3,* 103-115.

Zak, T. H., Huang, C. F., and Siegfried, J. J. (1979). Production efficiency: The case of professional basketball. *Journal of Business, 52*(3), 19-23.

Zhang, J. J., Lam, E. T. C., Bennett, G., and Connaughton, D. P. (2003a). Confirmatory factor analysis of the Spectator Decision Making Inventory (SDMI). *Measurement in Physical Education and Exercise Science, 7*(2), 57-70.

Zhang, J. J., Lam, E. T. C., and Connaughton, D. P. (2003b). General market demand variables associated with professional sport consumption. *International Journal of Sport marketing and Sponsorship, 5*(1), 33-55.

Zhang, J. J., Pease, D. G., and Hui, S. C. (1996). Value dimensions of professional sport as viewed by spectators. *Journal of Sport and Social Issues, 21,* 78-94.

Zhang, J. J., Pease, D. G., Hui, S. C., and Michaud, T. J. (1995). Variables affecting the spectator decision to attend NBA games. *Sports Marketing Quarterly, 4*(4), 29-39.

Zhang, J. J., and Smith, D. W. (1997). Impact of broadcasting on the attendance of professional basketball games. *Sport Marketing Quarterly, 6*(1), 23-29.

Zhang, J. J., Smith, D. W., Pease, D. G., and Jambor, E. A. (1997). Negative influence of market competitors on the attendance of professional sport games: The case of a minor league hockey team. *Sport Marketing Quarterly, 6*(3), 31-40.

Zillmann, D., Bryant, J., and Sapolsky, B. S. (1989). Enjoyment from sports spectatorship. In J. H. Goldstein (Ed.), *Sports, games, and play: Social and psychological viewpoints* (2nd ed.) (pp. 241-278). Hillsdale, NJ: Lawrence Erlbaum.

Zwerneman, B. (2002, August 25). Starting from scratch: Texas hopes to bake a recipe for success. *San Antonio Express News,* 10N.

Issues in Contemporary Athletics
Editor: James H. Humphrey, pp. 93-100

*Chapter 8*

# THE EMERGENCE OF SENIOR ATHLETES

## *George W. Knox*
Gahanna, Ohio, USA

## ABSTRACT

A 92 year-old senior athlete looks back through the events leading to and including senior athletes. In his narrative he includes personal experiences as they relate to the changing public attitude towards the inter-relationship between aging and physical exertion.

There was a time around four decades ago that for anyone over forty to go running was rather unthinkable. The real single event that led to athletic events of all ages, including seniors, happened about three decades ago in the state of California. An attorney, David Pain, arranged a one-mile race for people over forty. The public was strongly against it. "People would be having heart attacks all along the way." Nobody did. Instead, "older people" (over 40) began clamoring for another race, a shorter race, a longer race, a track meet including throws and jumps.

The desire was there, the avalanche started, track and field events emerged, road races began from the short 3K (1.8 miles) to the marathon and beyond (ultramarathons) for all ages. The "running craze" hit the road throughout the U.S. and around the world. The clamor instigated the recording of U.S. and around the world. The clamor instigated the recording of U.S. and world records of every age from forty into the nineties for each athletic event. California became the capital of masters and senior athletics. With the fast breaking of records, the booklet, Masters U.S. and World Age Records, had to be revised every year. Road races of all distances sprang up everywhere from 3K to the marathon for all ages. The "age gaps" of earlier years began to disappear. Senior olympics sprang up in many areas. For the first time, some athletic events were "just for seniors." The first World Masters (including senior championships) occurred in Toronto, Canada in 1975 and have continued bi-yearly throughout the world.

Perhaps the most important aspect of senior athletics is the effect on the senior athlete himself or herself. As for metal effects, the author, a still practicing psychologist, has been amazed at the improvement in his elderly patients who became athletes, while physiological measurements showed anti-aging effects.

# BEFORE THE EVENT

Before a certain event happened that led to an improvement of the lives of thousands of older people – their health, their enjoyment, perhaps event their longevity, there was a restrictive attitude toward physical activity of elderly people.

Let us regress in time to just a little over three decades ago. If we walked along the streets of any U.S. city or town, we would never see anyone over forty running, jogging, or purposely walking briskly unless they were in an urgent hurry for some reason. If we wanted to see anyone running, we would go to some high school or college track or cross-country route. Even then, the runners would be all young males, seldom any females.

This way of doing, or not doing, was a rather universal attitude. The elderly seemed to have the notion that at about the age of seventy or so you would either be ready to die or you would become feeble and, therefore, inactive. I always had the thought that because people became inactive, that was why they become feeble.

The elderly would tend to avoid stairs as much as possible, even forty-year-olds would not run to catch a bus unless it was absolutely necessary. This attitude even penetrated the medical profession. Doctors would advise people to be cautious of exertion. Bed rest was a common prescription. In contrast to today's approach to be described later, heart attack patients tended to be guided into being very inactive – to let the heart rest.

Whenever one makes statements that are almost universally true, they should consider any possible exertions. I do recall three runners of that era that were running after age forty. One exception was Clarence DeMar who had in his youth won the Boston Marathon, I believe it was seven times. He enjoyed running so much that he just wouldn't stop, no matter what anybody thought or said. When he was around forty-five, at a boys camp at Old Orchard, Maine (I believe it was 1931), he ran five mile distance against five boys, each running one mile in a relay – and he won!

Another was Larry Lewis, a waiter at a West Coast restaurant who ran every day. It is said that one day someone asked him why he always ran and he replied, "A hundred years ago (he was supposedly 106 at the time) an old Indian told him, "Keep moving (running) and you will move (live) longer," and that he always ran whenever he went ever since. It is said that at the time of his death at 110, someone said (and this represented the prevailing way of thinking), "No wonder the man died, straining his heart like that day after day."

The third was a forty-year-old or so attorney, David Pain, who liked to run at an age when you are not supposed to. It was he who brought on the event that changed the attitudes of millions of people concerning age and athletics.

# THE EVENT

A little stone can start an avalanche, a spark can start a forest fire, a single event can start the running craze, the masters program and senior athletes. But a stone alone is not enough, the mountain snow has to have reached a certain state. A single spark is not enough, the forest has to have reached a certain state of dryness. A single event did ignite the running craze, but a certain yearning caused the spread of a new attitude and a new way of being for older people.

It all started in California in the mind of David Pain who, contrary to the general public, liked to run. In his mind there came a strange but inviting thought. What would happen if he arranged a one-mile race just for people over 40? Would anybody come? Would anybody actually finish the race? Would anybody object? The answer to all three questions was a definite, "Yes!"

Many were strongly against it. "People would be dying along the way." However, nobody died, many came, many finished. What amazed David Pain the most was what happened afterwards. People started clamoring for more races – some wanted shorter races – some wanted longer races. Both began and both spread like wildfire. The people wanting shorter races went to the track which led to the Masters track and field program. The people wanting longer races led to road races, ranging from 3 Km to the ultra marathons.

## THE SHORTER RACES – BIRTH OF THE MASTERS TRACK AND FIELD PROGRAM

The shorter distance people who went to the track started with the traditional track runs. The format of the typical track meet, as far as runs are concerned, consists of 100, 200, 400, 800 meters, the mile (or metric mile) and the two mile (or metric). This wasn't enough, soon the meets extended to farther runs of 5 and 10 Km – to throws and to the jumps and race walks.

The masters track and field meets began to spread through California where the original "one mile for forties" took place, and quickly spread through the country and around the world. It became apparent that performance does vary relative to age, so ages from 40 to 95 were arranged in five year intervals. Later it was decided to invite the 35-39 age group into the track meets.

By 1975 the first masters and senior world championship took place in Toronto, Canada. About 1,500 older athletes aged up to 96 from twenty-seven countries took part in every existing track and field event, plus race walking events. The age world championships followed the pattern of the regular world olympics. The attitude perhaps was somewhat different, especially among some of the older athletes who never dreamed such a thing would happen to them. There was less stress and anxiety and more of a kind of naïve enjoyment. One 92-year-old British sprinter, for example, was beaten by two 85-year-olds. The 92-year-old won in his age group category but was somehow put in the same heat as the 85-year-olds. The 92-year-old was sure he could beat the two 85-year-old youngsters and he tried his best to get the officials to make it a two out of three race.

While the masters program included all athletes from 40 (or later 35) on up, an off-shoot of the masters included only senior athletes and was referred to as the "senior olympics." There were two types, local and national.

The local type is for every senior, regardless of skill, so the term "olympics" does not really apply. Many communities have their own "olympics" and winners do not proceed to any further location. These events, however, are very beneficial in getting the average senior to become more active. While some events are regular track and field strenuous events, others of lesser intensity are also included as horseshoes, table tennis, and dart throwing. This enabled almost all seniors a chance to participate.

The national program is arranged more like the olympics, focused more on traditional track and field events. In addition, it is organized so winners can advance to regional, state, and national meets.

With older athletes all over the world competing in many events, it set the stage for record keeping of best performances, thus the record book was born, *World and U.S. Age Records for Track and Field, Ages 35 and Above.* It turned out to cover a span of 60 years from 35 to over 95. Rather than hold to an age group span of every five years, records are kept for *every* age for each event, both world and U.S. record. Because records keep improving fast, a new edition is prepared each year. The record book of about fifty pages is published each year and takes each event, one at a time, and arranges the information as follows:

On the left is a vertical listing of ages from 35 to the oldest, usually somewhere in the nineties. To the right of the age is the record, followed by the name of the record-holding athlete, followed by the abbreviated name of the athlete's country. If the record holder is from the U.S., the abbreviation of his state is given. If the record holder is from a foreign country, then the U.S. record holder is also given. To the extreme right is the year and day the record was made.

To the senior athlete, the age of the oldest record holder is of interest. Following are the oldest record holders' ages for the usual standard track and field events: 100 meters, age 99; 200 meters age 99; 400 meters, age 96; 800 meters, age 95/ one mile age 95; two miles age 91; 5 Km, age 94; 10 Km; age 94; and one hour run, age 98. For the jumps: high jump, age 89; long jump, age 99; triple jump, age 94; pole vault, age 89. For the throws: shot putt, age 99; discus, age 99; hammer throw, age 96; and javelin, age 99. These figures were taken from an older book, if there are any changes in the most recent book, the only possible changes would be that the oldest record holder is still older.

How fast one runs or how far one jumps of throws is not the real important thing. The important thing is that these senior athletes could be doing these things at all. I remember the time when people thought they were supposed to become feeble at 70, and so with this acceptance they became inactive. If you are interested in keeping in touch with masters (and senior) athletics, write *National Masters News*, P.O. Box 50098, Eugene, Oregon 97405, or phone them at 541-343-7716 (the headquarters recently moved from California to Oregon).

## THE LONGER RACES – BIRTH OF THE ROAD RACES

Through the years the traditional races of a track meet were the sprints 100 and 200 meters, middle distance quarter and half mile and "long distances" of the mile and two mile. After the "Big Bang" (the one mile race for 40+ year olds), those that took to the track and started the masters track and field program, increased distances were made to 5 Km (3.1 miles), 10 Km (6.2 miles), and the one hour run.

For the road runners, the short and most frequent runs are 5 Km, 5 mile and 10 Km. Then there's the popular marathon, 26.2 miles. Would anybody possibly run any further than that? The answer is yes. A few runners do the 50 Km (31 miles), the 50 miles, and the 100 Km (62 miles). It may seem a bit senseless, but I have run each of these. I like these runs because you don't have to hurry. Just to complete the picture, there are two more, the 24 hour run and the 100 mile run. These ultra ultra marathons are usually run both at once since they often turn out to be about the same.

Having surveyed the array of track and road runs, let us consider the senior citizen of any age who is considering becoming a senior athlete with running as his specialty or as his means of keeping in top shape for other athletic activity.

For the beginner, the road is the easiest, most available place to start – it's everywhere. Of the various distances of road races, the shorter group of 5 and 10 Km and the 5 mile is the best place to start. Almost every town or city has one of these three as its special run. Each community has its special "day of the year" run. Sometimes half the town turns out for the

May Day Run, the Fire Cracker Five (a five mile run on July 4th), the Labor Day run, etc. During the summer months there may be two or three to choose from each weekend.

These village runs are for both sexes, all ages, sometimes family groups. There are the five year age groups with awards for each. In these little runs, although there are age categories relative to awards, the old "age gap" vanishes. The gap between youth and middle age and old age vanishes as all ages do the same thing. If you are considering becoming a senior athlete, whether it's to run the hurdles, throw the hammer or finish the marathon, I feel that these community road races are the easiest and most enjoyable way to start. In a year you will be able to do things you might now consider completely impossible and for several years your performance improves. You will feel like you are getting younger. In fact, some of your basic physiological processes will be getting better, just as if you were becoming younger – but more about that later.

But wait, just in case my description above has put you into a state of readiness to plunge into the line-up for the next 10 Km race --there are a few things to do first. First, of course, have a physical and get your doctor's o.k. Then and thereafter bear in mind – the big word is GRADUAL, even if your ultimate objective is one of those ultra marathons. If you do too much right off, your body and mind will balk, as they can't keep up with the modifications needed for your increased activity. Best to start walking, *gradually* increasing your distance and speed. When you have adjusted to his, during your walk start inserting brief intervals of jogging. *Gradually* increase the intervals of jogging until the jogging becomes the base with little intervals of walking. Finally, it's all jogging, gradually increasing to running. Increase the running distance until it equals the distance of your first race. All this time you should have been wearing *training* running shoes. Later on, use *racing* running shoes during races. Get both from a running shoe store. The training shoe is heavier but easier on the feet, the racers are much lighter and more flexible. Runners sometimes get real persnickety about every single ounce in their racing shoes. Frank Shorter, the night before winning the gold in the Olympic Marathon, was found trying to shave off another ounce of his running shoes. I was caught once by my wife and grandson trying to weigh my socks!

At first you may want to do your running every other day or so and later usually six days a week. You don't need to worry any more (in most communities) about running down the street, regardless of age, you will probably meet other runners, speed walkers, or race walkers of either sex and of any age.

Prior to entering races, a very easy, enjoyable, helpful way is to sign up and enter each of the charitable walk-run events to raise funds for a charitable cause. Most of the charities have a fund raising event once a year. In doing this you are doing several things all at once. You are getting your daily jog, you are reducing the age gap, and helping a cause at the same time. There is always a friendly atmosphere and you may get a lot of pleasant attention "running at your age."

The smaller communities have their 5-10 Km, 5 miles races, the big cities have the big race – the marathon. The marathon was at one time mainly Boston – a handful of young men, women not allowed, older or middle aged men wouldn't dare.

Just as the smaller communities go all out for a "little run," the big cities go all out for the "big run" – helicopters overhead, streets blocked off to traffic, sometimes millions lining the route and thousands – six thousands in Columbus, Ohio, forty thousand in Chicago recently, more yet at Atlanta and New York. Who are these runners – teenagers, housewives, doctors, old people, athletes in wheelchairs.

Should you some day wish to join the array of marathoners, you should first work up to the 10 K races. Then increase your daily runs to about a third the marathon distance, 8-9 miles, and do an easy 20 miles every couple weeks. Many people don't, but one should train for it for a half year or more.

For a beginning runner there is no greater help than to join a local running club. Anyone is welcome to join. There is one in most larger cities. They generally create and manage races and mail you a monthly newsletter including news or flyers of upcoming races. If you wish, they can line you up with a running partner or with a small group that often runs together. Sometimes weekly "fun runs" exist where you can run desired distances and time if you wish, but no competition. There are often meetings and an annual banquet.

In Columbus, Ohio, the "Columbus Roadrunners" started about three decades ago with a half dozen master male runners. Now there are about 400, both sexes, all ages. If there is no Roadrunner organization in your area and you and your friends want to start one, you can get some help and suggestions in organizing a Roadrunners club in your community by contacting the Columbus Roadrunners, P.O. Box 15584 ,Columbus, Ohio 43215-0584.

## THE ADVANTAGE OF BECOMING A SENIOR ATHLETE

Both in my practice of psychology and in my association with runners, I can not help but detect a big difference in the lives of senior citizens who became athletes. Many seniors, upon retirement from their life work, often find themselves with nothing to do or accomplish, everything lies behind, nothing seems to lie ahead. They often get bored, lonesome, and depressed. Many things they used to do, they are no longer able to do. Some start getting prescription anti-depressant treatment from their doctor.

A few of these older people have taken up running. For a few years, to their own surprise, they keep getting better and better. Every runner has his P.R. (Personal Record) for each distance. They keep beating themselves. Now, instead of not being able to do some things they used to do, they are doing things they never did and didn't think they ever could. It's an entirely reversed outlook. Combined with these psychological reversals there may also be contributing physiological effects such as the release of endorphins (the "happy chemicals") with exercise, sometimes producing "runners high."

In any case, the anti-depressants seem no longer needed. One psychiatrist, instead of either prescribing anti-depressants or administrating psychotherapy, took patients out for a jog, apparently producing a greater therapeutic effect than either the drugs or using the traditional "couch." Just as anti-depressant drugs often become un-needed, so do anti-anxiety drugs. Engrossed in their progress, patients become less anxious about the things older people often get anxious about. One senior patient found his agoraphobia and panic attacks constantly diminished as his running was increased.

The attitude about aging seems to also be reversed. Instead of being concerned about each advancing year, I remember a runner saying, "I just can't wait till I turn 65 (because he knows he can beat the runners in the next age group (65-69).

After several years of continually improving the P.R., aging finally begins to slow the performance. But senior runners are prepared for that eventuality as expressed in their frequent remark, "Age slows running but running slows aging."

Are these apparent, rather phenomenal changes, "just" psychological in nature, "just in the head," or are there also some "actual" measurable physiological changes that take place with running or other intensive exercises? The running seniors think, feel, act, and even perform for a number of years as if they are getting younger rather than older. Have they, as some would say, discovered the fountain of youth? There is a physical measurement that seems to come the closest to measuring the physiological changes of aging. This measurement is called the VO2 max. It measures the efficiency with which the body uses oxygen. In ordinary aging, the measurement reduces at the rate of one percent per year. Scientists studying the effects of exercise on aging concluded that an average would reach the level of those 15 years younger. However, if that individual should continue into and intensive program for athletes, he could eventually compare with sedentary people 40 years younger. The scientists felt that no substance or physician- oriented procedures could ever compare in anti-aging as does the effect of strenuous exercise.

However, many an elderly person may ask, "That's all well and good for some, but what if you have a handicap? A handicap, of course, may limit what one can do. I realize that since I have two handicaps myself. The best is to study the nature of your handicap, perhaps with your doctor, determine what exercise you can and can not do, what exercises will help and what may hinder.

Whenever I think of the word "can't," I always counter with memories of the Columbus Marathon wheelchair athletes who can whiz by the fastest runner. I talk with them every Columbus Marathon Day. In spite of whatever the nature of the handicap of each, each one is amazing and in as good physical condition as the best of runners. They are in a positive state of mind comparable to any, and unbelievably different than the state before they became an athlete.

For years I wrote a column for the *Ohio Runner Magazine*. The column was called "The Masters." I interviewed runners between ages 40 and 94. About a third of them were seniors. The objective was not on how fast or far they ran, rather it was how had running affected their lives. I was amazed at some of the results – an enthusiasm that replaced boredom and depression, and diminished anxiety and stress.

I can never forget the 94-year-old (who did the 100, 200, and long jump). I asked him, "How many more years would you like to live?" His reply, "If it's going to be like this, I'll take all I can get." He also recently got married – *after* he became a senior athlete.

Let me mention just briefly why I am so enthused in encouraging seniors to become more active, even to becoming an athlete. My family tree was full of males who died in their fifties and sixties of heart attacks. The longevity record I think was 68. My father died of his attack at age 52. Mind came at 55 and someone said I might have five more years. All the others were given the "be inactive" treatment. It wasn't working, so I took the opposite direction and started exercising gradually. Now at 92, I work six days a week and each February I climb a forty-story tower twice before noon in a charity event. Should you start (gradually) becoming a senior athlete, according to where you live, you may still encounter the way of thinking that was rather universal before those forty-year-olds ran the mile. I started before that time. My early encounters may be of some interest.

I started by running around our back yard pool. In spite of a fairly high hedge, neighbors could see me, "that old man that keeps running in circles every day." So I decided to run in a straight line for a change. I took off in my bedroom slippers into the streets of Gahanna where I live. After a good mile, the Gahanna police stopped me. They asked if someone was after me or was I chasing someone. When I replied neither, they thought I was just a little loony and they let me go. I then thought I should run legitimately somewhere. There was an open track meet at the City of Whitehall. I went there to register. They said, "Are you registering for your son or daughter?" I answered, "Neither, just for myself." They smiled and said, "This open meet is for teenagers, not for adults or, uh, older people." Then one friendly person reminded the others, "We do have an 18 and over age group." So I signed up with the 18 and over category and had a great time.

I figured I'd better just get away from people with my self-inflicted exercise program. So I went to the Adirondack Mountains in northern New York. My first mountain I picked to climb was Prospect Mountain near Lake George. The climb was enjoyable. At the top there was peace and quiet, no people. In the distance to the east I could see the Green Mountains of Vermont, to the north the Lake Placid area where the U.S. beat the Russians in ice hockey in the Winter Olympics.

Peace and quite...then came two large buses on the road to the op. Out of the buses poured senior citizens. I mingled among them. Finally, a bell rang and everybody loaded into the buses. The drivers came after me to get me on the bus. When I told them I climbed up they thought I was affected with senile delusions. I finally convinced them and the buses rumbled down the mountain. Later I heard they always boarded thirty seniors and would always recount upon their arrival back at the foot of the mountain. Their worst nightmare would be to count 29. I often wonder, had I entered the bus the confusion upon counting 31 at the foot of the mountain.

So as you (gradually) start your athletic program, depending on your location, you may still encounter the attitude that seniors should be inactive. Don't let it bother you. Just keep on running and remember, "Age slows running – but running slows aging."

Issues in Contemporary Athletics
Editor: James H. Humphrey, pp. 101-112

ISBN 1-59454-595-2

*Chapter 9*

# TERRORISM: A FORESEEABLE THREAT TO U.S. SPORT FACILITY OWNERS AND OPERATORS

## *Thomas Baker*

## ABSTRACT

September 11, 2001 immeasurably and permanently changed the United States. The events of that fateful day have made American life more complicated and uncertain. This is true even for those who work in the sports industry, and especially true for those who own or operate sport stadiums and arenas. What was once unimaginable and unforeseeable is now reality. This new foreseeable threat carries with it legal implications for those who own or operate sport facilities. If a sport facility is the target of a terrorist attack, then there is a possibility that the facility's owners and operators could be sued and subsequently held liable. Therefore, it is crucial for sport facility owners and operators to understand how liability can be imposed on them for the actions of third-party terrorists.

## INTRODUCTION

September 11, 2001 immeasurably and permanently changed the United States. The events of that fateful day have made American life more complicated and uncertain. This is true even for those who work in the sports industry, and especially true for those who own or operate sport stadiums and arenas. What was once unimaginable and unforeseeable is now reality and this new foreseeable terrorism threat carries with it legal implications for those who own or operate sport facilities.

Terrorism is the use of force or violence against persons or property in violation of the criminal laws of the United States for purposes of intimidation, coercion, or ransom. Terrorists typically use threats to create fear among the public, to try to convince citizens that their government is powerless to prevent terrorism, and to get immediate publicity for their causes. Acts of terrorism may include both threats and actions of terrorism, including assassinations, bombings, and the use of chemical, biological, and nuclear weapons. High-risk targets include military and government facilities, airports, large cities, and high-profile landmarks. Terrorists may also target large public venues such as corporate centers, holiday gatherings, and sports arenas (Federal Emergency Management Agency (FEMA), 2003).

Recently, CNN (2003) reported that "Attorney General John Ashcroft said reports indicated that so called 'soft' targets, those more lightly guarded, such as apartments, hotels, sports arenas, and amusement parks, are at an increased risk" for terrorist attack. Additionally, in 2002, the Federal Bureau of Investigation (FBI) issued a "very vague" alert warning that individuals with suspected ties to terrorist groups had used the Internet to access information on stadiums and arenas in the United States (Associated Press, 2002).

In our post-September 11, 2001 society, American sport remains a symbolic target of terrorism based on its association with the globalization of the American economy and culture (Tolbert, 2003). As such, sport venues carry an increased risk of terrorist attack (CNN, 2003). Professional sports leagues have recognized terrorism as a foreseeable threat and have acted accordingly. In fact, after September 11, 2001, event security became the number one priority of the National Football League (NFL). Supporting the increase in security, NFL Commissioner Paul Tagliabue stated that the league could survive a lot of mistakes and bad business decisions, but could not, perhaps, survive a terrorist attack (George, 2001).

In response to the risk of terrorism at U.S. sport stadiums and arenas, many governmental and sport organizations have taken proactive, precautionary measures. Examples of this include governmental agencies such as the FBI (Horn, 2002) conducting counter-terrorism training at Cinergy Field in Cincinnati, and the National Guard providing security at events such as the 2002 Olympic Winter Games held in Salt Lake City (Associated Press, 2003) and checking for chemical agents during the Major League Baseball playoffs (Prawdzik, 2002). In 2002, the U.S. Secret Service led forty-eight agencies in providing security at the NFL's Super Bowl XXXVI, which the federal government designated as a National Special Security Event, a status typically reserved for presidential and papal visits (U.S. Department of Homeland Security, n.d.; Pells, 2003). The following year, at Super Bowl XXXVII held in San Diego, military jets patrolled the skies to enforce a no-fly zone that included a 7-mile radius and an 18,000-foot ceiling over the stadium (Pells, 2003).

In an effort to manage the risks associated with terrorism, many sport leagues/associations such the National Hockey League (NHL, Wallace, 2002), the National Basketball Association (NBA, Tolbert, 2003), Major League Baseball (MLB, 2002), the NFL (Dohrmann, 2001; Fallon, 2003; Farley, 2004; Iwata, 2002), and the National Collegiate Athletic Association (NCAA, Pickle, 2003; Wingfield, 2002) have issued wide-ranging security rules and recommendations. Such measures have also been studied by researchers including Ammon, Southall, and Blair (2004) and Pantera et al. (2003) who identified many of the security/terrorism-related risk management practices recently employed at sport stadiums and arenas.

In addition to the governmental and sport agencies that have addressed the risks associated with terrorism, a number of industry organizations associated with sport and entertainment venue management have also addressed the issue. For example, in 2004, the International Association of Assembly Managers (IAAM) in cooperation with the U.S. Department of Homeland Security is offering a free *Terrorism Awareness Training Course*. This four-hour course focuses exclusively on stadiums and arenas to assist security personnel in recognizing and preventing terrorist activity (IAAM, 2004). Additionally, representatives from the NFL, NHL, MLB, NBA and NCAA collaborated with the IAAM and produced the *Best Practices Guide* that provides measures that can be taken by facility managers to protect against terrorism (IAAM, n.d.). However, sports leagues like the NFL do not dictate security policy to the stadiums and arenas that house their teams. After all, most sport stadiums and arenas are owned by individuals or municipalities (Fallon, 2003). Thus, sport facility managers are under no obligation to adopt these measures.

Other associations have also addressed the risks associated with terrorism at sport facilities. In 2003, Street and Smith's *Sports Business Journal* organized the 2nd annual *Sports Venue Safety and Security: Enhancing and Combating Complacency* forum. This meeting focused on examining and improving venue security, player safety, fan safety, and terrorism preparedness (SportsBusiness Journal, 2003). Likewise, the Worldwide Conventions and Business Forums (WCBF, 2003) organized a 2003 conference entitled *Venue and Event Security: Counter-Terrorism Strategies for Stadiums, Arenas, Live Events and Facilities*. This conference was designed to provide information regarding the threat of terrorist attack to companies responsible for staging live entertainment, public, or sport events in the U.S., and to owners and operators of stadiums, arenas, and convention and performing art centers (WCBF, 2003).

In the event of a terrorist attack on a sport venue, imposing liability on the owners and operators of sport stadiums and arenas for the actions of terrorists may seem unfair. Certainly, the terrorists are the ones to blame for their actions. However, it is also certain that the victims of terror will not be able to recover from the terrorists to any material degree (Gash, 2003). Accordingly, victims of terrorism will look to others for compensation. If a sports facility is the target of a terrorist attack, then there is a possibility that the facility's owners and operators could be sued and subsequently held liable. Therefore, it is critical that owners and operators of sport facilities understand how liability can be imposed on them for the actions of third-party terrorists. This article will examine the concept of foreseeability and determine whether victims of terrorism can establish liability by showing that terrorism is now a foreseeable threat to U.S. sport arenas and stadiums. In doing so, this article will address the role of foreseeability in the duty of care determination.

## THE DUTY OF CARE

The first question that must be addressed in assessing liability is whether the owners and operators of sport facilities owe spectators and participants a duty of care in negligence to protect them from third-party acts of terror. It is important to note that the existence of a duty of care is a question of law because it results in the conclusion that it is appropriate to impose liability for the injuries suffered (*Tarasoff v. Regents of University of California*, 1976). Thus, judges bear the responsibility of determining whether a duty of care exists because questions of law are decided by judges, not juries.

Generally, a person does not owe a duty to protect others from the acts of third parties or to warn said individuals that they are endangered by third party action. However, a duty may arise if either a special relation exists between the actor and the third person that imposes a duty upon the actor to control the third person's conduct, or if a special relation exists between the actor and the person that needs protection (Restatement (Second) of Torts § 35, 1965).

A special relation does exist between landowners and those who use their premises (Restatement (Second) of Torts § 344, 1965). Traditionally, this relationship would turn on whether the guest was deemed to be an invitee or licensee (62 American Jurisprudence 2nd Premises Liability § 81, 2003). However, the distinction between invitees and licensees in many jurisdictions is no longer followed. Instead, such jurisdictions recognize a duty of reasonable care owed by the occupier of land to all lawful visitors (62 American Jurisprudence 2nd Premises Liability § 81, 2003).

Owners or operators of sport stadiums or arenas, like any other owner or operator of a premises, are under a duty to exercise reasonable care under the circumstances to prevent harm to participants and spectators of activities that take place in their facilities (Hurst, Zoubek, and Pratsinakis, 2002). The imposition of liability under these circumstances is known as premises liability. So what is the reasonable duty of care for those who own and operate sport facilities in regard to participants and spectators? Section 344 of the Restatement (Second) of Torts defines the duty of reasonable care owed by property owners who allow others to enter their premises for business purposes. Section 344 states:

> A possessor of land who holds it open to the public for entry for his business purposes is subject to liability to members of the public while they are upon the land for such a purpose, for physical harm caused by the accidental, negligent, or intentionally harmful acts of third persons or animals, and by the failure of the possessor to exercise reasonable care to (a) discover that such acts are being done or are likely to be done, or (b) give a warning adequate to enable the visitors to avoid the harm, or otherwise to protect against it (Restatement (Second) Torts § 344, 1965).

Additionally, Comment (f) of section 344 provides further explanation of the duty of reasonable care owed by landowners to protect patrons from third party action. Comment (f) states:

> Since the possessor is not an insurer of the visitor's safety, he is ordinarily under no duty to exercise any care until he knows or has reason to know that the acts of the third person are occurring, or are about to occur. He may, however, know or have reason to know, from past experience, that there is a likelihood of conduct on the part of third persons in general which is likely to endanger the safety of the visitor, even though he has no reason to expect it on the part of any particular individual. If the place or character of his business, or his past experience, is such that he should reasonably anticipate careless criminal conduct on the part of third persons, either generally or at some particular time, he may be under a duty to take precautions against it, and to provide a reasonably sufficient number of servants to afford a reasonable protection (Comment (f) to Restatement (Second) Torts § 344, 1965).

Courts have interpreted the statements in Comment (f) to establish a duty on the part of landowners to protect customers from the foreseeable acts of third parties (*McClung v. Delta Square Limited Partnership*, 1996). In fact, most courts have followed Comment (f) by holding that while landowners are not the insurers of their customer's safety, they do owe a duty to take reasonable precautions to protect customers from foreseeable criminal acts (*McClung v. Delta Square Limited Partnership*, 1996).

At trial, the plaintiff bears the burden of providing facts that establish foreseeability (*Gill v. Chicago Park District*, 1980). In *Gill v. Chicago Park District*, the plaintiff sued the Chicago Park District, the Chicago Bears, and the owner of Soldier Field after being physically assaulted by a third party at a football game. The Appellate Court of Illinois found that the existence of a reasonable duty under the facts at issue does not exist unless the occurrence was reasonably foreseeable. The appellate court affirmed the trial court's decision that liability does not exist "unless there are sufficient facts to put defendants on notice that an intervening criminal act is likely to occur" (p. 673).

However, threats of violence can provide the requisite proof of foreseeability (Miller, 1993; van der Smissen, 1990). In fact, courts have held that facility managers bear the responsibility to act on threats of violence as if they had actually occurred (*Bishop v. Fair Lanes*, 1986). The fact that violence had yet to occur at the time of the threat will not protect facility owners and operators who know of credible violence yet refrain from taking reasonable preventative measures (*Ledger v. Stockton*, 1988).

Absent clear and credible threats, third-party action may still be deemed foreseeable. There are four basic tests that courts employ to determine whether a third-party criminal act was foreseeable. These tests are: (1) the specific harm test, (2) the prior similar incidents test, (3) the totality of the circumstances test, and (4) the balancing test (*Boren v. Worthen National Bank of Arkansas*, 1996; *Delta Tau Delta v. Johnson*, 1999; *Krier v. Safeway Stores 46, Inc.*, 1997; and *McClung v. Delta Square Limited Partnership*, 1996).

## The Specific Harm Test

The specific harm test provides that landowners do not owe a duty to those on their property unless the owner knew or should have known that the specific harm was occurring or was about to occur. Most courts do not follow this test based on an unwillingness to hold that a criminal act is foreseeable only in the aforementioned situations (*Boren v. Worthen National Bank of Arkansas*, 1996; *Delta Tau Delta v. Johnson*, 1999; *McClung v. Delta Square Limited Partnership*, 1996). Also, courts have found that the specific harm test is vague, offers too little protection to invitees, and too much protection to landowners (Mallen, 2001).

Under the specific harm test, it would be difficult, if not impossible, to impose liability on a facility owner or operator for the actions of terrorists absent a credible threat of terrorism or some other form of actual knowledge of the terrorist activity. It seems highly unlikely that a terrorist intending to strike a sport facility will enter the facility and announce his or her intentions, thereby providing the defendant with actual notice of the attack (*McClung v. Delta Square Limited Partnership*, 1996). Thus, jurisdictions that utilize the specific harm test afford sport facility owners and operators a great deal of protection.

## The Prior Similar Incidents Test

The prior similar incidents (PSI) test requires the plaintiff to introduce evidence of prior incidents of crime on or near the defendant's premises to establish foreseeability. Courts vary on whether the prior crimes must be of the same general type and nature as the present offense. The modern application of this rule does not require evidence of the same type of prior crimes occurring on or near defendant's premises. Instead, courts inquire into the location, nature and extent of previous criminal activities and their similarity, proximity or other relationship to the crime in question (*McClung v. Delta Square Limited Partnership*, 1996; *Polomie v. Golub Corporation*, 1996).

The PSI test has several limitations. First, the test has the effect of discouraging landowners from taking adequate measures to protect their premises from known dangers because under the test, the first victim loses while subsequent victims recover (*Delta Tau Delta v. Johnson*, 1999; see also, *Clohesy v. Food Circus Supermarkets, Inc.*, 1997; *Doud v. Las Vegas Hilton Corp.*, 1993; *Maguire v. Hilton Hotels Corp.*, 1995; *Seibert v. Vic Regnier Builders, Inc.* 1993; *Sharp v. W.H. Moore, Inc.*, 1990; *Small v. McKennan Hospital*, 1989; and *Whittaker v. Saraceno*, 1994). This result is unfair and contravenes the policy behind the test. After all, why should a landowner get one free assault before being held liable for third-party criminal acts (*McClung v. Delta Square Limited Partnership*, 1996)?

Second, the PSI test's limitation of evidence of foreseeability to prior similar criminal acts leads to arbitrary results and distinctions. This is because the test leaves open the question as to how similar the prior incidents must be. Other potential problems with the test include issues concerning the proximity of time and location of the incidents. The test also equates foreseeability of a specific act with previous occurrences of similar acts. Thus, landowners may ignore foreseeable dangers based on the absence of prior incidents. Finally, the test removes too many cases from jury consideration, because foreseeability is ordinarily a question of fact that is decided by juries (*McClung v. Delta Square Limited Partnership*, 1996).

Accordingly, the PSI test also affords sport facility owners and operators a substantial amount of protection against liability for third-party acts of terror. In the U.S., only a few sport venues are located near areas that terrorists have struck. Hence, it will be difficult for plaintiffs to meet the requirement of showing prior similar incidents. A plaintiff may be able to establish that the facility is in a high crime area of town. However, even the modern application of the rule requires that there be some similarity between the prior incidents and the crime at issue. The problem is that the nature and extent of terrorism typically differs from the nature and extent of most criminal activity. This is especially true when one considers the potential for mass injury and catastrophic damage that is associated with terrorism. Thus, any connection between most felonies committed near sports venues and terrorist activity is tenuous at best. Consequently, judges may not be convinced that prior incidents involving criminal activity create the requisite foreseeability necessary to sustain a cause of action. Therefore, absent a previous terrorist attack on or near the premises, facility owners and operators in jurisdictions that use the PSI test, may escape liability for an initial terrorist attack.

## The Totality of the Circumstances Test

In the totality of the circumstances test, a court considers all the circumstances surrounding an event to determine whether a criminal act was foreseeable. Prior similar instances are included in the equation along with the nature, condition, and location of the land. The advantage of the totality of the circumstances test is that it incorporates the specific harm test and the prior similar incidents test as substantial factors in the foreseeability determination. However, the absence of either prior similar incidents or knowledge of the specific harm will not preclude recovery. Thus, unlike the specific harm test and the PSI test, the totality of the circumstances test does not "artificially and arbitrarily" limit the determination (*Delta Tau Delta v. Johnson*, 1999, p. 972).

There is a drawback to the totality of the circumstances test. Courts have criticized the test for being too broad and unpredictable (*Delta Tau Delta v. Johnson*, 1999; *McClung v. Delta Square Limited Partnership*, 1996). The test tends to impose on landowners an unqualified duty to protect customers in areas that experience any significant level of criminal activity (*Ann M. v. Pacific Plaza Shopping Center*, 1993; *McClung v. Delta Square Limited Partnership*, 1996). The imposition of this duty seems to conflict with the general principle that landowners are not insurers of their customer's safety. However, courts have determined that the test does not impose upon landowners the duty to ensure their customers' safety, but simply requires landowners to take reasonable precautions to prevent criminal acts against their customers (*Delta Tau Delta v. Johnson*, 1999; see also, *Clohesy v. Food Circus Supermarkets, Inc.*, 1997; *Doud v. Las Vegas Hilton Corp.*, 1993; *Maguire v. Hilton Hotels*

*Corp.*, 1995; *Seibert v. Vic Regnier Builders, Inc.* 1993; *Sharp v. W.H. Moore, Inc.*, 1990; *Small v. McKennan Hospital*, 1989; and *Whittaker v. Saraceno*, 1994).

*Delta Tau Delta v. Johnson* (1999) and *Hayden v. the University of Notre Dame* (1999) provide examples of how courts can apply the totality of the circumstances test. These two cases both come from Indiana, a jurisdiction that adopted the totality of the circumstances test. In *Delta Tau Delta*, the plaintiff, an undergraduate student at Indiana University, brought suit against a fraternity, Delta Tau Delta, Beta Alpha chapter, after an alumnus of the fraternity sexually assaulted her at one of the fraternity's parties. The Supreme Court of Indiana found that the fraternity had prior similar incidents of both sexual assault and forced alcohol consumption at its parties. Further, the fraternity chapter had awareness of prior instances of date rape that occurred on campus. The court used these facts to reach the conclusion that the date rape was foreseeable based on the totality of the circumstances. Therefore, the court held that the fraternity owed a duty of care to the plaintiff to protect her from a third-party sexual assault while she was on the fraternity's premises (*Delta Tau Delta v. Johnson*, 1999).

In *Hayden v. University of Notre Dame*, Letitia Hayden brought suit against the University of Notre Dame after spectators injured her while she was attending a football game at Notre Dame's football stadium. Hayden and her husband, both season ticket holders, were seated in the south end zone of the stadium behind the goalpost. During the second quarter of the football game, one of the teams kicked the ball into the stands near Hayden. Several spectators lunged for the ball and one of them struck Hayden, knocking her down and injuring her shoulder (*Hayden v. University of Notre Dame*, 1999).

The court in *Hayden* found that there were several prior incidents involving fans being bumped or injured by other fans who were attempting to retrieve footballs. The court placed emphasis on Mrs. Hayden's testimony in which she stated that she had attended Notre Dame football games for many years and during this period she had witnessed balls land in the seats near her many times. Furthermore, Hayden testified that she had witnessed fans jump to retrieve balls on numerous occasions. Her husband also testified that the netting used to prevent balls from flying into the stands only worked about fifty percent of the time. When the netting did not work, the ball would fly into the stands and a scramble for the ball would ensue. He went on to state that he was even jostled by scrambling fans on several occasions. Finally, he stated that ushers were aware that fans were being jostled in scrambles for loose balls; however, the ushers did not aggressively attempt to retrieve the balls (*Hayden v. University of Notre Dame*, 1999).

Applying the totality of the circumstances test to the aforementioned facts, the court found that Notre Dame should have foreseen that injuries were likely to result from the actions of third parties lunging for balls kicked into the end zone seating area. Thus, Notre Dame owed a duty to protect Hayden from such injury (*Hayden v. University of Notre Dame*, 1999).

It is likely that the totality of the circumstances test could be used to establish liability against a sports facility for the actions of terrorists. This is because, unlike the first two tests, the totality of the circumstances test has broad applicability and is not limited only to instances where knowledge of the specific harm exists or situations similar to prior incidents.

It is true that the best two examples of the use of this test, *Hayden v. University of Notre Dame* and *Delta Tau Delta v. Johnson*, both place significant emphasis on the existence of prior similar incidents in their determinations. However, courts have recognized that the test can establish liability even in the absence of prior similar incidents (*Delta Tau Delta v.*

*Johnson*, 1999, p. 972). After all, the totality of the circumstances test permits the court to consider all the circumstances to determine foreseeability.

Accordingly, it seems likely that a situation could arise where the totality of the facts require the imposition of liability despite an absence of prior similar incidents involving terrorism at or near the sports facility. For example, what if a stadium or arena utilized grossly inadequate inspection procedures at admission gates despite a credible threat of terrorism? And what if one of the patrons that enters through the gates is armed with a bomb? The broadness of the totality of the circumstances test allows courts to consider an array of facts that can be used to establish liability. In fact, the test is so broad that it has been criticized as imposing an unfair burden on the part of landowners to protect their guests (*Delta Tau Delta v. Johnson*, 1999). Therefore, owners and operators of sport facilities in jurisdictions that use this test should realize that the duty they owe will be determined based on the totality of the facts including their actions, and not just whether they had actual knowledge of the terrorist activity or are located in areas that have had prior similar incidents.

## The Balancing Test

The fourth test used by courts is the balancing test. The balancing test weighs the foreseeable probability and gravity of harm posed by the defendant's conduct against the burden upon the defendant to take measures to prevent the harm. When the probability and gravity of harm outweigh the burden of preventative measures, a duty of care is established (*McCall v. Wilder*, 1995). Accordingly, as the foreseeability and degree of potential harm increase, so too, does the duty to prevent it (*Delta Tau Delta v. Johnson*, 1999).

Courts have developed factors to be considered in the balancing process. These factors include: the foreseeable probability of the harm or injury occurring; the possible magnitude of the potential harm; the importance or social value of the defendant's activity; the usefulness of the conduct to the defendant; the feasibility of safer alternative conduct; the relative costs and burdens associated with the alternative conduct; and, the relative safety of the alternative conduct. Also, courts must consider the location, nature and extent of previous criminal activities and their similarity, proximity, or other relationship to the crime at issue. These factors provide an analytical framework by which courts employing the balancing test can determine the duty owed (*McClung v. Delta Square Limited Partnership*, 1996).

The main criticism of the balancing test is that it requires the judge to decide whether the defendant took reasonable precautions given the circumstances. This is a question that is typically left for a jury to decide. Another criticism lies in the fact that the test places significant emphasis on prior similar incidents (*Delta Tau Delta v. Johnson*, 1999; *McClung v. Delta Square Limited Partnership*, 1996).

Like the totality of the circumstances test, the balancing test also seems favorable to plaintiffs harmed by third-party terrorists because it too permits courts to consider all the circumstances surrounding the event. However, the foreseeability aspect of the balancing test may pose a problem for plaintiffs. This is because foreseeability under this test places more emphasis on prior similar instances than what is required under the totality of the circumstances test. With that said, the flexible nature of the balancing test could offset this problem. In fact, it is possible that the gravity of the harm posed by terrorists may tip the balancing scale in favor of finding a duty of care.

## General Foreseeable Risk

A plaintiff may be able to establish a duty of care without being subjected to one of the four tests under premises liability. Some courts have found the requisite special relationship needed for a duty of care based on the finding that the defendant's conduct gave rise to a general foreseeable risk. The existence of a duty of care under this approach also turns on the foreseeability of the risk of harm (*Stanford v. Kuwait Airlines Corporation*, 1996). However, foreseeability is not determined by using any of the four tests that courts use to establish a duty of care under premises liability. Instead, the courts must determine whether the defendant's conduct created a broader "zone of risk" that poses a general threat to others (*McCain v. Florida Power Corporation*, 1992).

In *Stanford v. Kuwait Airlines Corporation*, the United States Second Circuit Court of Appeals found a duty of care on the part of the airline to protect passengers on connecting flights based on a general foreseeable risk of terrorism. The facts establishing the general foreseeable risk included the airline's knowledge of (1) threats made by Hezbollah terrorists, (2) the fact that terrorists were already boarding flights in "dirty" airports so that they could infiltrate other airlines, (3) the poor security measures in place at the Beirut airport, and (4) the fact that the hijacker's tickets "teemed with suspicion" (p. 125). The court found that the defendant's failure to act in the face of these facts created a general foreseeable risk. Thus, a special relationship existed between the airline and the passengers that gave rise to a duty of care on the part of the airline to take reasonable precautions necessary to protect the innocent passengers from the terrorists boarding connecting flights.

Similarly, it is quite possible that a situation could develop in which sport facility owners and operators are faced with a general foreseeable risk of terrorism. If this happens, a corresponding duty could be found that would require the facility managers to take reasonable preventative measures to protect their patrons and participants from the foreseeable risk. However, the applicability of the general foreseeable risk theory to plaintiffs in an action against a sport facility owner or operator is not clear. There are very few cases that support the use of this concept as a separate method for establishing a duty of care. Thus, some jurisdictions may not recognize the concept of a general foreseeable risk as an alternative to the four tests used under premises liability.

## CONCLUSION

Foreseeability is a difficult concept to define. This article provides examples of how courts in different jurisdictions have developed methods to determine foreseeability in terms of a duty of care analysis. Unfortunately, despite these efforts, foreseeability remains an amorphous concept. However, the existence of foreseeability is essential for a plaintiff to prevail in a case against owners and operators of sport facilities for the actions of terrorists. Thus, the question of liability turns on whether terrorism is a foreseeable threat to sport facilities.

Steps taken by sports leagues such as the NFL, professional organizations like the IAAM, as well as other for-profit associations such as Street and Smith show that industry leaders believe that terrorism is a foreseeable threat to sport facilities. Further, these steps could factor into the duty of care determination of a lawsuit involving a sport facility owner or operator who allegedly did not adopt adequate anti-terrorism procedures. The broad nature of both the totality of the circumstances test and the balancing test under premises liability could allow courts to consider measures taken by industry leaders to determine whether a duty of care was owed. Additionally, the concept of general foreseeable risk is also very broad in application; thus, courts using this theory could look to what other organizations are doing to decide whether the defendant's lack of security created a "zone of risk."

Accordingly, it is critical for those who operate sport arenas and stadiums to develop and implement risk management strategies aimed at reducing the risks associated with terrorism. Today, Americans are more concerned about security and expect reasonable measures to be in place when they attend large sporting events (Palumbo, 2004). Sport facility owners and managers should take note of what sport leagues, relevant professional associations, and other arenas and stadiums are doing to guard their patrons and facilities against terrorism. After all, if other sport facility managers believe that terrorism is a foreseeable threat to sport venues, then courts of law may reach the same conclusion.

## REFERENCES

American Jurisprudence (2nd.). (2003). *Premises Liability*, 62 § 81.

Ammon, R., Southall, R.M., and Blair, D.A. (2004). *Sport facility management: Organizing events and mitigating risks.* Morgantown, WV: Fitness Information Technology.

Ann M. v. Pacific Plaza Shopping Center, 863 P.2d 207 (Cal. 1993).

Associated Press. (2002, July 4). FBI alert on stadiums. *CBSNEWS.com.* Retrieved May 28, 2004, from http://www.cbsnews.com/stories/2002/07/03/attack/main514252.shtml.

Associated Press. (2003, November 3). FBI director to get firsthand look at Athens Olympic security. Retrieved January 30, 2004, from http://www.ksdk.com/sports/olympics _article_new.asp?storyid=49540.

Bishop v. Fair Lanes, 803 F.2d 1548 (11th Cir. 1986).

Boren v. Worthen National Bank of Arkansas, 921 S.W.2d 934 (Ark. 1996).

Clohesy v. Food Circus Supermarkets, Inc., 694 A.2d 1017 (N.J. 1997).

CNN. (2003, February 9). Official: Credible threats pushed terror alert higher. *CNN.com.* Retrieved May 28, 2004, from http://www.cnn.com/2003/US/02/07/threat.level/.

Delta Tau Delta v. Johnson, 712 N.E.2d 968 (Ind. 1999).

Dohrmann, G. (2001, September 18). In the wake of the Sept. 11 attacks, going to a game won't be the same. *SI Online.* Retrieved May 28, 2004, from http://sportsillustrated. cnn.com/features/scorecard/news/2001/09/18/sc/.

Doud v. Las Vegas Hilton Corp., 864 P.2d 796 (Nev. 1993).

Farley, G. (2004, January 30). Security blankets Patriots once again. *The Enterprise.* Retrieved May 28, 2004, from http://enterprise.southofboston.com/articles/2004/01/30/ news/sports/sports03.txt.

Federal Emergency Management Agency. (2002). *Are you ready? A guide to citizen preparedness.* FEMA Publication H-34. Washington, DC: FEMA. Retrieved May 28, 2004, from http://www.fema.gov/areyouready/.

Fallon, R.H. (2003). Fordham sports law forum: Legal issues in sports security. In L. Freedman (Ed.), *Fordham Intellectual Property, Media and Entertainment Law Journal, 13*(2), 349-403.

Gash, J. (2003). At the intersection of proximate cause and terrorism: a contextual analysis of the (proposed) Restatement Third of Torts' approach to intervening and superseding causes. *Kentucky Law Journal, 91*(3), 523-612.

George, T. (2001, September 18). NFL is tightening security as games resume on Sunday. *New York Times*, C18.

Gill v. Chicago Park Dist., 407 N.E.2d 671 (Ill. App. 3rd. 1980).

Hayden v. University of Notre Dame, 716 N.E.2d 603 (Ind. App. 1999).

Horn, D. (2002, November, 7). FBI asked to stop blasts at stadium, Counter-terrorism training frightened city. *The Cincinnati Enquirer*. Retrieved May 28, 2004, from http://www.enquirer.com/editions/2002/11/07/loc_kaboom07.html.

Hurst, R., Zoubek, P., and Pratsinakis, C. (2002). American Sports as a target of terrorism: The duty of care after September 11th. *Sport and the Law Journal, 10*(1), 134-139.

IAAM. (no date). Center for venue management studies. *Iaam.org*. Retrieved May 28, 2004, from http://www.iaam.org/CVMS/CVMSsafety.htm.

IAAM. (2004). Department of Homeland Security presents terrorism awareness training course for stadiums and arenas. Retrieved May 28, 2004, from http://www.iaam.org/2004_meetings/DHS/DHS.htm.

Iwata, E. (2002, March 17). Stadium security gets serious. *USA Today*. Retrieved May 28, 2004, from http://www.usatoday.com/money/general/2002/03/18/stadiums-security.htm.

Keeton, W.P. (1984). *Prosser and Keeton on the law of torts*. St. Paul, MN: West.Krier v. Safeway Stores 46, Inc., 943 P.2d 405 (Wyo. 1997).

Ledger v. Stockton, 249 Cal.Rptr. 688 (Cal. App. 3rd. 1988).

Maguire v. Hilton Hotels Corp., 899 P.2d 393 (Hawaii 1995).

Major League Baseball. (2002, April 25). MLB implements new security measures. *MLB.com*. Retrieved May 28, 2004, from http://mlb.mlb.com/NASApp/mlb/mlb/news/mlb_news.jsp?ymd=20020425andcontent_id=14313andvkey=news_mlbandfext=.jsp.

Mallen, S.A. (2001). Touchdown! A victory for injured fans at sporting events? *Missouri Law Review, 66*(2), 487-504.

McCall v. Wilder, 913 S.W.2d 150 (Tenn. 1995).

McCain v. Florida Power Corp., 593 So.2d 500 (Fla.1992).

McClung v. Delta Square Limited Partnership, 937 S.W.2d 891 (Tenn. 1996).

Miller, L.K. (1993). Crowd control. *Journal of Physical Education, Recreation and Dance, 62*(2), 31-35.

Palumbo, L. (2004). Counterterrorism measures: An essential part of venue security. *Public Venue Security*. Retrieved May 28, 2004, from http://www.publicvenuesecurity.com/articles/391feat4.html.

Pantera, M.J., Accorsi, R., Winter, C., Gobeille, R., Griveas, S., Queen, D., et al. (2003). *The Sport Journal, 6*(4). Retrieved May 28, 2004, from http://www.thesportjournal.org/2003Journal/Vol6-No4/security.htm.

Pells, E. (2003, January 24). Super Bowl security to be less intrusive. *Athens Banner-Herald*. Retrieved January 30, 2004, from http://www.onlineathens.com/stories/012403/spo_20030124026.shtml.

Pickle, D. (2003, January 6). New premium placed on insurance. *The NCAA News*. Retrieved May 28, 2004, from http://www.ncaa.org/news/2003/20030106/active/4001n04.html.

Polomie v. Golub Corporation, 226 A.D.2d 979 (NY. 1996).

Prawdzik, C. (2002, November). Civil support teams: Protecting the pastime. *National Guard Magazine*. Retrieved May 28, 2004, from http://www.ngaus.org/ngmagazine/protectingpastime1102.asp.

Restatement (Second) of Torts. (1965). § 35.

Restatement (Second) of Torts. (1965). § 344.

Seibert v. Vic Regnier Builders, Inc., 856 P.2d 1332 (Kan. 1993).

Sharp v. W.H. Moore, Inc., 796 P.2d 506 (Idaho 1990).

Small v. McKennan Hospital, 403 N.W.2d 410 (S.D. 1987), aff'd, 437 N.W.2d 194 (S.D. 1989).

SportsBusiness Journal. (2003). *Sports venue safety and security: Enhancing performance and combating complacency* [Brochure]. Charlotte, NC: Author.

Stanford v. Kuwait Airlines Corporation, 89 F.3d 117 (2d Cir. 1996).

Tarasoff v. Regents of University of California, 17 Cal. 3rd 425 (Cal. 1976).

Tolbert, B.A. (2003, January 24). Playing it safe: NBA's security chief addresses New York City law alumni. *UB Law Links*. Retrieved May 28, 2004, from http://www.law.buffalo.edu/Alumni_And_Giving/ub_law_links/02-2003/default.asp?ll=5andf=NYCLunch.

U.S. Department of Homeland Security. (no date). Threats and protection: National security special events. Retrieved May 28, 2004, from http://www.dhs.gov/dhspublic/display?theme=30andcontent=55.

van der Smissen, B. (1990). *Legal liability and risk management for public and private entities* (Vols. 1-3). Cincinnati: Anderson.

Wallace, K. (2002, June 3). Stanley Cup finals mean more security for ESA: State, federal officials will be on hand to help with security efforts. *WRAL.com*. Retrieved May 28, 2004, from http://www.wral.com/sports/1489953/detail.html.

Whittaker v. Saraceno, 635 N.E.2d 1185 (Mass. 1994).

Wingfield, K. (2002, February 14). Final Four security considered. *The State.com*. Retrieved May 28, 2004, from http://www.thestate.com/mld/thestate/sports/2672352.htm.

Worldwide Conventions and Business Forums. (2003). Venue and event security: Counter-terrorism strategies for stadiums, arenas, live events and facilities. Retrieved January 30, 2004, from http://www.wcbf.com/security/6003/news.php.

Issues in Contemporary Athletics
Editor: James H. Humphrey, pp. 113-121

ISBN 1-59454-595-2
© 2007 Nova Science Publishers, Inc.

*Chapter 10*

# THE ECONOMIC IMPACT OF PROFESSIONAL TENNIS

## *Brian Bianco, George B. Cunningham,*[1]
## *and Michael Sagas*

Texas A and M University, College Station, Texas, USA

## ABSTRACT

Though there are several benefits to hosting a professional sport event, tangible, monetary benefits are often thought of as most important. Economic impact analysis represents one method of measuring such effects. The purpose of this study was to conduct an economic impact analysis of a professional tennis tournament. Data were collected on-site from 638 spectators. Results indicate the tournament had a $16.92 million in local economic activity (sales multiplier), $8.11 million in residents' personal income (income multiplier), $11.38 million in personal income, property income, and indirect business taxes (value-added multiplier), and 203.6 new jobs (employment multiplier). The benefits and pitfalls of the various multipliers used and of economic impact analysis in general are discussed.

## THE ECONOMIC IMPACT OF
## PROFESSIONAL TENNIS

There are many justifications for the subsidization of public sporting events. Some analyses of benefits focus on intangible effects such as increased community visibility, enhanced community image, stimulation of other development, and psychic income (Crompton, 2004). *Increased community visibility* refers to the specific media coverage and national attention afforded to a community due to the presence of a specific team or event. This coverage provides millions of dollars worth of public relations for the community involved (Crompton, 2004). *Enhanced community image* refers to the actual image the city invokes in another person's mind. Teams are used to help brand the city and sell an image to prospective citizens and employers alike (Crompton, 2004). The impact of the team on image is inversely proportional to the size of the community; in other words, a small community like

[1] Address all correspondence to George B. Cunningham, PhD, Department of Health and Kinesiology, Texas Aand M University, TAMU 4243, College Station, TX 77843-4243, Phone: (979) 458-8006, FAX: (979) 847-8987

Green Bay would receive a greater image benefit than Los Angeles or New York (Crompton, 2004). *Stimulation of other development* refers to the idea that a team, arena, or event will attract other businesses and attractions near the event, thereby expanding the community's tax base (Crompton, 2004). Many communities see sport as a centerpiece for a downtown development or renewal plan to expand the local economy. Finally, *psychic income* is an internal benefit that encompasses the positive emotional and psychological impact an event or team can create within the community (Crompton, 2004). This benefit is unique in that members of the community can derive these benefits simply by following the team or event, regardless of whether they pay for tickets or merchandise. Teams allow a community that is divided on other issues to unite and rally around the success or outcomes of local sporting events (Crompton, 2004).

Although the above mentioned benefits are important to assessing the total value of a sporting event, the key factor is always money. Like most businesses, those involved want to know how each particular event impacts the bottom line. Money is a universally tangible indicator of success that is easier to quantify than the previously mentioned, and less direct, benefits. Given the primacy of money in justifying the support of sport and leisure events, it is necessary to delineate methods by which the monetary impact of an event on an economy can be examined. One such method is *economic impact analysis*. Economic impact analysis has also been labeled "an effective tool in the 'battle' to maintain existing tax support" (Kanters, Carson, and Pearson, 2001, p. 43). The process can be used to show both government and the general public that tax money has been spent prudently and allow a better comparison of the costs and benefits produced by a project (Kanters et al., 2001). Thus, economic impact analysis provides a fiscal rationale for the support of various sport and recreation events. Below, we present the rationale for economic impact and the basic tenets behind such analyses.

# ECONOMIC IMPACT ANALYSIS

## Basic Principles

Economic impact analysis measures the new monies injected into a host community as the result of a specific event, such as a tennis tournament. New money is defined as money from persons from outside the host community who came to the community for the sole purpose of attending the event, or who stayed longer in the community because of the event (Howard and Crompton, 2004). The concept of new money is extremely important because it defines the scope of money used to calculate the final impact of the event. Money spent by members of the community and visitors who came for reasons other than the event and simply changed their entertainment plans do not add any further value to the event. Failure to exclude these monies is a common abuse of economic impact analysis that can create large over-estimates of value (Crompton, 1995).

In conducting an economic impact analysis, it is possible to determine the impact the event had on four sources: (a) economic activity within a host community; (b) the personal income of the community's residents; (c) new jobs within the community; and (d) value added to the community through personal income, property income, and indirect business taxes (Crompton, 1995). Hudson (2001) uses these definitions to create a loosely described typical approach to economic impact studies, which includes estimating the direct impact and then determining how it circulates in other ways throughout the area of study (indirect and induced effects). Hudson (2001) also found that almost every study he came across was funded by a state or municipal government or an interest group. This creates a conflict of interest that calls into question the validity of such studies.

Once the proper sources of money have been identified, economic impact analysis calculates their trickle effect through the economy. Once the total money spent is calculated, it is analyzed through multipliers. Multipliers take the initial direct expenditure made by visitors and examine its effect on business turnover, personal income, employment, and government revenue. Since a local economy is an interdependent entity, the initial expenditure will travel through not only the business it is made to, but to its suppliers and then the supplier's suppliers, and so forth (Crompton, 1995). As this money trickles through the local economy, the money that escapes or leaks out (i.e., monies that go to sources outside the local economy), must also be accounted for a removed to avoid overestimation.

Four multipliers are commonly used in economic impact analysis, and thus, were incorporated in this study: sales (or output), income, value added, and employment (Howard and Crompton, 2004). The *sales* multiplier measures how an extra unit of visitor spending affects economic activity within the local economy. The *income* multiplier measures how an extra unit of visitor spending affects the personal income of local residents. The *value added* multiplier, like the income multiplier, measures how an extra unit of visitor spending affects the personal income of local residents, but also includes indirect business taxes, employee compensation, and proprietary income. Finally, the *employment* multiplier measures the effects of a unit of visitor spending of the number of jobs (full time and part time) created within the local economy (Howard and Crompton, 2004). Using these four multipliers on only new money introduced to the economy provides an accurate picture of the true economic impact of the event.

## Potential Abuses

In an ideal world, economic impact analysis would be performed by an unbiased, neutral third party that is interested only in an accurate reflection of the impact of each event. In actuality, most studies are a reflection of the researcher's personal perception and choice of methodology. Most economic impact analyses are funded by an interested party, and therefore there is an enormous question as to whether any study done by a party with such a vested interest can be considered an objective quantification of an event (Crompton, 1995). Hudson (2001) has stressed that many previous studies are done by individuals who have to make discretionary decisions that can severely alter results. Studies should be examined with a "very critical eye" (Hudson, 2001, p.20) cast towards possible discrepancies. Studies are often tools for sport organizations to seek tax support, government funding, or even to justify an attempt at relocation or adding a new team or event. With so many possible conflicts of interest at hand, it is important to create a consistent and scientifically sound way of examining economic impact. There is a strong need for academic research in the area of economic impact analysis; however, few studies have addressed this need. This is a void that desperately needs to be addressed.

## Purpose of the Study

Given the need for accurate and systematic approaches to economic impact analysis, the purpose of this study is to conduct an economic impact analysis on a professional tennis tournament while being mindful of the abuses and miscalculations that have marred past studies. This paper will hopefully provide the basis of a framework for an academic understanding and application of economic impact analysis in sport that can be further applied in different types of sport events and organizations. Despite the volume of previous studies conducted, there remains a great need for honest, unbiased, and accurate assessments of economic impact within the field of sport.

## METHODS

### Participants

Participants were 638 spectators at a professional tennis tournament. Participant demographic characteristics are presented in Table 1, with information provided for in-town participants, out-of-town participants, and the total sample. The sample consisted of 58.3% women. There was a relatively equal distribution of persons age 41-50 years (27.4%), 51-60 years (25.1%), and over 61 years (25.6%). The sample was predominantly Caucasian (85.1%), with Hispanic representing the second largest demographic group (7.1%). Most participants had an undergraduate (44.1%) or graduate (36.8%) education. Finally, the household income of the participants was relatively high, with 63.2% having a household income greater than $75,000.

### Measures

The items used to measure the economic impact of the tennis tournament mirrored that presented by Howard and Crompton (2004, see p. 146). Specifically, the questionnaire requested participants to (a) provide the zip code of their home address; (b) indicate the days which they attended or planned on attending the tournament; (c) indicate how many people (including themselves) were in their immediate group; (d) list how much money their group spent, both inside the locale of interest and outside the locale, on admission, food and beverages, night clubs and lounges, retail shopping, lodging expenses, private automobile expenses, rental automobile expenses, and "other" while they were at the tournament; (e) indicate whether they would have been in town had the tournament not been held at this time (used to identify casuals); (f) indicate whether they would have come to the city in the next three months had they not come at this time for the tournament (used to identify time-switchers). The questionnaire also requested the participants to provide their demographic information, as listed in Table 1.

## Table 1. Participant Demographics

| Category | Local Spectators | | Out-of-Town Spectators | | Total | |
|---|---|---|---|---|---|---|
| | N | % | N | % | N | % |
| *Gender* | | | | | | |
| Male | 70 | 36.1 | 184 | 44.3 | 254 | 41.7 |
| Female | 124 | 63.9 | 231 | 55.7 | 355 | 58.3 |
| *Age* | | | | | | |
| 18-30 years | 16 | 8.2 | 30 | 7.2 | 46 | 7.6 |
| 31-40 years | 29 | 14.9 | 58 | 14.0 | 87 | 14.3 |
| 41-50 years | 57 | 29.5 | 110 | 26.5 | 167 | 27.4 |
| 51-60 years | 45 | 23.2 | 108 | 26.0 | 153 | 25.1 |
| 61 or more years | 47 | 24.2 | 109 | 26.3 | 156 | 25.6 |
| *Ethnicity* | | | | | | |
| African American | 3 | 1.5 | 11 | 2.7 | 14 | 2.3 |
| Asian | 11 | 5.7 | 8 | 1.9 | 19 | 3.1 |
| Caucasian | 168 | 86.6 | 347 | 83.6 | 515 | 85.1 |
| Hispanic | 12 | 6.2 | 31 | 7.5 | 43 | 7.1 |
| Other | 0 | 0 | 14 | 3.4 | 14 | 2.3 |
| *Education* | | | | | | |
| High School | 7 | 3.6 | 22 | 5.3 | 29 | 4.8 |
| Some College | 21 | 10.7 | 66 | 16.0 | 87 | 14.3 |
| College | 98 | 50.0 | 170 | 41.3 | 268 | 44.1 |
| Graduate School | 70 | 35.7 | 154 | 37.4 | 224 | 36.8 |
| *Household Income* | | | | | | |
| Under $25,000 | 3 | 1.7 | 14 | 3.6 | 17 | 3.0 |
| $25,000-$50,000 | 21 | 11.8 | 53 | 13.7 | 74 | 13.2 |
| $50,001-$75,000 | 27 | 15.2 | 95 | 24.5 | 122 | 21.6 |
| $75,001-100,000 | 27 | 15.2 | 68 | 17.6 | 95 | 16.9 |
| $100,001-$150,000 | 49 | 27.5 | 56 | 14.5 | 105 | 18.6 |
| $150,001 or more | 51 | 28.6 | 101 | 26.1 | 156 | 27.7 |

## Procedures

Data were collected on-site during two days of the tournament. Questionnaire packets (N = 3000) containing a questionnaire, pencil, and postcard were distributed to spectators as they entered the tournament facility. The cover of the packet contained a label that informed spectators that completion of enclosed questionnaire would enter them in a drawing for a Palm Zire pocket PC. Spectators were requested to complete the questionnaire and provide their correspondence on the postcard. In this way, responses to the questionnaire items remained anonymous. Both were returned to a table set up near the entrance of the facility. A winner of the Palm Zire was randomly selected after all data were collected and subsequently mailed the prize. In all 638 completed questionnaires were returned, for a 21.3% response rate. The sample size was large enough to make generalizations to the overall population of spectators at the event (Krejcie and Morgan, 1970).

## Data Analysis

Means and standard deviations were calculated to determine the average amount of money spent by each spectator *within the locale of interest*. The tournament took place in a large metropolitan city located in the southern United States. Because persons within the county usually visited the city, we used the county as the locale of interest. In calculating the data, we excluded responses from persons who (a) were from the county; (b) would have come to the county during that time even if the tournament had not been taking place (i.e., casuals); and (c) planned on visiting the county within the next three months even if the tournament had not taken place (i.e., time-switchers) (see Howard and Crompton, 2004). IMPLAN Pro Version 2.0—the software package recommended by Howard and Crompton (2004)—was then used to calculate the economic impact of the event. In doing so, we used four multipliers: sales, income, value-added, and employment. The advantages and disadvantages of each of these multipliers are discussed later in the paper.

# RESULTS

## Spectator Spending

A total of 638 persons completed the questionnaire. Results indicated that 421 of the 638 respondents were from the county. We then deleted the responses from persons (a) whose primary reason for visiting Harris County was *not* to attend the tournament, but decided to attend the event rather than doing something else (i.e., casuals) and (b) who would have come to the county in the next three months if they had not come at this time for this event (i.e., time-switchers). A total of 278 persons remained, or 43.6% of the original sample. Based on data obtained from tournament organizers and estimates from our data, it was estimated that 12,001 spectators from outside Harris County attended the event. This figure was used in estimating the economic impact of the event.

As noted above, participants were asked to provide information related to their spending in the county and outside the county. For the purposes of the economic impact analysis, we were only concerned with monies spent *in the county*. Finally, the results reported below are for the spectators who visited the county for the expressed purpose of attending the tournament; that is, the 278 spectators described above.

During their stay at the tournament, out-of-town spectators spent, on average, $446 on admission, $97 on food and beverages, $20 on lounges and bars, $88 on retail shopping, $176 on lodging, $19 on private automobile expenses, $40 on rental car expenses, and $23 on other expenses. Many listed airfare costs in the "other" category on the questionnaire; however, these expenditures were not included in the data analysis because the monies were spent outside the county. The average out-of-town spectator spent $910.33 during his or her visit to the county.

## Economic Impact

In calculating the economic impact of the tournament, we used four multipliers: sale, income, value-added, and employment. Results indicate that the impact of the tournament on the economic activity within the host environment (sales multiplier) was $16,922,581. The impact of the tournament on the personal income of the county's residents (income multiplier) was $8,109,322, while the value added with respect to the personal income of the residents, property income, and indirect business taxes (value-added multiplier) was $11,382,824. Finally, results indicated that the tournament generated an additional 203.6 jobs in the county.

## Additional Analyses

As noted above, economic impact analyses are sometimes used for mischievous purposes with the intent of providing inflated economic figures (Crompton, 1995; Howard and Crompton, 2004). For example, there have been recent reports in Houston, Texas, concerning the economic impact of Super Bowl XXXVIII. According to these reports, the Super Bowl was expected to generate $336 million for the city—a figure that prompted state officials to appropriate $8.7 million to help finance the event. However, economic impact analysis experts have estimated that this figure is at least two times too large (John Crompton, personal communication).

This information is brought to light because it is useful to assess the economic impact of the Tennis Masters Cup in the appropriate context. Indeed, failure to exclude all out-of-town residents from the analysis yields much different results: Sales (Output) = $38,459,996; Income = $18,429,601; Value Added = $25,869,102; Employment = 462.6. These figures, consistent with what some economists refer to as an *economic surge*, fail to exclude in-town spectators or those persons who would have been in the county even if the tournament had not taken place. Obviously, these spectators' expenditures do not represent new monies injected into the county's economy, and thus, it is inappropriate to consider such inflated numbers. Again, these numbers, oftentimes deceitfully used for political gain, *are not* the accurate numbers to report in an economic impact analysis.

## DISCUSSION

Our study underscores the need for accurate and unbiased economic impact studies within the sport industry. Economic impact analysis provides the best way to measure and compare the investment of local residents, municipalities, and other entities into a project and the total benefits they receive for their expenditures (Howard and Crompton, 2004). Accurate and unbiased measures can then be used in areas ranging from organizational improvement to seeking alternative means of funding. This will be discussed in further detail later. The key point, however, is that accurate economic impact analyses benefit local residents, local government, various stakeholders, and, most importantly, the parties running the event itself.

One of the keys to the accuracy of the study is the use of the multiplier coefficients. These coefficients provide the most accurate estimates of the tournament in this study's effect on sales, personal income, value added, and employment, but they each still have their own individual strengths and weaknesses. These strength and weaknesses are important to consider when analyzing the results of economic impact studies.

The sales multiplier is the most commonly abused of the four multipliers used within the study. The sales numbers provide the largest bottom line numbers (the multiplier is often three times or larger than the others) and is often misused to create "inaccurate, exaggerated, [and] spurious inferences" (Howard and Crompton, 2004, p.120). Our study is concerned only with the impact on residents' personal incomes. Sales do not have the highest effect on residents' personal income and may in fact have a negligible total local impact. Since the impact to local residents is so slight, the sales multiplier should not be used to show public benefits, but can show benefits to other parties, such as business proprietors, economists, or government officials who want to see how funds affect particular sectors (Howard and Crompton, 2004).

The personal income multiplier specifically shows have the tax resources invested by local residents translates into actual local economic benefits (Howard and Crompton, 2004). Specifically, it reflects the impact of employee compensation and proprietor income. The value added is a more expansive indicator than personal income because it also includes income from other property and indirect business taxes on top of what the personal income multiplier measures (Howard and Crompton, 2004).

Finally, the results of the employment multiplier calculation also need to be carefully interpreted. The multiplier measures the number of jobs per million dollars in direct sales (Howard and Crompton, 2004). There are a few caveats that need to be attached to this number, however. Most of the jobs created by the event are not actual full-time jobs. In fact, the first assumption of the multiplier is that existing employees are fully occupied and cannot take on extra hour or responsibility. According to Howard and Crompton (2004), the most likely result is in fact an expansion of hours and duties of current employees. Even if new jobs are created, they will most likely be part time or seasonal jobs that occur only when the event is occurring. Examples of these positions are food vendors within an arena and temporary security around an event. These jobs have relatively low pay and would not produce any overall large, long term economic gains. Even if new jobs are created, there is no guarantee that they will be filled by local residents. The lucrative front office positions will mostly likely be taken from a nationwide search, not simply residents who live around the event itself. Jobs are created, however, and these jobs still play a role within the local economy.

Although the employment multiplier seems flawed, many of the above caveats are related more to professional sports franchises. Howard and Crompton (2004) mention that when the focus is on a sports facility or something long term the jobs are more likely to be full time. The tournament studied here would likely fall into the former category (with professional sport franchises), as although it will be held for a number of years in the current location, it only takes place for two weeks a year. Like all other aspects of economic impact analysis, the employment multiplier should be interpreted cautiously but can provide a good estimate of value.

Finally, the final results of an economic impact analysis can have several possible policy implications. Since government funding is a common occurrence for sporting events, it is not unreasonable to use economic data as part of a request for partial subsidization. The current locale has shown a past willingness to subsidize local teams and events, such as professional sport franchises, and the impact numbers of the tennis tournament show a substantial effect on the city's economy. The organizers of the event could make a good case to government officials for subsidization. Impact numbers can also be used to show local business the overall quantifiable success of the tournament and how it helps their interests as well. This could be a tool to secure additional sponsorships or funding. An accurate and correctly performed economic analysis can be a powerful tool to both cultivate and create a successful and efficiently funded event.

# REFERENCES

Crompton, J. L. (1995). Economic impact analysis of sports facilities and events: Eleven sources of misapplication. *Journal of Sport Management, 9*, 14-35.

Crompton, J. L. (2004). Beyond economic impact: An alternative rationale for the public subsidy of major league sports facilities. *Journal of Sport Management, 18*, 40-56

Howard, D. R., and Crompton, J. L. (2004). *Financing sport* (2nd ed.). Morgantown, WV: Fitness Information Technology.

Hudson, I. (2001). The use and misuse of economic impact analysis. *Journal of Sport and Social Issues, 25(1)*, 20-39.

Kanters, M. A., Carter, D., and Pearson, B. (2001). A community based model for assessing the economic impact of sport and recreation services. *Journal of Park and Recreation Administration, 19(2)*, 43-61.

Krejcie, R. V., and Morgan, D. W. (1970). Determining sample size for research initiatives. *Educational and Psychological Measurement, 30*, 607 – 610.

*Chapter 11*

# STUDENT ATHLETES' PERCEPTIONS OF CONFERENCE CODES OF ETHICS

*T. Christopher Greenwell,[1,\*] Angela J. Grube,[2]*
*Jeremy S. Jordan[3] and Daniel F. Mahony[4]*

[1, 4]University of Louisville, Louisville, Kentucky, USA
[2]Western Carolina University, Cullowhee, North Carolina, USA
[3]University of Miami, Coral Gables, Florida, USA

## ABSTRACT

Within intercollegiate athletics, a popular strategy to encourage ethical decision-making and behavior has been to create codes of ethics. Despite the importance placed on codes of ethics, little is known about how student-athletes feel about their codes of ethics. To better understand student-athletes' perceptions of the content and purposes of their codes of ethics, a sample of student-athletes from one NCAA Division I conference (n = 336) was surveyed. Results revealed student-athletes' general perceptions of toward codes of ethics and their positions on responsibility for conduct, enforcement, and penalties. Further, results revealed student-athletes' feelings toward important ethical ideals. Findings from this research should help conferences in writing codes of ethics that are more effective.

## STUDENT ATHLETES' PERCEPTIONS OF CONFERENCE CODES OF ETHICS

The need for improved ethical behavior has been an issue in intercollegiate athletics since its early days (Smith, 1988). Despite efforts over the last century, there remains the perception among the general public in the United States that intercollegiate athletics is out of control (Frey, 1994). Reports in the media about problems such as academic fraud by athletes with the support of coaches (Wertheim and Yaeger, 1999; Wolff and Yaeger, 1994), gambling by athletes (Girard, 1998), and handouts to college athletes (Steptoe and Swift, 1994), as well as prior research that found an increase in the number and severity of NCAA rules violations (Mahony, Fink, and Pastore, 1999), appear to support the perception held by the general public.

In fact, concerns about unethical behavior in intercollegiate athletics has led to calls for reform by many leaders in higher education (Shulman and Bowen, 2001). The first Knight Commission (1991) suggested the concerns over unethical behavior had the potential to not only impact the image of athletics, but also tarnish the reputation of higher education institutions. While the Knight Commission (1991) issued a major call for national reform, ten years later the second Knight Commission (2001) stated that despite some positive changes, the overall state of intercollegiate athletics had become worse during the last decade. With over half of the Division I institutions being sanctioned or put on probation for rules violations in the 1990's, the Knight Commission (2001) suggested that violating NCAA rules was not unusual and instead appeared to be the norm. The question facing those who would like to see real changes is: how do we increase ethical behavior among those involved in intercollegiate athletic programs?

# CODES OF ETHICS

Those involved with intercollegiate athletics programs face a wide variety of ethical dilemmas. Therefore, it is critical to find ways to provide guidance to this group in order to promote increased ethical behavior. In professions that face similar concerns over the possibilities for unethical behavior (e.g., law, medicine), governing bodies have developed codes of ethics that provide such guidance. Governing bodies in intercollegiate athletics have also attempted to use codes of ethics to influence the behavior of administrators, coaches, athletes, and fans. Despite the existence of these codes, unethical behavior still appears to be prevalent in college sports. This suggests codes of ethics vary in their impact on behavior in a variety of contexts, including intercollegiate athletics (Mahony, Geist, Jordan, Greenwell, and Pastore, 1999). Therefore, another important question is: what are the criteria for an effective code of ethics?

## Criteria for an Effective Code of Ethics

Mahony et al. (1999) reviewed the literature in order to develop a list of criteria that should be considered when developing a code of ethics. It is important to briefly review their suggestions for developing an effective code of ethics. First, Mahony et al. said the code of ethics must be distributed to the organization's membership and be referred to on a regular basis. If the code is going to be effective and influence behavior, it must be immersed into the culture of the organization (Chonko and Hunt, 1985). Too often codes are developed, but rarely distributed or discussed. Second, codes must be neither too specific nor too vague (e.g., DeSensi and Rosenberg, 1996; Kretchmar, 1993). Codes that are too vague tend provide very little guidance as organization members face a variety of ethical dilemmas, while those that are too specific either ignore a number of possible ethical dilemmas or become too long to be easily remembered. In fact, some recommend that the best codes are based on a few overriding principles that provide guidance in a variety of situations faced by organization members (Fraleigh, 1993).

Third, Mahony et al. (1999) said the organization should be clear about the application of the code to various groups. In intercollegiate athletics, there are a variety of groups to whom the codes could apply (e.g., athletes, coaches, administrators, fans). The code should clearly state which groups are the focus of a particular code of ethics. For example, the defunct Association of Intercollegiate Athletics for Women had separate codes of ethics for different groups, including student-athletes (Kroll, 1976), coaches (Kroll, 1977a), spectators (Kroll, 1977b), and officials (Kroll, 1977b). Fourth, Mahony et al. suggest codes must have the support of the leadership and membership of the organization. Individuals are less likely to follow a code of ethics if they fundamentally disagree with the principles behind it. One of the ways to avoid this problem is to allow input from these groups during the process of developing the code of ethics (DeSensi and Rosenberg, 1996).

Finally, Mahony et al. (1999) said codes should include consequences for those who violate the standards within the codes. Otherwise, the codes become merely suggestions and are unlikely to have an impact on behavior (DeSensi and Rosenberg, 1996). In general, the code of ethics should be supported by enforcement procedures that are clear, an individual or group in charge of enforcing the code, and a system of the penalties. Using a neutral third party, who will be unaffected by the severity of the penalties, to be in charge of enforcement will further enhance the effectiveness of the code of ethics.

## Codes of Ethics in Intercollegiate Athletics

While there is a growing body of research on ethical behavior in sport (Hums, Barr and Gullion, 1999; Volkwein, 1995) a void of information has existed on codes of ethics used by intercollegiate sport organizations. Despite the lack of inquiry in this area, organizations within collegiate athletics have recognized the need to address ethical problems and thus have developed codes of ethics intended to serve as guidelines for various stakeholder groups. In an attempt to further understanding of collegiate codes of ethics, Greenwell, Geist, Mahony, Jordan and Pastore (2001) examined codes of ethics being used by intercollegiate athletic conferences at NCAA Divisions I, II, and III. One goal of this project was to identify what standards and ideals were incorporated into these codes and for which groups they were written. In addition, based on the work of Mahony et al. (1999) which identified criteria necessary for a code to be influential, Greenwell et al. (2001) sought to determine if intercollegiate codes of ethics included these criteria when constructing codes of ethics.

Despite the fact that codes included in the study by Greenwell et al. (2001) varied with regards to length and specificity, several themes emerged. First, the ideals of sportsmanship, integrity, healthy environment, and compliance with conference rules were most often included in conference codes of ethics. Second, groups most often addressed by the codes were coaches, administrators, and student-athletes. These groups were often provided with standards intended to provide guidance for what constituted appropriate behavior on and off the field. Third, over half of the codes examined contained information on enforcement policies such as which groups were responsible for enforcing the codes and penalties for violating its standards. Similar to the groups addressed by the codes, athletic administrators, coaches, and member institutions were most often identified as being responsible for assuring ethical behavior of those involved with collegiate sport.

Greenwell et al. (2001) also found several inconsistencies between the codes being used by collegiate conferences and the prescriptions for effective codes of ethics identified in the literature (DeSensi and Rosenberg, 1996; Fraleigh, 1993; Kretchmar, 1993; Mahony et al., 1999). First, many of the codes provided by athletic conferences closely resembled policies and procedures as opposed to a code of ethics. Standards within these codes had the appearance of rules, leaving little room for interpretation or the possibility of application in a variety of settings. As discussed by Mahony et al. (1999), codes should be more general and designed to provide a foundation for ethical decision-making appropriate for multiple situations. Second, many of the codes did not identify enforcement policies and consequences for violation of prescribed standards. Furthermore, when enforcement policies were addressed there was a general lack of consistency with regards to enforcement procedures. Finally, many of the codes attempted to address too many groups resulting in unclear or ambiguous standards. This lack of clarity makes adhering to the standards of the codes somewhat difficult for athletic stakeholder groups. Despite these shortcomings, Greenwell, et al. (2001) surmised that many conferences were attempting to address ethical behavior in college sport by creating codes intended to provide standards to promote ethical decision-making.

## Coaches Perceptions of Codes of Ethics

The fact that coaches were often identified as one party responsible for encouraging ethical behavior in collegiate sport (Greenwell et al., 2001) identifies the importance of this group understanding and adhering to the standards of conference codes of ethics. Campbell (1998) indicated that teams often reflect the character and personality of the coach who normally has the best opportunity to teach student-athletes how to compete fairly and develop ethical decision-making skills. Because much of the responsibility for assuring ethical behavior in intercollegiate athletics is placed on coaches, Jordan, Greenwell, Geist, Pastore, and Mahony (in press) felt it important to gain an understanding of coaches' perceptions of conference codes of ethics. Based on the research of Mahony et al. (1999) and Greenwell et al. (2001) a survey questionnaire was developed which solicited information from coaches pertaining to their knowledge and perceptions of codes of ethics. Findings from this study revealed coaches felt it was necessary to include all seven standards identified by Greenwell et al. (2001) in a code of ethics. With regards to importance, coaches in Jordan et al. (in press) rated the standards of sportsmanship and integrity the highest. This is consistent with Greenwell et al. (2001) who found that these two standards where most often included in conference codes of ethics.

Another finding consistent with previous research related to what groups should be addressed by a code of ethics and what parties are responsible for enforcing its standards. Coaches identified themselves, athletic administrators, and student-athletes as the main groups that should be addressed in conference code of ethics. In dealing with enforcement of standards, respondents indicated athletic administrators and coaches were in the best positions to promote ethical behavior among those associated with college sports. Finally, consistent with findings from Greenwell et al. (2001), coaches felt suspension was the best way to deal with those who violate the standards of a code of ethics. Interestingly, coaches identified institutional administrators and conference commissioners as the groups who should be responsible for enforcing the code and dispensing punishment. However, Mahony et al. (1999) argue that codes should be enforced by individuals who are neutral due to inherent conflicts of interest faced by conference commissioners and athletic department administrators.

In addition to exploring what coaches thought should be included in codes of ethics, Jordan et al. (in press) examined coaches' perceptions of their own conference code of ethics. Chonko and Hunt (1985) said that in order for a code to be effective, members must understand and agree with its standards. In general, coaches supported their conference code of ethics and felt it encouraged ethical behavior among groups associated with college sport. In fact, over 90% of respondents felt it was important for athletic conferences to have and enforce a code of ethics. However, only 70% of the coaches in Jordan et al. (in press) were familiar with their conference code of ethics and nearly half of the sample felt other coaches in the conference had not examined the code. These findings indicate codes are likely to be less effective in curbing unethical behavior because of coaches' lack of knowledge of identified standards. Finally, coaches indicated a preference for codes that contained both specific and general standards. While in theory this would appear to be the best way to develop an effective code, there is minimal support in the literature for writing codes in this fashion (DeSensi and Rosenberg, 1993; Greenwell et al. 2001; Kretchmar, 1993; Mahony et al. 1999). Codes that are both specific and general in nature tend to be lengthy and potentially difficult to manage and understand by members.

Although coaches are often entrusted with the ethical conduct of their programs, the student-athletes themselves bear some responsibility for their own conduct. Despite this responsibility, student-athletes are often not included when codes are written, and little is known about how they feel about the content and purposes of these codes of ethics. Therefore, the purpose of the current study was to (a) identify what student-athletes feel should be included in a conference code of ethics and (b) examine student-athletes' perceptions and understanding of their own conference code of ethics.

## METHOD

### Sample

The sample was selected from a NCAA Division I conference that included a mix of public and private institutions and a mix of non-football schools and schools participating at the IAA level. A cluster sampling method was used to select the sample where two teams (one men's team and one women's team) were selected at random from each conference institution. The advantage of this method is that it can be used when it is difficult to obtain a random sample of individuals. Questionnaires were distributed to each institution's NCAA Faculty Athletics Representative who administered the questionnaire to the selected teams.

### Instrument

The instrument for the study was developed from the questionnaire used by Jordan et al. (in press) to study coaches' perceptions of codes of ethics. In Jordan's et al. study, items were developed from a review of relevant literature (Mahony, et al., 1999) and a content analysis (Greenwell et al., 2001) of actual codes of ethics. For the current study, items were reworded to make them applicable for student-athletes rather than coaches. To further ensure items were appropriate for student-athletes and represented themes found in codes of ethics, items were worded utilizing language from actual codes of ethics wherever possible. In order to identify and correct any misunderstandings, ambiguities, or other inadequacies with the ways the items were worded, a field test was administered to undergraduate students enrolled at a large Midwestern University.

To begin, student athletes were asked "yes/no" questions pertaining to their general perceptions and understanding of codes of ethics in general. In order to measure student-athletes' perceptions of conference ideals, three to five statements were used for each ideal. Student-athletes were asked to rate the importance of each statement on a 7-point Likert scale, and mean scores were generated for each ideal. Items for each ideal were averaged to provide an overall measure for that ideal. For items questioning responsibility for conduct, responsibility for enforcement, and means to curb ethical violations, student-athletes were presented with a list of options generated from the literature and allowed to select multiple options. With regards to warnings against unsportsmanlike acts, student-athletes were asked to indicate the importance of each warning by rating the items on a 7-point Likert scale.

# RESULTS

Eight of the twelve member institutions in the conference responded, yielding 336 total student-athlete participants. Responses represented eight men's teams and eight women's teams in seven different men's sports and seven different women's sports. In terms of gender distribution, 206 of the respondents were male, 123 were female, and seven chose not to answer. Of the respondents, 109 of the respondents were on full scholarship, 157 were on a partial scholarship, 62 were non-scholarship athletes, and eight chose not to respond. The average age of the respondents was 19.7 years.

## General Opinions about Codes of Ethics

Student-athletes were asked general questions pertaining to their knowledge and understanding of their codes of ethics. Nearly all student-athletes agreed a code of ethics is effective in encouraging ethical behavior (91.5%) and almost as many felt it important for a conference to have a code of ethics (91.2%). Further, 88.2% considered it important for student-athletes to be familiar with their conference's code of ethics. However, only 22.0% admitted to having read their conference's code of ethics. Student-athletes were also asked to indicate whether a code of ethics should be general (list general guidelines intended to provide proper guidance on how to handle a variety of ethical dilemmas), specific (list specific rules and regulations for student-athletes to follow), or a combination of the two. More than half of the student-athletes (50.3%) responded that codes of ethics should be a combination of the two. Specific was indicated by 26.1% and general was favored by 23.6%.

## Conference Ideals

Data was first analyzed pertaining to ideals presented in codes of ethics. Student-athletes were asked to rate the importance of the seven ideals commonly found in codes of ethics on a 7-point Likert scale. Promotion of values ($M$ = 6.34) had the highest means. Professional conduct of coaches ($M$ = 6.18), sportsmanship ($M$ = 6.14) and healthy environment ($M$ = 6.08) followed closely. Welfare of student-athletes ($M$ = 5.93), compliance with conference rules ($M$ = 5.59), and equitable treatment ($M$ = 5.47) had the lowest means among the seven ideals. Means and standard deviations are presented in Table 1.

**Table 1. Means and Standard Deviations of Conference Ideals by Gender and Ethnicity**

| Variable | | Sample | Males | Females | White | Non-white |
|---|---|---|---|---|---|---|
| Values | M | 6.34 | 6.16 | 6.63 | 6.34 | 6.36 |
| | SD | 0.87 | 0.95 | 0.63 | 0.86 | 0.88 |
| Professional conduct of coaches | M | 6.18 | 6.00 | 6.45 | 6.18 | 6.16 |
| | SD | 0.84 | 0.90 | 0.65 | 0.82 | 0.89 |
| Sportsmanship | M | 6.14 | 5.92 | 6.46 | 6.14 | 6.13 |
| | SD | 0.94 | 1.00 | 0.71 | 0.95 | 0.92 |
| Healthy environment | M | 6.08 | 5.84 | 6.47 | 6.08 | 6.09 |
| | SD | 0.95 | 1.01 | 0.67 | 0.93 | 0.98 |
| Welfare of student athletes | M | 5.93 | 5.73 | 6.25 | 5.87 | 6.04 |
| | SD | 0.93 | 0.93 | 0.81 | 0.91 | 0.96 |
| Compliance with conference rules | M | 5.59 | 5.34 | 5.99 | 5.59 | 5.61 |
| | SD | 1.07 | 1.12 | 0.86 | 1.10 | 1.04 |
| Equitable treatment | M | 5.47 | 5.03 | 6.16 | 5.33 | 5.71 |
| | SD | 1.27 | 1.34 | 0.72 | 1.31 | 1.16 |

MANOVA was used to determine whether the means of dependent variables varied due to the demographic variables of gender, ethnicity, or class rank. In the MANOVA model, the demographic variables were entered as the independent variables, and the seven ideals were entered as the dependent variables. Ethnicity was converted into a dichotomous variable: white student-athletes ($n = 216$) and non-white student-athletes ($n = 120$). Class rank was also converted to a dichotomous variable: underclass ($n = 183$) and upper class ($n = 145$).

Results of the multifactorial MANOVA were significant for the main effects of gender, Wilks' Lambda $= .852$, $F (7, 310) = 7.664$, $p < .001$, indicating the combined dependent variables varied between genders. Significant differences did not exist for the main effects of ethnicity or class rank. Additionally, significant differences did not exist for any of the interaction effects meaning the main effects could be interpreted directly.

Subsequent analyses were performed to examine differences in each conference ideal attributable to gender. Univariate tests revealed gender was significant for each of the ideals and a comparison of means revealed women reported higher mean scores than men for each ideal. Although the MANOVA was not significant for ethnicity, the univariate tests are interpreted as a guide for future research (Tabachnick and Fidell, 1996). Univariate tests did reveal significant differences among white and non-white student-athletes in the importance of equitable treatment $F (1, 316) = 5.654$, $p = .038$. Comparisons of mean scores revealed only that non-white student-athletes felt equitable treatment was more important to include in a code of ethics than white students.

## Responsibility for Conduct

Student-athletes were asked to identify who they felt should be responsible for the ethical conduct of student-athletes. Respondents were allowed to select multiple groups. A vast majority of student-athletes felt they should be responsible for their own conduct (82.4%). Coaches/assistant coaches (64.0%), athletic administrators (38.7%), and game officials (20.2%) received fewer responses.

## Responsibility for Enforcement

Student-athletes were asked to identify who should be responsible for dealing with ethical violations and/or misconduct of student-athletes. Again, student-athletes were allowed to make multiple selections. Coaches were the most popular selection (85.7%) followed by school administrators (42.0%), conference commissioner (28.3%), and independent committee (14.9%).

## Unsportsmanlike Conduct

Student-athletes were asked to indicate how important it is to include certain warnings against specific unsportsmanlike acts in a code of ethics. All warnings were rated highly, with physical abuse ($M = 6.18$) having the highest mean. Warnings against inciting abusive action ($M = 5.82$), negative recruiting ($M = 5.44$), obscene gestures and profanity ($M = 5.23$), and gambling ($M = 5.12$) followed. Warnings against taunting or verbal abuse ($M = 4.94$), tobacco or alcohol usage ($M = 4.91$) and public criticism of officials, conference, or opponents ($M = 4.75$) received the lowest ratings.

## Penalties for Curbing Ethical Violations

Student-athletes were asked to identify which penalties they perceived to be effective in curbing ethical violations. Respondents were allowed to select multiple penalties. Student-athletes selected player suspension (75.6%) most often. Probation (48.2%), reprimand (33.0%), team suspension (30.4%), letter (30.1%), termination from the team (21.1%), institutional fine (11.0%) and institutional expulsion (7.1%) all were listed much less often.

## DISCUSSION

The first purpose of this study was to assess student-athletes' general opinions about codes of ethics. Although student-athletes felt strongly about the efficacy of codes of ethics, very few had actually read their conference's code of ethics. This seems to indicate either not enough is done to encourage student-athletes to read their conference's code of ethics or reading a code of ethics stands as a lower priority compared to many of the demands placed on a student-athlete. Based on prior research (Chonko and Hunt, 1985), it appears clear that athletic departments need to do a better job to incorporate these codes of ethics into the culture. A number of things could be done to improve this including posting them in the locker rooms and other prominent places and incorporating them into discussions involving coaches and athletes.

An important part of a code of ethics is the list of ideals or themes they include which are designed to guide the actions of the members. Student-athletes in this study tended to rate each of the seven ideals commonly found in intercollegiate codes as important, and women rated each ideal as more important than did men. Promotion of positive values such as honesty, integrity and fair play were rated the highest. Interestingly, equitable treatment was rated lowest. Upon further investigation, the item rated lowest in this area concerned treating student-athletes the same as the rest of the student population. Many of the subjects in this study indicated they felt student-athletes should be treated differently than the general student population. In fact many wrote additional comments in the margin of the questionnaire to indicate they felt student-athletes should receive preferential treatment as compared to other students. This ideal also had the greatest disparity between men and women (women felt it was more important to add than did men). And, it was the only difference found between white and non-white students (non-white students felt it was more important to add than did white students). The literature suggests that successful athletes often begin to have feelings of entitlement and expect better treatment because of their status as athletes (Schulman and Bowen, 2001; Sperber, 2000; Zimbalist, 1999). This may be due to the increased demands placed upon their time, their larger role in the community, or their role in generating income for the athletic department. This can raise major concerns when attempting to teach them ethical principles because they are more likely to believe that principles established for others do not apply to them (Wolff, 1988).

When asked about who should be responsible for conduct, student-athletes overwhelmingly put the responsibility on themselves and much less responsibility on their coaches. This seems counter to what is heard from the popular media, which often excuses young athletes of responsibility while chastising coaches and administrators for not providing enough control. In terms of responsibility for enforcement, student-athletes overwhelmingly listed coaches as the entity they felt should be responsible for dealing with ethical violations and/or misconduct of student-athletes. For both questions, student-athletes listed athletic administrators much less often than coaches. These findings seem to indicate athletes put their trust in their coaches, but are somewhat distant from administrators. There may be a general feeling that in-group members understand the issues and the group better than do outsiders. This is not surprising given the heavy emphasis placed on, and time spent with, the in-group (i.e., team). Distrust of outsiders is not unusual in these conditions.

Many codes list specific acts of unsportsmanlike conduct and specific penalties designed to stop unethical acts, so it was of great interest to investigate student-athletes perceptions in these areas. In terms of unsportsmanlike conduct, physical abuse and inciting abusive action, as expected, were rated as the most important warning to include in a code of ethics. Interestingly, gambling was only the fifth most important despite the emphasis the NCAA places on educating athletes about the dangers of gambling. Also rated relatively low were rules against taunting/verbal abuse and public criticism of officials, conference, or opponents. This seems consistent with the "trash-talk" culture that has invaded college athletics. In fact, younger athletes have generally grown up in that culture, while the older generation in charge of college athletics' rules and codes of ethics are more likely to have grown up in a time when "trash-talking" was not acceptable. While the older generation is likely to focus on such rules, the athletes are less likely to see this as unethical because they are used to it and have done it themselves, which means they would have to admit they are themselves unethical. In terms of penalties student-athletes feel are effective in stopping ethical violations, player suspension was listed as the most effective. No other penalty was listed by at least half of the respondents. The penalty being suggested here is fairly strong, which would suggest that many athletes do not see themselves as involved in ethical violations but want strong penalties to stop others from committing unethical acts.

Since this study parallels the study of coaches by Jordan et al. (in press), a comparison of results is warranted. Several key comparisons are worth noting. First, more coaches (71%) had reported reading their conferences' code of ethics compared to only 22% of athletes. It looks as if coaches are taking on the responsibility of ethical conduct themselves, but may not be doing enough to get their student-athletes to read their code of ethics and entrust their athletes with their own conduct. In fact, a common criticism of coaches is that they are too controlling and are unwilling to let athletes make decisions for themselves (e.g., Coakley, 2004; Eitzen and Sage, 1997). If the coach is in control of the athlete, they may only be concerned about making sure the athlete is following his or her rules and this may be the only thing they commonly present to the athlete. Second, professional conduct of coaches was among the most important ideals for the athletes, but not as important for the coaches. It appears student-athletes feel a greater emphasis should be put on the ethical conduct of their coaches, whereas coaches feel they are doing a good job of policing themselves. Third, athletes and coaches agreed that physical abuse was the most important act of unsportsmanlike conduct to address, and they both rated public criticism of officials, conference, or opponents among the lowest. However, rules against negative recruiting were important to athletes, but not as important to coaches. Again, student-athletes felt coaches needed regulation in this area, while coaches did not see this as an issue. Similar to some of the other items in this study and the Jordan et al. (in press) study, both athletes and coaches were more offended by things done by others and were less likely to see actions that they were more likely to engage in as unethical.

## LIMITATIONS AND FUTURE RESEARCH

The first limitation of this study is that it only addresses NCAA Division I student-athletes. Although these student-athletes tend to have the highest profiles, ethical problems are not exclusive to Division I. Future research should be directed toward examining opinions of other levels of athletics and comparing those with the opinions of Division I athletes. Second, the current study examines student-athletes perceptions of what is actually included in codes of ethics. This study does not examine what may be missing. Future study should take a more in-depth exploration into what student-athletes feel is not included in a code of ethics but should be included to make codes more effective. Also, it would be of interest to investigate what student-athletes think could be done to encourage them to read and follow their conference's code of ethics.

## REFERENCES

Campbell, D. E. (1998). Developing an athletic code of conduct. *Strategies, 11(5)*, 10-12.

Chonko, L. B., and Hunt, S. D. (1985). Ethics and marketing management: An empirical examination. Journal of Business Research, 13, 339-359.

Coakley, J. J. (2004). Sports in society: Issues and controversies (8th ed.). New York: McGraw-Hill.

DeSensi, J. T., and Rosenberg, D. (1996). Ethics in sport management. Morgantown, WV: Fitness Information Technology, Inc.

Eitzen, D. S., and Sage, G. H. (1997). Sociology of North American Sport (6th ed.). Dubuque, IA: Brown and Benchmark Publishers.

Fraleigh, W. P. (1993). Codes of ethics: Functions, form and structures, problems and possibilities. *Quest, 45*, 13-21.

Frey, J. H. (1994). Deviance of organizational subunits: The case of college athletic departments. *Journal of Sport and Social Issues, 18*, 110-123.

Girard, F. (1998, April 2). Sports wagering a "critical" issue for NCAA: Point-shaving incident at Northwestern forces university officials to take action. *Detroit News*, p. D1.

Greenwell, T. C., Geist, A. L., Mahony, D. F., Jordan, J. S., and Pastore, D. L. (2001). Characteristics of NCAA conference codes of ethics. *International Journal of Sport Management, 2,* 108-124.

Hums, M. A., Barr, C. A., and Gullion, L. (1999). The ethical issues confronting managers in the sport industry. *Journal of Business Ethics, 20,* 51-66.

Jordan, J. S., Greenwell, T. C., Geist, A. L., Pastore, D. L. and Mahony, D. F. (in press). Coaches' perceptions of conference code of ethics. *Physical Educator*

Knight Foundation – Commission on Intercollegiate Athletics. (1991). *Keeping faith with the student-athlete.* Charlotte, NC.

Knight Foundation – Commission Intercollegiate Athletics (2001). *A call to action: Reconnecting college sports and higher education.* Charlotte, NC.

Kretchmar (1993). Philosophy of ethics. *Quest, 45* (1), 3-12.

Kroll, W. (1976). Psychological scaling of AIAW code of ethics for players. *Research Quarterly, 47,* 126-133.

Kroll, W. (1977a). Psychological scaling of AIAW code of ethics for coaches. *Research Quarterly, 48,* 233-238.

Kroll, W. (1977b). Psychological scaling of AIAW code of ethics for officials and spectators. *Research Quarterly, 48,* 475-479.

Mahony, D. F., Fink, J., and Pastore, D. (1999). Ethics in intercollegiate athletics: An examination of NCAA violations and penalties -1952-1997. *Professional Ethics, 7* (2), 53-74.

Mahony, D. F., Geist, A. L., Jordan, J., Greenwell, T. C., and Pastore, D. (1999). Codes of ethics used by sport governing bodies: Problems in intercollegiate athletics. *Proceedings of the Congress of the European Association for Sport Management, 7,* 206-208.

Shulman, J. L., and Bowen, W. G. (2001). *The game of life.* Princeton, NJ: Princeton University Press.

Smith, R. A. (1988). *Sports and freedom: The rise of big-time college athletics.* New York: Oxford University Press.

Sperber, M. (2000). Beer and circus: How big-time college sport is crippling undergraduate education. New York: Henry Holt Publishers.

Steptoe, S., and Swift, E. M. (1994, May 16). Special report: Anatomy of a scandal. *Sports Illustrated,* pp. 18-28.

Volkwein, K. A. (1995). Ethics and top level sport – a paradox? *International Review for Sociology of Sport, 30,* 311-319.

Wertheim, L. J., and Yaeger, D. (1999, June 14). *The passing game.* Sports Illustrated, pp. 90-102.

Wolff, A. (1998, February, 23). The young and the restless. Sports Illustrated, pp. 70-73.

Wolff, A, and Yaeger, D. (1995, August 7). *Credit risk.* Sports Illustrated, pp. 46-55.

Zimbalist, A. (1999). *Unpaid professionals: Commercialism and conflict in big-time college sports.* Princeton, N.J.: Princeton University Press.

Issues in Contemporary Athletics
Editor: James H. Humphrey, pp. 135-144
ISBN 1-59454-595-2
© 2007 Nova Science Publishers, Inc,.

*Chapter 12*

# INFLUENTIAL FACTORS IN THE COLLEGE SELECTION PROCESS OF BASEBALL STUDENT-ATHLETES

*Jeffrey S. Pauline*[*], *Gina A. Pauline and Adam J. Stevens*
Ball State University, Muncie, Indiana, USA

## ABSTRACT

The purpose of this investigation was to evaluate the factors that may be influential in the college selection process of baseball student-athletes. A second purpose was to investigate the differences between baseball student-athletes from each of the National Collegiate Athletic Association (NCAA) Divisions (Division I, II, and II). The participants in this study were 320 collegiate baseball student-athletes from 12 colleges and universities in the Midwest. The participants completed the Influential Factors Survey for Student Athletes (IFSSA). The IFSSA was a 32-item survey that can be separated into five sections (athletics, coaching staff, academics, social, and financial aid). Results of the study were analyzed using descriptive statistics and a multivariate analysis of variance (MANOVA). Descriptive statistics showed the five most influential factors to be a winning program, opportunity to play early in career, baseball specific facilities, coach's personality/philosophy, and tradition of the athletic program. The MANOVA revealed factors related to athletics as the most influential for baseball student-athletes. Results also showed that Division III baseball student-athletes viewed academics significantly more influential than Division I and II student-athletes. Division II baseball student-athletes viewed financial aid to be significantly more influential than Division I or Division III student-athletes.

The recruitment of quality student athletes is one of the most important responsibilities of a collegiate coach. Stanford baseball coach Mark Marquess, who's teams have won 2 NCAA national championships and qualified for 11 college world series, makes this point clear when he stated "recruiting is the lifeblood of a successful college baseball program" (Kindall and Winkin, 2000, p.84). The importance of recruiting has also been reiterated by such coaching legends as John Wooden, Pat Summit, Joe Paterno, and Dean Smith. These coaching legends indicated that a team needs a high level of talent in order to be successful (Packer and

[*]Please send correspondence to: Jeffrey S. Pauline, Ed.D, School of Physical Education, Sport and Exercise Science, Ball State University, Muncie, IN 47306-0270, (765) 285 – 3286, jpauline@bsu.edu

Lazenby, 1999). Furthermore, they point out that attracting high level talent is not the only factor in developing a successful program; however it is extremely unlikely to consistently win without it. An athletic program acquires this high talent level through successful recruiting. Therefore, it is vital that coaches are excellent recruiters in order to attain a high level of talent among his or her team.

It is apparent that a coach's recruiting efforts have a direct impact on the success of their program (Kindall and Winkin, 2000). Due to the importance of recruiting, a coach must understand and be aware of the factors prospective student-athletes evaluate when deciding on what college to attend. Previous studies have evaluated the factors involved in the non-athlete or general student college selection process (Hodges and Barbuto, 2002; Christiansen et al., 2003; Pope and Fermin, 2003). However, few studies have been conducted on the factors that influence the student-athlete's decision process (Mathes and Gurney, 1985). Furthermore, the few studies that have been conducted on this topic present conflicting results.

Mathes and Gurney (1985) in their survey of 231 student-athletes from the same university found that academics were rated as the most important factor in their college selection process. Baumgartner's (1999) assessment of Division II female soccer players also showed academics as the most important factor in selecting a college to attend. These results are in contrast to what Doyle and Gaeth (1990) found in their investigation of NCAA Division I baseball and softball players. They found the amount of scholarship offered to be the most important factor, followed by the reputation of the athletic team, and then the academic reputation of the school. Baldwin (1999) evaluated the college selection process of Division I football players at one mid-western university. The results indicated that the coaching staff was rated as the most important factor. The coaching staff was also rated as above average in importance in Mathes and Gurney (1985). This is in contrast to Doyle and Garth (1990) which found the coach as the fifth most important factor and Baumgartner (1999) found the coaching staff to not be an influential factor in the college selection process.

Klenosky, Templin, and Troutman (2001) conducted a unique study that focused on why particular factors are deemed important in the college selection process of student-athletes. They utilized a means-end theory as a basis for their study and interviewed 27 Division I football players using an interview technique known as laddering. The student-athletes in this study indicated that the coaching staff, competitive schedule, athletic facilities, location, and academics were important factors. The coaching staff was important because they created a comfortable atmosphere and could assist them with improving their skills. The competitive schedule was an important factor because of the possibility of playing on television. The athletic facilities were influential due to the resources at their disposal. The location of the university was influential because of the familiarity of the region and accessibility for their family and friends to watch them play. Academics were also an important factor due to the desire to find a good job after graduation.

It has become apparent to the researchers of the current study that previous research conducted on this topic was often not sport specific or the student-athletes in the investigation were from the same school. Additionally, no previous research incorporated student-athletes from all three NCAA Divisions (I, II, and III) into their investigations.

With the above information in mind, it seems important for a coach to know what factors are most likely to influence a prospective student-athlete's decision making process when selecting a college or university to attend. Having this information at their disposal will assist coaches in the development of a recruiting plan. Furthermore, when a coach has an understanding of the reasons that factor into a student-athlete's decision process, he or she can tailor their recruiting efforts with this in mind. By tailoring their recruiting efforts to meet the desires of potential student-athletes in their sport they are more likely to attract the type and quality of student-athletes they need to establish a successful program. Therefore, the purpose of this study was to assist baseball coaches at NCAA Division I, II, and III institutions in tailoring their recruiting efforts to attract highly desirable student-athletes and to aid the student-athletes in their school selection process. The following research questions were addressed through this study: 1) What were the common factors that most influenced the college selection process of collegiate baseball players, and 2) What differences exist in the factors that influenced the decision making process of collegiate baseball players at the different NCAA Divisions?

# METHODS

## Participants

The participants consisted of a purposeful sample of 320 collegiate baseball players from 12 colleges and universities in the Midwest. The institutions in the study included four schools from each of the NCAA Divisions (I, II, and III). All participants were members of their varsity collegiate baseball team and were at least 18 years of age. The average age of the participants was 20.3 years old. The sample was fairly balanced between NCAA Division I, II, and III institutions. There were 105 (32.8%) Division I, 102 (31.9%) Division II, and 113 (35.3%) Division III student-athletes that completed the survey. Additionally, the sample included 85 freshmen (26.6%), 90 sophomores (28.1%), 78 juniors (24.4%), and 67 seniors (20.9%).

## Instrument

To address the purposes of this study, participants completed the Influential Factors Survey for Student Athletes (IFSSA) (see Table 1). The IFSSA was developed by the researchers, with the assistance of a panel of experts, and was based on surveys from other similar studies (Baumgartner, 1999; Doyle and Gaeth, 1990; Mathes and Gurney, 1985). The IFSSA consisted of 32-items with the responses on a 5-point Likert-type scale ranging from 1 (*not important*) to 5 (*very important*). The items on the survey were separated into five sections that included athletics, academics, social atmosphere, coaching staff, and financial aid. The average score for each section was calculated by summing the responses for each section and dividing by the number of questions related to that section.

A review of literature was conducted prior to the development of the questionnaire to reduce measurement error. Information derived from existing research literature helped form the initial questions. A panel of experts (four coaches, two administrators, and two faculty members each with over 10 years of collegiate athletics experience) was then consulted to acknowledge that the information being collected was relevant to the college recruiting process. During a pilot test, ten collegiate baseball student-athletes (not included in the study) completed the questionnaire. The purpose of the pilot test was to help determine the validity of each question used to evaluate important factors in college selection process of baseball student-athletes. Pilot testers were asked to make suggestion and/or changes that would help ensure that the questions represent important aspects in the recruitment process. Only minor changes were made to the original version of the questionnaire.

Reliability was further tested through the use of a field test. Ten collegiate baseball players who were not included in the study completed the questionnaire. The same players then completed the questionnaire again 7 days later. Questionnaires were compared to determine if any questions were not answered consistently on both administrations. A Cronbach's alpha determined each item's contribution to measurement of the constructs. If reliability on any question was below .80, that question was eliminated. Two questions were eliminated from the questionnaire due to their lack of contribution, and two questions believed to be necessary were reworded.

## Procedures

Following IRB approval, 12 head collegiate baseball coaches throughout the Midwest were contacted regarding the purpose of the study and their willingness to participate in the study. After indicating their willingness to participate, each head coach was mailed a packet that included 35 surveys, a stamped envelope for returning the completed surveys, and a cover letter detailing the instructions on how to complete the survey. Each head coach was responsible for distributing, collecting, and mailing the surveys back to the researchers. Upon the receipt of the surveys, each head coach was mailed a letter thanking them for their team's participation and informed that they would receive a copy of the results after the completion of the study.

## Statistical Design and Analysis

The descriptive survey was designed to provide information for collegiate coaches regarding the factors that were influential in college selection process of baseball student-athletes. The statistical package SPSS Version 12.0 was used for the statistical analyses for this study (SPSS, 2003). Means and standard deviations were calculated for the scale scores by NCAA Division affiliation. A multivariate analysis of variance (MANOVA) compared NCAA Division I, II, and III baseball student-athletes on each of the five sections (athletics, academics, social atmosphere, coaching staff, and financial aid) of the survey. Follow-up univariate tests and pairwise comparisons were calculated when appropriate. The level of significance was set at $p < .05$ for all analyses.

How important were each of the following items in the selection of the school that you currently attend? (1 = Not important, 5 = Very important)

## Table 1. Influential Factors Survey for Student Athletes

| | Not Important | | | | Very Important |
|---|---|---|---|---|---|
| Winning Program | 1 | 2 | 3 | 4 | 5 |
| Conference | 1 | 2 | 3 | 4 | 5 |
| Tradition of athletic program | 1 | 2 | 3 | 4 | 5 |
| Opportunity to play early in career | 1 | 2 | 3 | 4 | 5 |
| NCAA Division (I, II, or III) of school | 1 | 2 | 3 | 4 | 5 |
| Athletic facilities (Weight room, track, training room, etc.) | 1 | 2 | 3 | 4 | 5 |
| Baseball specific facilities (Field, batting cages, locker room, etc.) | 1 | 2 | 3 | 4 | 5 |
| Spring trip location | 1 | 2 | 3 | 4 | 5 |
| Number of alumni in professional baseball | 1 | 2 | 3 | 4 | 5 |
| Academic reputation of institution | 1 | 2 | 3 | 4 | 5 |
| Specific academic major/discipline of interest | 1 | 2 | 3 | 4 | 5 |
| Faculty at institution | 1 | 2 | 3 | 4 | 5 |
| Academic facilities (Library, computer labs, etc.) | 1 | 2 | 3 | 4 | 5 |
| Graduation rate of athletes | 1 | 2 | 3 | 4 | 5 |
| Know someone on the baseball team | 1 | 2 | 3 | 4 | 5 |
| Hove other friends at the institution | 1 | 2 | 3 | 4 | 5 |
| Know other athletes at the institution | 1 | 2 | 3 | 4 | 5 |
| Size of institution | 1 | 2 | 3 | 4 | 5 |
| Close to home | 1 | 2 | 3 | 4 | 5 |
| Regional location of school | 1 | 2 | 3 | 4 | 5 |
| Extracurricular activities (Fraternities, intramural, etc.) | 1 | 2 | 3 | 4 | 5 |
| Religious affiliation | 1 | 2 | 3 | 4 | 5 |
| Social environment | 1 | 2 | 3 | 4 | 5 |
| Coaching staff's time spent recruiting you | 1 | 2 | 3 | 4 | 5 |
| Promises made during recruiting process | 1 | 2 | 3 | 4 | 5 |
| Reputation of coach/coaching staff | 1 | 2 | 3 | 4 | 5 |
| Coach's personality/philosophy | 1 | 2 | 3 | 4 | 5 |
| Coach's number of years at institution | 1 | 2 | 3 | 4 | 5 |
| Amount of athletic scholarship | 1 | 2 | 3 | 4 | 5 |
| Overall cost of school | 1 | 2 | 3 | 4 | 5 |
| Opportunities for additional financial aid | 1 | 2 | 3 | 4 | 5 |
| Other: _____ | 1 | 2 | 3 | 4 | 5 |
| Other: _____ | 1 | 2 | 3 | 4 | 5 |
| Other: _____ | 1 | 2 | 3 | 4 | 5 |

# RESULTS

Descriptive statistics revealed the top five influential factors for all participants in the study were a winning program ($M = 4.43$), the opportunity to play early in career ($M = 4.16$), baseball specific facilities ($M = 4.06$), coach's personality/philosophy ($M = 4.04$), and tradition of the athletic program ($M = 4.04$). The five least influential factors were religious affiliation of the school ($M = 1.96$), knowing other athletes at the school ($M = 2.39$), having other friends at the school ($M = 2.45$), extracurricular activities ($M = 2.51$), and knowing someone on the team ($M = 2.53$).

A MANOVA revealed significant differences between each of the five sections of the questionnaire, [Wilk's $\Lambda = .341$, $F (4, 314) = 76.93$, $p < .001$]. A univariate test of within-subject effects was significant $F (4, 314) = 62.73$, $p < .001$. The means and standard deviations for the scale scores by NCAA Division affiliation are presented in Table 2. Pairwise comparisons showed that the athletic scale was significantly different from the academic ($p = .043$), social ($p < .001$), and financial aid scales ($p = .001$). This result indicates that athletic factors appear to be more influential in the college selection process of baseball players than academic, social, and financial factors. The social scale was significantly different from the academic ($p < .001$), coaching staff ($p < .001$), and financial aid scales ($p < .001$). This result indicates that social factors were not as influential in the college selections process as academic, coaching staff, and financial aid factors. The coaching staff was also significantly different from the financial aid scale ($p = .031$) indicating that the coaching staff was seen as more important in the decision making process than financial aid factors.

**Table 2 Mean Numbers and Standard Deviations by Sections and Division Affiliation**

| Section | Division | Mean | SD | N |
|---|---|---|---|---|
| Athletic | I | 3.77 | .43 | 105 |
| | II | 3.81 | .47 | 102 |
| | III | 3.59 | .55 | 113 |
| | Total | 3.72 | .49 | 320 |
| Coaching Staff | I | 3.66 | .82 | 105 |
| | II | 3.73 | .71 | 102 |
| | III | 3.54 | .83 | 113 |
| | Total | 3.64 | .79 | 320 |
| Academics | I | 3.19 | .85 | 105 |
| | II | 3.51 | .87 | 102 |
| | III | 3.89 | .65 | 113 |
| | Total | 3.53 | .85 | 320 |
| Financial Aid | I | 3.20 | .99 | 105 |
| | II | 3.63 | .87 | 102 |
| | III | 3.43 | .83 | 113 |
| | Total | 3.42 | .91 | 320 |
| Social | I | 2.61 | .74 | 105 |
| | II | 2.76 | .85 | 102 |
| | III | 2.70 | .60 | 113 |
| | Total | 2.69 | .73 | 320 |

The second research question addressed any differences between baseball players at the NCAA Division levels and the five sections of the survey. The MANOVA revealed a significant interaction effect between the NCAA Division levels and the sections of the survey [Wilk's $\Lambda$ = .803, $F$ (8, 628) = 4.457, $p$ < .001]. A test of within-subjects effects was also significant, $F$ (8, 628) = 4.590, $p$ < .001. The means and standard deviations for the scale scores by division affiliation are presented in Table 2. Pairwise comparisons revealed that Division I and Division III baseball student-athletes viewed academics significantly different ($p$ < .001) and Division II and Division III baseball student-athletes viewed academics significantly differently ($p$ = .043). Division III baseball student athletes viewed academics ($M$ = 3.90) as more influential in their college selection process than Division I baseball student-athletes ($M$ = 3.19) and Division II baseball student-athletes ($M$ = 3.51). Pairwise comparisons further revealed that Division II baseball student-athletes viewed financial aid significantly different than Division I baseball student-athletes ($p$ = .049). Division II baseball student-athletes viewed financial aid as more important ($M$ = 3.63) than Division I baseball student-athletes ($M$ = 3.20)

## DISCUSSION

This study was unique compared to the previous investigations of this topic by incorporating baseball student-athletes from the different NCAA Divisions (I, II, and III). Furthermore, this study was unique due to the sampling of only baseball student-athletes. These unique factors will be addressed when discussing the results of the current study in comparison to previous research, conclusions, and implications for future research.

The first research question investigated which factors would be influential in the college selection process of baseball student-athletes from all three Divisions (I, II, and III) of the NCAA. The most influential factor in the current study was a winning program. This is in contrast to Doyle and Gaeth (1990) who found athletic scholarship to be most important and Baumgartner (1999), Fielitz (2001), and Mathes and Gurney (1985) who found academics to be the most important factor. The second and third most influential factors in the current study included the opportunity to play early in career and baseball specific facilities (field, batting cages, locker rooms). These factors are related to athletics and are also inconsistent with previous investigations.

These inconsistencies may be due to the fact that the current study focused solely on baseball student-athletes while most of the previous research included student-athletes from multiple sports. While the inclusion of different sports in the sample may add to the generalizability of the results, it also lacks the specificity required for a coach to tailor his or her recruiting plan to attract the desired student-athletes to their program. When a coach and their staff are able to focus their efforts and emphasize the factors that attract the type of student-athletes that fit their program's goals and expectations, they are more likely to have satisfied players that are cohesive and successful.

Furthermore, most of the published research includes both male and female student-athletes in their samples (Doyle and, Gaeth, 1990; Mathes and Gurney, 1985). The current study included only males. Males may take different factors into consideration when deciding on what school to attend when compared with females. Even with the dramatic increase in the number of female student-athletes over the past twenty-five years (Acosta and Carpenter, 2002) and the opportunities for females to continue their athletic career beyond college (e.g. Women's National Basketball Association and Women's Professional Softball League), males still have many more opportunities to continue their athletic career beyond college. Therefore, many more male student-athletes may value athletics as an important factor when selecting a college due to their aspirations and opportunities to continue their athletic career beyond college.

When comparing the five sections (athletics, academics, social atmosphere, coaching staff, and financial aid) of the survey, without separating the sample into their appropriate NCAA Division level, the athletic section was shown to be the most important factor in the college selection process. Furthermore, the importance of athletic factors for the participants in this study were indicated by rating individual athletic survey items as four of the top five most influential factors. This is not congruent with previous research but is not very surprising due to the high-level of importance placed on athletics in our society. The importance of sport and athletics in our society often establishes athletic identity as an important part of the self-concept in athletes and non-athletes (Cornelius, 1995; Murphy, Petitpas, and Brewer, 1996; Perna, Zaichowsky, and Bocknek, 1996). However, individuals currently participating in organized sports manifest higher levels of athletic identity than non-participants (Brewer, Van Raalte, and Linder, 1993). It would then seem natural for many of these young athletes, like the ones that participated in the current study, to focus on athletic factors when selecting a college to attend for the next four years of their life.

Currently, when evaluating the factors involved in the college selection process of student-athletes there is no published research comparing the different NCAA Divisions (I, II, III). Therefore, the current study evaluated if there were any differences in the decision making process of colligate baseball players between the NCAA Divisional levels. The current study did reveal significant differences in the way collegiate baseball student-athletes viewed academics. Division III baseball student-athletes viewed academics significantly more important in the college selection process than Division I or Division II baseball student-athletes. The importance of academics indicated by the Division III baseball student-athletes is consistent with the NCAA Division III philosophy (National Collegiate Athletic Association, 2003). Athletics are not stressed beyond the direct impact on the student-athletes' overall quality of the educational experience at the NCAA Division III level (National Collegiate Athletic Association, 2003). It is also very unlikely that Division III student-athletes, including baseball players, will have much of an opportunity to continue their athletic careers' beyond college due to limited exposure and talent. Unlike NCAA Division I and II student-athletes who are eligible to receive athletically based financial aid, Division III student-athletes are not eligible to receive athletically based financial aid. By not receiving athletically based financial assistance, Division III student-athletes need to evaluate other factors when deciding what school to attend. For the current study the most important factors for Division III baseball student-athletes were related to academics.

The results revealed another differences between the NCAA Division levels. Division II baseball student-athletes were found to be significantly different than Division I student-athletes in their perspective of financial aid. Division II baseball student-athletes viewed financial aid as more important than Division I student-athletes. A plausible explanation for this result is that most student-athletes want to play at the Division I level which is the highest collegiate level. Therefore, many student-athletes might be willing to accept a higher financial burden to be able to compete at the highest level. Division II student-athletes may feel the need for more financial assistance because they are not playing at the highest collegiate level of competition.

This descriptive survey was delimited to only collegiate baseball student-athletes in the Midwest, which may appear to limit the generalizability or the results to other collegiate sports and other areas of the country. Nevertheless, by including only baseball student-athletes from the NCAA Division I, II, and III institutions these results can be directly applied to the recruiting efforts of collegiate baseball coaches. Based on this investigation the recommendations for collegiate baseball coaches are: (1) structure their recruiting plan based on athletic related factors such as success of program, opportunity of play, baseball specific facilities, and tradition of athletic programs, (2) Division III coaches should also emphasize the academic strengths of their institution, and (3) Division II coaches should attempt to maximize the amount of financial aid assistance available.

The results of this study can also be useful for prospective baseball student-athletes and their parents. The college selection process can be a very exciting time for prospective student-athletes but it can also be very hectic and overwhelming for student-athletes and parents who are not prepared (Koehler, 1996). Prospective student-athletes begin their preparation by completing the Influential Factors Survey for Student-Athletes and utilize the results to guide their college selection process. Collegiate athletic administrators can utilize the information garnered through this study to assist their coaches with structuring a recruiting plan to maximize the likelihood of attracting the highest quality student-athletes. Utilizing empirical information could increase an athletic department's ability to not only attract but also retain high quality student-athletes because these student-athletes will match the athletic department's goals and philosophy. Athletic administrators can also utilize this information in directing their financial resources to the appropriate areas to assist with the recruitment of potential student-athletes.

Future research should continue to explore the factors involved in the college selection process of student-athletes. A deeper understanding of this process can lead to many benefits and can be far reaching for all parties involved in this process. Future points of emphasis should evaluate differences between revenue and non-revenue sports, males and females, while focusing on freshmen student-athletes because they are not far removed from the factors that influenced their college selection.

# REFERENCES

Acosta, and Carpenter, (2002). *Women in intercollegiate sport: A longitudinal study – twenty-five year update, 1977 – 2002.* Unpublished manuscript. Brooklyn College, Department of Physical Education.

Baldwin, B. (1999). *The factors that Division I college football players considered most important when deciding which university to attend during the recruiting process.* Unpublished master's thesis, Ball State University, Muncie, IN.

Baumgartner, A. (1999). *Factors that influence Division II recruited female intercollegiate soccer student-athletes in selecting their university of choice.* Unpublished master's thesis, Slippery Rock University, Slippery Rock, PA.

Brewer, B., Van Raalte, J., and Linder, D. (1993). Athletic identity: Hercules' muscles or Achilles heel? *International Journal of Sport Psychology, 24,* 237 – 254.

Christiansen, D., Davidson, C., Roper, C., Sprinkles, C., and Thomas, J. (2003). Getting personal with today's prospective students: Use of the web in the college selection process, *College and University, 79*(1), 9 – 14.

Cornelius, A. (1995). The relationship between athletic identity, peer and faculty socialization, and college development. *Journal of College Development, 36,* 560 – 573.

Doyle, C., and Gaeth, G. (1990). Assessing the institutional choice process of student-athletes. *Research Quarterly for Exercise and Sport, 61,* 85 – 92.

Fielitz, L. (2001). *Factors influencing the student-athletes' decision to attend the United States Military Academy.* Unpublished manuscript. United States Military Academy.

Hodges, T., and Barbuto, J. (2002). Recruiting urban and rural students: Factors influencing the post-secondary education institution choices of rural and urban high school students. *College and University, 77*(3), 23 – 26.

Kindall, J., and Winkin. (Eds.). (2000). *The baseball coaching bible.* Champaign, IL: Human Kinetics.

Klenosky, D., Templin, T., and Troutman, J. (2001). Recruiting student athletes: A means-end investigation of school-choice decision making. *Journal of Sport Management, 15,* 95 – 106.

Koehler, S. (1996). *Advising student athletes through the recruitment process: A complete guide for counselors, coaches, and parents.* Englewood Cliffs, NJ: Prentice Hall.

Mathes, S., and Gurney, G. (1985). Factors in student athletes choices of colleges. *Journal of College Personnel, 3,* 327 – 333.

Murphy, G., Petitpas, A., and Brewer, B. (1996). Identity foreclosure, athletic identity, and career maturity in intercollegiate athletes. *Sport Psychologist, 10,* 239 – 246.

National Collegiate Athletic Association (2003). *NCAA Division III Manual.* Indianapolis, IN: Author

Packer, B., and Lazenby, R. (1999). *Why we win: Great American coaches offer their strategies for success in sports and life.* Chicago, IL: Masters Press.

Perna, F, Zaichowsky, l., and Bocknek, G. (1996). The association of mentoring with psychosocial development among male athletes at termination of college career. *Journal of Applied Sport Psychology, 8,* 76 – 88.

Pope, M., and Fermin, B. (2003). The perceptions of college students regarding the factors most influential in their decision to attend post secondary education. *College and University, 78*(4), 19 – 25.

SPSS, Inc. (2003). *SPSS 12.0 guide to data analysis.* Chicago, IL: SPSS, Inc.

ISBN 1-59454-595-2
© 2007 Nova Science Publishers, Inc.

*Chapter 13*

# GENDER DIFFERENCES IN SPORT CONSUMER BEHAVIOR AMONG COLLEGE STUDENTS

## *Dean F. Anderson,[1] Hyungil (Harry) Kwon and Galen T. Trail*
### Iowa State University, Ames, Iowa , USA

## ABSTRACT

Demographic research shows that the percentage of female spectators for many sports is growing. Some experts suggest that, as sport spectators, females differ from males. If such differences do in fact exist, then it is critical to identify them in order to develop more effect marketing schemes. This investigation examined gender differences in sport consumer behavior among a convenience sample of 484 college students (male = 225, female = 259). Ninety-three percent of the respondents self-identified as Caucasian. MANCOVA results showed that after controlling for level of respondent's team identification, the effect of gender was statistically significant ($F = 18.6$, $p < .00$; $\eta^2 = 0.19$) on combined sport consumer behaviors. Results indicated that female respondents were more likely to have purchased team merchandise in the past, more likely to purchase team merchandise in the future, and were more likely to wear team apparel than male respondents. Male respondents were more likely to read about the team and watch the team on television than female respondents. No gender differences were found for plans to attend home football games.

Research indicates that most Americans, approximately 70%, are at least a little bit interested in professional and collegiate sport (ESPN Sports Poll, 2001). Sport marketers are extremely interested in converting this interest into consumption behavior. Until recently, many believed that the rapid expansion in sport consumption would continue. However, recent economic events have cast doubts upon this belief of continued expansion. Attendance figures for several sports leagues have plateaued or even shown a decrease (Pro Sports Tracker, 2002). At times, the purchase of sports licensed merchandise has shown a similar trend. Although retail sales of sports licensed merchandised topped $11 billion in 2001, this represented a decline of about 13% since 1999 (Sweet, 2002). Indications are that the market may be becoming saturated with choices for sport consumers. Until about a decade ago,

---
[1] Correspondence concerning this article should be addressed to Dean F. Anderson, Department of Health and Human Performance, Iowa State University, 207 Forker Building, Ames, IA 50011. Electronic mail may be sent via Internet to deanf@iastate.edu.

sports marketers typically viewed sport consumers as a homogeneous male segment and generally ignored the possibility that females were or could be an important sport consumer segment (Burnett, Menon, and Smart, 1993). The simple recognition that women may be an important sport consumer segment is starting to pay positive dividends in some areas. Recent research indicated that females make up 46% of Major League Baseball and National Football attendees as well as 38% of the attendees for the National Basketball Association games (Yerak, 2000). In addition, findings suggest that the percentage of female spectators for these and other professional sports may be growing (McCarthy, 2001).

## GENDER DIFFERENCES

Some have suggested that, as spectators and fans, females differ from males (Lopiano, 1997; Brennan, 2001). However, research findings have been mixed and many times differences have been relatively small. For example, in a study of spectators at both men's and women's intercollegiate basketball games, no gender differences were found for the importance of four pre-event environmental factors (ticket pricing, friend influence, family involvement, advertising/promotions) while gender of team was significant (Fink, Trail, and Anderson, 2002). In contrast, results for present behaviors and future intentions displayed both gender and team gender differences. Although gender differences were statistically significant, they may not be meaningful as effect sizes showed that gender explained 2% or less in any of the present behaviors or future intentions (Fink et al., 2002).

Other empirical research also points to conflicting results regarding gender. Zhang, Smith, Pease, and Lam (1998) found no gender differences in ticket-service satisfaction while Zhang, Pennington-Gray, Connaughton, Braunstein, Ellis, Lam, and Williamson (2003) found that individual sociodemographic variables such as gender explained less than 4% of the variance in game consumption variables. Greenwell, Fink and Pastore (2002) found no gender differences for the evaluation of the physical facility or the service personnel, but Pope, Brown, and Forrest (1999) reported that men showed greater intentions to purchase sport team products on the internet than did women. Some research indicated that females were less likely to consume sport media than men (Gantz and Wenner, 1991). They reported differences for both reading about sport and watching sport on television. However, because their data were collected in 1987, it is reasonable to suggest that changes may have occurred over the past fifteen years and these findings may no longer be accurate.

## TEAM IDENTIFICATION

Team identification has frequently been found to be a strong predictor of sport fan consumption behavior. Fans high in team identification are more likely to attend games, pay more for tickets, spend more money on team merchandise, consume more media, be satisfied with the game experience, and stay loyal to the team during periods of poor performance (Kwon and Armstrong, 2002; James and Trail, 2005; Madrigal, 1995; Wakefield, 1995; Wann and Branscombe, 1993). Fan identification is one of the most important aspects for sport teams to foster. Indeed both Mitrano (1999) and Sutton, McDonald, Milne and Cimperman (1997) noted that fans with high levels of identification behave differently than those with lower levels because highly identified fans are more likely to have a strong sense of attachment and belonging to the team. In fact, Wann and Branscombe (1990) have suggested that the differences in team identification levels explained the phenomena of die-hard and fair-weather fans. Fair-weather fans only associate with the team when it is performing well, while die-hard fans show allegiance regardless to performance. They have suggested that fair-weather fans are the cause of attendance fluctuations that occur as the result of winning or losing seasons. Murrel and Dietz (1992) have reported similar findings that as identification with a team increases, so does the level of support exhibited by the individual. They, too, suggested that less identified individuals were the cause of attendance fluctuations. Further, Wann and Branscombe (1993) have found that identification influenced several other sport spectator consumption variables. Highly identified individuals reported attending more home games than less identified individuals. Highly identified fans also reported a greater likelihood of attending away games. In addition, they reported a willingness to spend more money to obtain regular season, playoff, and championship tickets. Highly identified fans also reported that they would be willing to spend greater amounts of time waiting in line for tickets than those people that were less highly identified.

## RELATIONSHIP BETWEEN GENDER AND FAN IDENTIFICATION

Thus, fan identification is vitally important to a team's economic success. Sport managers should do all they can to foster and draw upon its strength. While a great deal is known regarding the consequences of fan identification, research examining the relationship between gender and identification has shown conflicting results. Branscombe and Wann (1991), Wann and Branscombe (1993), and Wann, Tucker, and Schrader (1996) found no significant gender differences for team identification among college students. Likewise, Lough and Kim (2004) found no significant gender differences for spectators at women's professional basketball games in South Korea and Robinson and Trail (in press) found no gender differences on team identification for spectators of collegiate basketball and football games. In addition, Kolbe and James (2000) found that in the final stages of loyalty, males and females were equal. In contrast, Wann, Dolan, McGeorge, and Allison (1994) found significant gender differences among college students on identification and Pan, Gabert, McGaugh, and Branvold (1997) found gender differences on fan identification of season ticket holders.

Thus, because of the aforementioned relationship between gender and identification, gender differences on present sport consumption behavior and future consumption intentions actually may be moderated by identification. To date, there have been no studies to test for gender differences while controlling for level of team identification. Thus, the purpose of this study was to examine the relationship between gender and both present and future sport consumer behavior, while controlling for level of team identification with the university football team.

## METHOD

### Participants

Data were collected at the beginning of fall semester from a convenience sample of 466 college students (female = 259, male = 225) taking classes in the Department of Health and Human Performance at a large Mid-western university. Ninety-three percent of the respondents self-identified as Caucasian. Average age was 20.5 years ($SD$ = 14.6) and respondents reported having attended the university for an average of 1.9 years.

## Instrumentation

The questionnaire included four aspects of past sport consumer behavior: merchandise consumption (three items), print media consumption (three items), television consumption (three items), and wearing of team paraphernalia (three items). A 3-item factor was used to examine the plans for future merchandise consumption. All items had a 7-point response format ranging from "Strongly Disagree" (1) to "Strongly Agree" (7). The alpha coefficients ranged from .82 to .94 for these subscales. A single item asking, "How many of the seven home games do you plan to attend" was also included as an indicator of future attendance intentions. Lastly, the three-item, Team Identification Index (TII), was used to measure the level of identification with the university football team. The TII has also shown good reliability previously (Trail and James, 2001) and the Cronbach's alpha was again high ($\alpha$ = .88) in this study. A demographic section was also included.

## Data Analysis

We used a one-way MANCOVA to test for the effects of gender upon the four past consumer behavior subscales, the consumer behavior intention subscale, and the single attendance item, while controlling for level identification with the university team.

## RESULTS

With the use of Wilks' criterion, MANCOVA results showed that the combined dependent variables were significantly related to the covariate of team identification, $F(6, 476)$ = 133.05, $p$ < .000, and the association was large ($\eta^2$ = .63). After adjustments for the covariate, the results indicated that there was a significant gender effect, $F(6, 476)$ = 18.60, $p$ < .000 on the combine DVs, and the association was large $\eta^2$ = .19.

The univariate tests indicated that five of the six dependent variables significantly differed by gender (Table 1). Female respondents indicated that they were more likely to have purchased team merchandise ($\eta^2$ = .04) and were more likely to have worn team paraphernalia ($\eta^2$ = .05) than male respondents. Male respondents indicated that they were more likely to have consumed both print media ($\eta^2$ = .08) and television media ($\eta^2$ = .03) than female respondents. Although these univariate results were statistically significant, the variance gender explained in each of these past sport consumption behaviors was small.

The univariate tests indicated for future sport consumer behavioral intentions, only future merchandise consumption intentions differed significantly by gender, but the variance was small ($\eta^2$ = .03). These results indicated that females expressed greater intentions to purchase team merchandise in the future than male respondents. No gender differences were found for respondents' plans to attend future home football games.

**Table 1. Means, Standard Deviations, F-values, Significance Levels, and Effect Size for Sport Consumption Behaviors by Gender**

|  | Men | | Women | | | | |
|---|---|---|---|---|---|---|---|
|  | M | SD | M | SD | F | $p$ | $\eta^2$ |
| Merchandise consumption | 4.94 | 1.50 | 5.23 | 1.39 | 21.58 | .000 | .043 |
| Print media consumption | 5.32 | 1.50 | 4.43 | 1.56 | 43.77 | .000 | .083 |
| Television consumption | 5.35 | 1.50 | 4.78 | 1.54 | 12.41 | .000 | .025 |
| Wearing paraphernalia | 5.02 | 1.56 | 5.35 | 1.46 | 25.95 | .000 | .051 |
| Games plan to attend | 4.92 | 2.52 | 4.61 | 2.44 | 0.01 | .916 | .000 |
| Future consumption | 5.54 | 1.49 | 5.65 | 1.36 | 12.07 | .001 | .025 |
| Team Identification Index | 4.83 | 1.58 | 4.48 | 1.33 | 7.56 | .006 | .015 |

## DISCUSSION

The purpose of the study was to determine if, after controlling for team identification, both past sport consumption behavior and future sport consumption intentions still differed by gender. The results indicated that team identification explained 63% of the variance in the combination of past and future consumption behaviors. After controlling for team identification, gender explained 19% of the variance in the combined past and future consumption behaviors. However, the gender differences on each of the separate behaviors, although significant except for future attendance, were small to medium.

These results are similar to past research. James and Trail (2005) reported that team identification explained 16% of the variance in future attendance and about 65% of the variance in media and merchandise consumption intentions. In our study, team identification explained 7% of the variance in future attendance and 23% in future merchandise consumption. This also supports the findings of Kwon and Armstrong (2002) and Wann and Branscombe (1993) who found similar results.

For the gender differences, our results support the findings of Gantz and Wenner (1991), who found that men were more likely to consume media than were women. We found that men consumed both more print media and more TV media. This differed slightly from Fink et al. (2002) who found no significant differences on print media consumption, but did find that men consumed more TV media. However, relative to purchasing and wearing consumption behavior, our results contradicted those of Fink et al., who found that men bought more merchandise and wore more team clothing than did the women. In our study, women bought more and tended to wear more team apparel than men did. This could be due to the different samples, as Fink et al.'s was a spectator sample and ours was a student sample.

Our results also differed from Fink et al.'s (2002) relative to future attendance intentions. We found no difference between men and women and their intention to attend games in the future. In Fink et al.'s sample, women were more likely to indicate that they would attend games in the future than men. However, our results were similar to Fink et al.'s in that we found women were more likely to purchase team apparel in the future than men were. In both studies, the amount of variance explained in both past and future sport consumption behavior was negligible. Fink et al. explained less than 2% of any dependent variable and we explained anywhere from 3-5%, with the exception being print media consumption at 8%.

## Implications to Organizations

These results, and those of past research, indicate that although in some cases gender differences may be significant and even meaningful, what is more important is the concept of team identification. Because of the small differences evidenced between genders, it may make little sense to market to men and women differently. On the other hand, as Trail, Robinson, Gillentine, and Dick (2003) noted, marketers should focus on two different segments of potential and actual attendees: fans and spectators. They noted that fans, those who have high team identification, seem to be motivated by vicarious achievement, whereas spectators, those lower on team identification, seem to be motivated by aesthetics, physical skills of athletes, eustress/drama, and acquisition of knowledge.

This was echoed by Robinson and Trail (in press) who noted that sport marketers should focus on two different communication strategies. One strategy focuses on the relationship between team identification and vicarious achievement, which works as long as the team is successful. The second strategy is less success contingent. It focuses on the aesthetic qualities of the event and the sport in-and-of-itself. As Robinson and Trail suggested, with the focus on the sport and its aesthetic and dramatic qualities, there are fewer negative consequences (relative to the marketing plan anyway) if the team is not successful.

## Limitations and Suggestions for Future Research

Our results suggest that gender differences in sport consumption behaviors may have decreased since Gantz and Wenner (1991) conducted their research in the 1980s. Clearly, more resent research shows inconsistent results concerning gender differences in sport consumption behavior. For example, results reported here for college students differ somewhat from the results reporter by Fink et al. (2002) for spectators at a sporting venue. These differences may merely be a function of sample differences. Consequently, future research investigating gender differences in sport consumer behavior should utilize general community samples in order to decrease the effect of sampling bias.

## REFERENCES

Branscombe, N. R., and Wann, D. L. (1991). The positive social and self-concept consequences of sports team identification. *Journal of Sport and Social Issues, 15,* 115-127.

Brennan, C. (2001, May 8). Talking about a revolution. *USA Today,* p. C3.

Burnett, J., Menon, A., and Smart, D. T. (1993). Sport Marketing: A new ball game with new rules. *Journal of Advertising Research,* 21-35.

ESPN Sports Poll. (July, 2001). The ESPN Sports Poll Newsletter and Trend Report. Retrieved, July 12th, 2002, from http://www.sportspoll.com/press/ewsletter- Example.pdf

Fink, J. S., Trail, G. T., and Anderson, D. F. (2002). Environmental factors associated with spectator attendance and sport consumption behavior: Gender and team differences. *Sport Marketing Quarterly, 11,* 8-19.

Gantz, W.,and Wenner, L. A. (1991). Men, women, and sports: Audience experiences and effects. *Journal of Broadcasting and Electronic Media, 35,* 233-243.

Greenwell, T. C., Fink, J. S., and Pastore, D. L. (2002). Perceptions of the service experience: Using demographis and psychographis variables to identify customer segments. *Sport Marketing Quarterly, 11,* 233-241.

James, J. D., and Trail, G. T. (2005). The relevance of team identification to sport consumption behavior intentions. *International Sports Journal, 9(1).*

Kolbe, R. H., and James, J. D. (2000). An identification and examination of influences that shape the creation of a professional team fan. *International Journal of Sports Marketing and Sponsorship, 2(1),* 23-36.

Kwon, H. H., and Armstrong, K. L. (2002). Factors influencing impulse buying of sport team licensed merchandise. *Sport Marketing Quarterly, 11,* 151-162.

Lopiano, D. (1997). Tomorrow in women's sports: Now is just the tip of the iceberg. Paper presented at the Summit 1997 (Women's Sports Foundation National Conference), Bloomingdale, IL.

Lough, N. L., and Kim, A.R. (2004). Analysis of sociomotivations affecting spectator attendance at women's professional basketball games in South Korea. *Sport Marketing Quarterly, 13,* 35-42.

Madrigal, R. (1995). Cognitive and affective determinants of fan satisfaction with sporting event attendance. *Journal of Leisure Research, 27,* 205-227.

McCarthy, M. (2001, Jan. 25). The changing face of Super Sunday marketers, NFL focus on game's audience of 40 million women. *USA Today,* p. B-1.

Mitrano, J. R. (1999). The "sudden death" of hockey in Hartford: Sports fans and franchise relocation. *Sociology of Sport Journal, 16,* 134-154.

Murrell, A. J., and Dietz, B. (1992). Fan support of sports teams: The effect of a common group identity. *Journal of Sport and Exercise Psychology, 14,* 28-39.

Pan, D. W., Gabert, T. E., McGaugh, E. C., and Branvold, S. E. (1997). Factors and differential demographis effects on purchase of season tickets for intercollegiate basketball games. *Journal of Sport Behavior, 20,* 447-463.

Pope, N., Brown, M., and Forrest, E. (1999). Risk, Innovativeness, Gender, and Involvement Factors Affecting the Intention to Purchase Sport Product Online. *Sport Marketing Quarterly.* 8(2). 25-31.

Pro Sports Tracker (2002, April 22nd and 29th). *Sport Business Journal,* pp.33 and 35.

Robinson, M., and Trail, G. T. (in press). Relationship among spectator gender, motives, and points of attachment in selected intercollegiate sports. *Journal of Sport Management.*

Sutton, W. A., McDonald, M. A., Milne, G. R., and Cimperman, J. (1997). Creating and fostering fan identification in professional sports. *Sport Marketing Quarterly, 6(1),* 15-22.

Sweet, D. (2002). Licensed Goods. *Street and Smith's sportbusiness Journal, 4(47),* 33.

Trail, G. T., and James, J. D. (2001). The Motivation Scale for Sport Consumption: Assessment of the Scale's Psychometric Properties. *Journal of Sport Behavior, 24,* 108-127.

Trail, G. T., Robinson, M.J., Dick, R. J., and Gillentine, A. J. (2003). Motives and points of attachments: Fans versus spectators in intercollegiate athletics. *Sport Marketing Quarterly, 12,* 217-227.

Wakefield, K. L. (1995). The pervasive effects of social influence on sporting event attendance. *Journal of Sport and Social Issues, 19,* 335-351.Wann, 1995

Wann, D. L., and Branscombe, N. R. (1990). Die-hard and fair-weather fans: Effects of identification on BIRGing and CORFing tendencies. *Journal of Sport and Social Issues, 14,* 103-117.

Wann, D. L., and Branscombe, N. R. (1993). Sports fans: Measuring degree of identification with their team. *International Journal of Sport Psychology, 24,* 1-17.

Wann, D. L., Dolan, T. J., McGeorge, K. K., and Allison, J. A. (1994). Relationships between spectator identification and spectators' perceptions of influence, spectators' emotions, and competition outcome. *Journal of Sport and Exercise Psychology, 16,* 347-364.

Wann, D. L., Tucker, K. B., and Schrader, M. P. (1996). An exploratory examination of the factors influencing the origination, continuation, and cessation of identification with sports teams. *Perceptual and Motor Skills, 82,* 995-1001.

Yerak, B. (2000, Oct. 16). Baseball makes pitch to women. League isn't the only sport to court female fan base. *USA Today,* p. B-3.

Zhang, J. J., Smith, D. W., Pease, D. G., Lam, E. T. (1998). Dimensions of spectator satisfaction toward support programs of professional hockey games. *International Sports Journal, 2,* 1-17.

Zhang, J. J., Pennington-Gray, L., Connaughton, D. P., Braustein, J. R., Ellis, M. H., Lam, E. T., and Williamson, D. (2003). Understanding women's professional basketball game spectators: Sociodemographic, game consumption, and entertainment options. *Sport Marketing Quarterly, 12,* 228-243.

# INDEX

## G

## H

## I

## J

## K

## L

## M

## N

## O

## P